BEADS

of

LIGHT

BEADS

of

LIGHT

A Story of Alignment

By Enrica Ferruzzi

Briton Publishing, LLC
810 Eastgate North Dr., Suite 200
Cincinnati, Ohio 45245
www.britonpublishing.com

ISBN 978-1-956216-14-1

Cover illustrations by Verena Wild, www.verena-wild.com.

Briton Publishing books are distributed by Ingram Content Group and made available worldwide.

To my mom, Lorraine Rae Weil.
Thank you for always encouraging me and for showing me
the way.

ACKNOWLEDGMENTS

I want to extend my heartfelt gratitude to Jason for his unconditional love and patience.

Carrie Hewitt for her genuine friendship, warm support, and for being there for me throughout the creation of this project.

Master Anita Ahn, for helping me rediscover the art of listening to my own voice.

Jennifer Wrobel, for the gentle yet powerful expression of healing love.

The following individuals for sticking with me all this time: Jennie, Edith, Carolina, Lynn, Marie, Sue B., Liz, Carlos, Terry, Fredora, Jennifer R., Marlene, Sue L., Theresa O., Robin, and the late Theresa Seley for her generosity, warm heart, creative spirit and delightful sense of humor. The extended Prescott community for their support over the years, holding a special place in my heart.

Valentina and Alessandra for over thirty-five years of unwavering and authentic friendship.

My inspiring, and wise aunt, Anna, my incredibly talented sister Angelica, and my father, Massimo Ferruzzi, a great teacher, and pillar in life.

PREFACE

Embark on a captivating journey of transformation, where the themes of refinement, regeneration, and renewal converge into a story of understanding and discovery. This story is a heartfelt exploration of how inspired practices can serve as guiding lights, illuminating the path toward a profound connection with our inner selves.

Imagine a path that takes you through the labyrinth of life's twists and turns, symbolizing the process of refinement. As we encounter challenges and experiences, we're offered opportunities to revise our perspectives and attitudes, shaping us into more resilient beings. This journey isn't just about conquering obstacles; it's about embracing the idea that each experience has a purpose, and that purpose is to lead us toward greater self-awareness.

Regeneration is the beating heart of this story. It's the magic that unfolds when we allow ourselves to heal and rejuvenate. Through insightful practices and moments of stillness, we tap into our innate ability to replenish our spirits. The narrative encourages us to listen to the whispers of our intuition, to understand that there's immense power in surrendering to the currents of renewal.

Renewal isn't just a far-off concept, it's the very fabric of this story. Inspired practices become the bridge that connects us with our own minds, helping us deepen our understanding of who we are and what we're capable of. These practices serve as anchors, grounding us in the present moment while guiding us toward the transformation we seek.

INTRODUCTION

Throughout my life, I've always had an incredible passion for learning new things, and what brings deep fulfillment is the opportunity to share my experiences with others. I've seen how my love for learning and teaching has become the heart and soul of everything I do, both in my work and personal life. I am wholeheartedly dedicated to being a lifelong student and a catalyst for change. When I acquire new understanding or undergo any form of personal growth, I instinctively gravitate toward sharing based on my firsthand experiences. My purpose in life is to continuously learn while inspiring and empowering those around me.

In this book, I aspire to share my personal growth journey and the process of alignment with my authentic self. Throughout this narrative, I will use my unique style of expression. Drawing from the wisdom of my guides and higher selves, I will convey inspired messages in various ways. Sometimes, these messages will be presented through dreams, inspired journeys, encouraging words, clarification, and instructions in the second person. At other times, they will be delivered as direct packets of information, such as power words, helpful pointers, symbols, and teaching exchanges in sessions and workshops. I have transcribed these messages verbatim from my handwritten notebooks, preserving their authenticity.

I prefer to avoid using the word 'channeling' due to its frequent usage, which has led to a certain level of misunderstanding or expectations. In my view, each individual possesses their own distinct manner of connecting with higher consciousness, as this process is inherent to all beings. We constantly receive messages from various sources of consciousness. We all channel. The key to maintaining a strong and reliable *signal*, so to speak, similar to a high-quality antenna, lies in the dedicated commitment to both internal and external purification practices. The nature and extent of these practices vary depending on specific needs at any given moment.

I will describe and delve into some of these practices that have supported my understanding of the invisible worlds and share insights on energy systems being upgraded in our evolution.

As we strive for purity, our connection to our own essence, which encompasses our entire being, strengthens. This results in clearer, higher-quality signals and messages. There is no room for doubt or confusion regarding the intention of the messages and their place of origin, which is pure consciousness, presenting us with the gift of wisdom. Therefore, I refer to these messages as inspired *indicators* that show up through different levels of sensory perception, including the physical form and energy-spiritual bodies. At times, I discern the presence of my higher self, my inner teacher and healer, while on other occasions, it's apparent to me that the source of these messages is an extension of myself, such as a guide, a guardian angel, my mother, or even the Earth herself.

The book begins by recounting the initial spark that led to its formation. It started with a single idea I received one morning on how to put my writing together. It quickly expanded into over five hours of dedicated writing as I sat down at my laptop that afternoon, allowing my inspired outline to flow guided by my inner compass.

From there, I will delve into the background information of my journey, revealing the significant catalysts that have shaped my path and influenced my personal growth.

The nudges about writing have always been there, I just chose to ignore them. Since I can remember, I've always had this persistent belief that I would become a writer. Even during past-life regression sessions and through messages from my guides, I was consistently told that writing was my calling and that I had done it before, but what was running in the background was a sense of restriction on many levels.

For years, I lived in the shadow of self-doubt, feeling buried under the weight of not being educated enough or lacking mastery over the

English language, let alone my native Italian. Communication was an area where I always felt inadequate, despite building a thriving career in hospitality and being successful in great part thanks to my communication skills, there were two strong conflicting voices deep down.

I excelled as a team leader in Operations and trained countless individuals. I loved what I did and blossomed in it, though I also made many mistakes and learned valuable lessons along the way. Communication became my superpower, so why did I still harbor a sense of inadequacy deep down? That feeling remained even during my time in Mexico, where I led an incredible team and experienced tremendous self-confidence and success, recognizing my ability to flourish while becoming proficient in a third language and noticing that perfection is indeed a devastating block that has nothing to do with creating and leading a joyful life.

Over the past seven years, the messages kept encouraging me repeatedly in various ways, but I chose to ignore them or look the other way. It wasn't until a few years ago that I began contemplating how I could bring those messages to life. How could I gather my thoughts and weave them into a book? What would I write about? Would anyone even care about my story? I could focus on sharing my experiences, but then again, there seems to be an overwhelming amount of content already out there. I struggled to find the right way to convey deep and meaningful concepts.

But the message grew stronger and clearer. I recognized and accepted that I was meant to transmit the vibration and frequency of my heart through my writing, and it was time to stop avoiding it like the plague.

While words hold immense power, I understood that the essence of my story was to share my unique soul vibration. Many could learn and discover more about themselves through the experiences and teachings and find the motivation to gracefully move forward in their own lives. This calling was not just for me, but for others.

So here I am, extending an invitation. It is an invitation to open your heart to receive these words instead of relying solely on the intellectual mind.

I've incorporated active dreaming into my spiritual practice for a long time. When I was young, I began to keep this side of my life to myself, not speaking about dreams with my family or friends. However, I always paid close attention to the messages I would receive through visionary journeys, symbols, sounds, and colors.

I will weave some of my dreams and visionary journeys into my story. Some of the healing journeys, in particular, may be helpful to others. Exercising our visualization gifts supports us in creating the lives we want to experience. Through dreams and visions, we can become aware of different perspectives, our own authentic voice, and what she wants us to focus on, allowing us to create consciously. This way of life is a gift we all carry and must restore.

I would also like to take a moment to clarify my language and explain how I use the term "minds." Minds refer to our multidimensional selves, encompassing various levels and layers. The mind of the body, for instance, consists of multiple dimensions. Our heart-mind serves as the center of consciousness, housing our soul. On the other hand, the head-brain represents the mind of the spirit. When I use the term "minds' in the plural form, I will make every effort to describe its intended meaning and convey the imagery and energy codes that I envision delivering these insights and experiences.

Consciousness, Life, Change, and Movement are all one being, constantly offering new perspectives and expanded views, reminding us of the many resources we hold and may not recognize. Accepting only a partial view of who we are is simply no longer good enough. It's an incomplete picture, and we are ready for much more.

It is with deep commitment that I will provide another set of lenses and perspectives.

CONTENTS

1

A NEW BEGINNING

Clarity In Moving Forward

It's about an hour to drive to my dad's house. It's a calm Sunday morning, and I'm enjoying the quiet drive alone. I am about halfway there when I experience an unusual feeling in my body. Strong buzzing sensations rush through me. I know I'm driving, but not fully in my body. I become aware I'm having a meeting with my higher self and spiritual guides. The formal conversation is occurring beyond my conscious awareness until I wake up right in the middle of it. I think I'm participating, maybe I'm just observing. I try not to get in the way. There is a beautiful floating sensation all around me, but I remain fully present as my body drives and focuses on the road and peaceful landscape. There is more of *me* here, beyond my physical form.

I experience what feels like a frozen time capsule. Nothing moves. I enter an expanded state, as if I am a large being that cannot be contained. I am moving through a jelly-like substance with iridescent edges. It is a *Seba*, a gateway, but I don't see it until I am going through it. Passing through the round gateway, I look to the side and notice the liquid border resembles a thick, multi-faceted glass lens that moves with fluidity, reminding me of a prism. My body is vibrating, and my mind is very still. I know I am somewhere else, but I'm still driving the car peacefully. My body's mind is perfectly stable and calm while my consciousness is in this other space.

I am fully aware, and just as if some dear friends are sitting in the car with me, I hear suggestions. I agree that it would be a good start, reminding me that it's just the beginning and that it would help me open up the floodgates. There is a visual image of a huge waterfall and the *Nefer* hieroglyph, and I hear this message: *the heart is connected to the throat, the heart holds the memories and lessons, tell your stories, here is the outline. It's time.*

I witness the communication between guides, angels, and higher self. This is how you should plan it out. Right now, is the moment when you have clarity. Then it simply appears to me in the next moment. An outline of the book. It's my story of alignment. I know how it should flow and where I should insert some guided messages, dreams, and details about growth experiences. There is no sense of doubt or worry about the fact that I'm not a writer, and that I know nothing about how to go about writing. The logical mind is displaying all of the limitations one may encounter. I receive this sense of assurance that the heart story needs to be shared.

The visit with my father was pleasant. My spirits were lifted, not weighed by anything at all. The drive home was peaceful. As soon as I got home, I sat in front of my laptop and wrote the exact outline I was given. Honestly, I couldn't wait. During my 5-hour visit with my sister and father, my thoughts kept going back to writing this book. As I opened up to this process, I followed my body's mind to record my thoughts that day, trusting that electric-buzzing feeling running through me. This is the feeling I've learned to recognize as a signal of a higher frequency of intelligence; it's a signature-calling whisper. The entire afternoon was spent writing. It was surreal and magical.

Create Joy - Inspired Message

I've been hearing this melody for a while. Awake within the dream, I recognize the melody all around me, and begin to see some words. They become very clear, shown to me as a title, The Story of You, Remembering *- a suggestion for what I'm supposed to share. My mind goes into how, what, when, and all the details. One part of me* *thinks everything can be worked out, feeling reassured. I don't need to know, I hear, just need to be myself, be inspired, and record messages upon receiving them. Then collect stories of remembering. Bring together these links into the story and refine it. Start to put the little pieces together; the way and the inspired structure will be shown. There is a warm, encouraging fire in the heart - enthusiastic about this process as a healing journey through this medium. I can do it, I hear. It is a sign of what my heart's Fire and Will desire most for inspiring others.*

I see myself looking out a cave opening. It's so beautiful and bright out there. Courage pushes me to leave the cave and see what is there. We hold you. You can't do it wrong, as that is an incomplete view. You can take the steps forward in love. Create joy. Love your process. The order, structure, the foundation of truth, balance, and harmony is your signature. This is the aligned signature of your vibration. We hold, counsel, and show you. Be you. See us through you.

Light language transmissions came through and as I woke up, I could hear it in the room. So beautiful. Thank you.

Concept of Sharing

Strong messages surface here and there throughout the years. At times, these messages encourage me, and I feel a big *yes* inside. *I know it's right.* An intelligence from within is showing me that it comes from my true self.

Other times I completely look the other way. Here is the message: how about you share your story? It's a good story, and as you share it, you run a new frequency through your being. This is the process of transformation. The sharing itself.

My other self, who wants to look the other way, says, well, that's totally hideous, nobody cares about my story, no one is listening, and there is nothing special about it.

The light bead inside simplifies this for me, for my left brain-ego mind. You're right, there is nothing special, but sharing the story and experiences makes it special. Special means holding more light. The light expands into a new frequency, not just for you, but to support someone else's empowerment journey and growth on all levels. You may look at it as a *spiral staircase* (concept explained later).

There is no beginning or end, a spiral-like structure gracefully ascending. You keep going up the stairs and reach another round. Each step represents one version, one level, or one layer. You experience a collection of life versions. Once you complete the set, you continue on to the next, and so on. The movement is endless. So, as you share, you cultivate energy, which is then circulated throughout the spiral, allowing you to complete one set, then step up to the next, and see the series of steps in the next set, the next collection.

This concept of sharing has been difficult for me my entire life.

In my professional corporate career, I found myself to be influential and able to bring the message across. Sharing personal experiences would help people see a different point of view and improve ways of handling situations, especially because I had the privilege of working and learning from individuals of many different cultures.

As I navigated the spiritual training programs and learned different techniques, I found myself a bit annoyed when it was *sharing time* at the end of each training session. I mean, really? Why do we have to share? This is absurd. Nobody cares; actually, this is my personal experience, it's hard to put into words, and I'm pretty sure I'll butcher it as I open my mouth and try to express what's happening inside with *words*; words are so limited.

Sometimes when I refused to share, I became very annoyed with myself. My teacher could be seen taking a mental note of this. I received her messages telepathically so many times. *You're like a baby over here whining about your sharing.* I knew it was not only directed at me, but the teachings and reprimands definitely included me. Yes, that's right. I am behaving like a baby, and I just want to sit here and whine about it. I will not share. Why the hell do I have

to share!? This went on for a while. It was the beginning of openi
up into something I hadn't experienced before.

I suddenly got it, even if only intellectually at first. Sharing
circulates energy. Others listening will receive your energy, your
vibration, even if you're able to communicate only 1% of what you're
experiencing. I later understood in more depth that energy expands
and creates different qualities of vibration when we share - when
we express and communicate. Instead, when we hold it, it's like we
don't want to shine the light along this dark path we're walking.
Sharing is not for others to really listen (or not) to what you have to
say. It's for you and only you. If you circulate and contribute, you
expand and can hold more energy gathering from the Earth and the
Cosmos. An equal amount of giving and receiving will allow
improved energy circulation. Then, it can positively affect others
around you in a way that we cannot comprehend with our *thinking
processes*. The ripple effects are remarkable.

Without circulating energy, we become more discordant and
continue to create more *noise* - the implosion of dissonant sounds
our minds constantly make. Yes, minds in the plural. We have many
minds, which I like to explain as dimensions of self. When I speak of
mind, it is intelligence beyond thinking. I have always seen *thinking*
and emotions as two friends holding hands or interlocking arms,
walking, skipping around, and running together. One feeds the other
in a loop; that's their role (more on this later).

So, what happened? I still didn't want to share. My left brain-ego
mind was stubborn and persistent; that's her job. But I knew that
expressing anything at all was helpful anyway. So, I watched the
more experienced student-teachers. I copied their sharing: *my body
feels this and that, I experienced opening here and there, and this feels
tight, thank you so much for the training. That's it.* Simple. My head-
brain continued to chat about how much I was talking too much.
Simplify what's happening up there already!

I talked too much. Sometimes I still do. I struggled with this, as I had
a habit of going around and around, wow, so many words. As I was
awakening some parts of myself that led me to recognize I didn't
need so many words, I was experiencing conflict with the mind that

7

wanted to overly explain in multiple ways so that I could be understood, but with this crew, my teacher especially, there was no need for so much talking. Just like a slap in the face, I got it: wow, I do know the power of circulating energy through words. I now need to refine the use of this tool. The communication and expression energy were making noise. Why don't they teach us this when we're little?!

I've been experiencing a recalibration of the voice for the last 13 years. The voice as in frequency, light-sound, and vibration of my intention. As it is refining more, it can behave more like a *transfer device* that I am. Reflecting on the calculated experiences I placed myself in throughout my life, it's all so beautiful.

I see my higher self, one version of the higher self I have access to, as a giant being holding me in her hands as a precious gem. She's placing me in this and that scenario as if gently lowering me to the Earth and allowing me to navigate, look around, give, and receive, like when we have a puppy. She doesn't know any better, so sweet, walking this way, oh you can't go there, let's turn around and go this other way now. I feel such tenderness in my heart when I see my higher-self following me and watching after me as she placed me in particular situations to gain understanding and other situations to absorb other series of teachings.

I forgot when I started looking at a picture of myself as a small child. I was 2 years old in the picture I am referring to, maybe earlier. My mom is super cute, with her 70's hair, holding me in a bare kitchen in the apartment in Rome. I'm just so lovable, as I look at my eyes in this picture. I know so much. Then look at my mom's eyes, knowing she knows so much too. For a while, I kept returning to this picture to allow myself to be more compassionate toward who I am and how I choose to live; to look into those blue eyes, mine and my mom's, and say, you're doing so good; how lovable are you? You can do anything. Just keep going. I put that picture on my fridge so I could be reminded more often.

I have a vivid memory of me as a small child. It's bedtime. Dad was on the ship, and mom was in the bathroom getting ready for bed while I was already in her bedroom. I could sleep in my mom's bed when my dad was gone for an overnight trip. For me, this was wonderful because I didn't like to sleep alone. My father was a captain on a large ship. He was a strong leader, generous and flexible but firm. He met mom when he navigated the great oceans on oil tankers, a bit of a movie story. Years later, he worked locally in the Tyrrhenian Sea. Some of my most cherished moments were going on the ship with him for an overnight trip to Sardegna. It was the best for me; being pushed by the wind on the bridge, learning about the constellations, and eating delicious food. I loved it.

So, I often got to sleep with mom. On this occasion, I remember clearly, I was talking to *some friends*; this is what they felt like to me. There was a distinct feeling that more than one was there. We were having a full-on conversation as I was listening and responding, saying something about the blanket, and that it's ok they can sit here, as well as some other bits and pieces of a conversation. My mom entered the room and approached slowly as she heard me speaking. I was a bit startled by her, but didn't think anything of it. Mom was definitely freaked out at this point. She asked, are you ok? Who are you talking to? She was probably thinking I was talking to some ghost, something dark and evil. I could actually see it on her face. It was obvious that she was concerned about some entity swirling around, clearly worried, and scared. So, I played it down like I was just talking aloud and making lists or something. Don't worry, mà, I told her, it's nothing. I just like to talk out loud sometimes. I'm not talking to anyone, just myself.

As I spoke those words, the communication I received through my mind from these *friends* was something like this: ok, we got the message that it's risky to keep contact this way, she doesn't want to scare her mother. She is closing this door. We will communicate in other ways. I only nodded, afraid to speak through my voice out loud, but I was agreeing, quietly saying something like, I can hear you, totally aware of this inner conversation. I remember very distinctly that I thought this was something everyone does and knows how to do, but I simply figured my mom was afraid because of something I didn't know and left it at that, realizing then, that I had to be *careful*, whatever careful meant. I didn't overthink back then. Such glorious times - not to overthink!

I remember lying down and feeling embarrassed and sorry for being so stupid. My fantasy world created this situation where I would be seen as a freak-show while I just wanted to be accepted. At that moment, I closed parts of my heart, the vibration of a higher voice throughout my body, and I created a life on a different energy line. It literally felt like I grew a new energy line - parallel to the current pillar, toward the right side affecting the two right chambers of the heart, the three lobes of the right lung, the right kidney and adrenal, right arm and hand.

There is a great deal of multidimensional information revolving around the energy line - the pillar of light that runs along our spine, connecting us to the whole universe.

In the past few years, being reminded of these pillars of connection, I gained clarity on the development or simply awareness of other energy lines. This is true for me, which means it must also be true for others. We do have many levels of energy systems.
What is alignment? There are so many dimensions of *alignment*. Each individual is so unique, so the alignment path for one person may differ from the alignment path and choice for the other. Alignment is usually seen as a straight line and power spots connecting to each other on this one line, similar to the seven internal chakras and our spine; but I see it as much more complex than that.

The signature vibration of what is more predominant in the choices we make in life directs which path we are on. It's so fascinating to me that I was shown these other dimensional energy lines, not only what I can call a vertical line but also horizontal energy lines. Alignment is multi-faceted and multidimensional as the quality of the vibrations of each of our minds, which are the energy-spiritual bodies and higher dimensional energy systems. It's an exciting time to ignite the coming back online of these ancient guiding forces within and around ourselves.

2

ALIGNMENT

The Three Fires

It's early Sunday morning. I'm purifying and preparing my mind and body to receive as I practice shaking the body, also called total body vibration, while listening to beautiful Native American drumming. These sounds feel so comfortable and nurturing. They inform the mind of my body to recalibrate. It calms my heart and connects me to the deeper or, I should say, vaster aspects of who I am and what I hold.

This is something that I do daily. After shaking or tapping my whole body, I allow her to move with the energy flowing within and around me. Connecting with the sweetness inside, with my soul's bright, joyful voice merging with my spirit. Energy dance is soul language. Movement, sound, and vibration have been the key to the gates and doorways within and without.

A message enters my awareness, and my body experiences the same vibration and buzzing sensations I feel when I just know something is right, true, something I should record right away. A nudge from my guidance system. This is the signature. *I got it. Ok, I will write it down now.*

The three alignments. Three dimensions of alignment. *Sekhem,* the ancient hieroglyph for the lion goddess Sekhmet, beautifully represents these three qualities of fire energy.

The three fires symbolize the mind of the *body*, the mind of the *heart*, the mind of the *brain*. I see a correlation with the ancient Taoist teachings of the three dahnjons or dantiens. The lower abdomen holds the mind of the body, the center of the chest holds the soul, and the center of the brain holds the spirit. These three fires carry qualities of energy, we can't simplify by calling them *fires* although the vision shows a flame. It's an intense energy of potential, holding the balance between yin and yang.

The three alignments show the depth of our being. When we say alignment, many of us think of a straight line and things perfectly lined up with each other, like diligent soldiers. And that is true, but that's not the entire picture; it's one level of alignment.

This vision presents another way to view the phenomenon of alignment. On the physical level, alignment includes the internal energy centers, such as the seven chakras, the physical body's function, nervous systems, endocrine system, and so on. Preparing the expanded minds to commune and merge with the body's mind requires physical alignment.

Heart-mind or soul alignment represents the ongoing journey of opening to our entire range of emotions - the continuous refinement of purifying filters of heart-fire. One way to align the heart-mind is to feel energy with the five primary physical senses first, then expand to our energy and spiritual senses. Opening to our emotions does not mean reliving experiences that made us contract and create armors. It's more about bringing back all the parts of ourselves that we lost. Practicing neutrality is the primary work of the heart-mind. When we let the pendulum swing gracefully from side to side without huge swings. This is a universal law. It will inevitably swing right after it swings left. The degree of the swing toward the left depends on how much it swung toward the right. The more significant swings cause disruption, misalignment to the mind of the body, and uneasiness in our hearts.

Creating the space for neutrality is key, consciously observing the outpouring of opinions and making fewer evaluations. This includes mindfulness practice, noticing our bodies without judgment or distracting internal arguments. Then, seeing how the energy moves inside and outside our body. Here we practice refining the energy of the heart-mind, then allow it to expand effortlessly.

Soul alignment is a process that goes beyond the physical body. It was shown as a sphere pulsating outward in all directions. As it grows and matures, it expands more and more. The expansion allows the beads of light that were discarded in the past to come back as if we were a magnet for parts of ourselves that we lost along the way. We may not need the old framework of healing - we can try a less *mental* approach now - this is evolution. Expanding to the heart sense perceptions, the first layer of spiritual senses, well beyond the five or six senses - as thinking is a sense perception just like touch or smell.

I want to clarify that I absolutely value therapy work of any kind, although I refer to it as an *old framework* - this is simply my opinion. I have significantly benefited by finding support through a few excellent medical professionals. There was a time in my life when it was a necessary process. A wonderful therapist introduced me to mindfulness-based stress reduction (MBSR) through a multi-week program, which marked the beginning of the rest of my life.

The practice of *feeling energy* sounds simplistic, and we have so much wonderful information out there on how to do it. Each person will resonate with a particular teacher and follow this or that method. You're probably very familiar with yoga, breathwork, qigong, tai chi, and many other meditation practices. I feel that the work for us to go deeper and expand even more is advancing. These practices are truly outstanding and allow us to connect deeply.

The concept of what we hold, including our physical form, is so vast that I don't think our head-brain can fully grasp it. Actually, our way of thinking can't process it, and when I speak of *thinking* it's purely brain processing through filters of incomplete information.

We may get glimpses of our light vibration during memorable experiences of communing with spirit. The ethereal worlds are part of us just as a cell is part of our body. We ignore the cells because we can't see them. We only pay attention to our outer layers, such as dressing our bodies or what we surround ourselves with - meaning our possessions and what others see. The *invisible* aspects of our lives are awakening in so many, and fully stepping into this natural flow of life requires our systems to consciously dis-continue, de-construct, and re-generate.

Back to alignment. Soul alignment can be facilitated when the mind of our body is grounded, when we feel that gravity - the invisible force of Earth pulling us toward her. We are her; she is us. We can grow when we feel part of the Earth, know we have a purpose here, our body is strong, and we take care of it mindfully. Our bodies are the bridge to connecting to our higher minds. Through movement - internal and external - we can prepare our bodies to release discordant energies and allow communication from the depths of the Earth to merge with the mind of the body. This is very powerful and needed for our growth.

The head brain hosts specific functions of consciousness as it is an instrument of mastery including two currents of light, yin and yang. Two qualities of vibration and information. The mind of the spirit can descend as we expand awareness through the soul-mind, the heart-mind.

The head-brain processes information. Communication and energy packets travel upwards toward the brain as we get input through the funnel of our gut-brain and the heart's electromagnetic field. It is then processed like little boxes on a conveyor belt. But this conveyor belt has layers and layers of opinions, primarily unconscious thick layers that simply change the quality of these energy packets. The head-brain is extremely impressive but also causes enormous difficulties in our lives. In our modern world, we are taught that thinking is the master of all processing systems. We choose to place ourselves in this or that *box,* which comes with a specific type of thought process, anything else would be *out of the box* and interpreted as *wrong.* Allowing thinking to be the sole leader inevitably causes us to sever the connection to the heart-mind, and the body-mind suffers.

We presume that as we become older, we're deteriorating, and the body loses its vitality. And yes, that may occur, but vitality can be restored and sustained by other aspects of ourselves and our other minds. Vitality as a sense perception can be paid attention to, nurtured, and allowed to do its work. We all know the body heals naturally. That is the natural process of life. When our soul and spirit are completely disconnected, that is when we are not well, which results in increased loss of vitality, of life-force-energy.

We don't need to feel bad and blame ourselves. This is a journey we chose to experience. I am convinced we wanted to challenge ourselves, to see if we could wake up to all our beauty and light, and see what direction we would take. Our souls and spirit think our journey is all so interesting and impressive. They are hugging us, kissing us on the forehead, and holding our hand all the time. We're just a bit stubborn, let's say - walking around with inaccurate prescription lenses.

The brain holds so much power we can't really fully understand. As ancient hermetic alchemists experienced, only when our soul and spirit meet can we then experience the fullness of our being.

There are so many similarities with Taoist alchemical practices. They are very ancient and were only allowed to surface in the Western world in the last 50-60 years. Many wisdom teachings were held secret because humanity wants to grasp concepts with the head-brain, process, and then evaluate with outdated filters. Still, just like the language of light through sounds, movements, light, and vibration, these wisdom teachings can only be captured by the heart-mind, which is the direction we are heading and have been for quite some time.

The heart-mind has a unique intelligence. A specific quality of vibration that awakens the inner teacher and healer. It will direct energy exactly where it is needed and will guide our lives just like directing light to parts of the body or outer layers of the energy fields, here and in other dimensions. The heart-mind is a multi-layered compass, time capsule, and light technology instrument.

True alignment is aligning the three minds. Body, soul, spirit. Understand that these three words cannot fully encompass the vastness of what each represents. As we merge three fires in one, we can hold a new quality of light vibration. The body is deeply connected to Earth's wisdom, able to give and receive in equal amounts, purifying the vessel by upgrading this connection to Earth.

The soul has room; there is space in deep presence. Shining the brightness between light and dark, between future and past, this is the timeless space where we in-gather the scattered and lost beads of light - the spirit, the purest form of intelligence connected to our source of guidance. It can merge with the soul, providing clear vision, the lighthouse overlooking the vast ocean, increasing our ability to see our promises lying under the waves.

We have everyday lives. We have to go to the bank, and the post office, do house chores, deal with work, engage with family, friends, etc. etc.

So, this alignment stuff is all great and beautiful, but I'm busy; how do I get there? Well, just like anything else, it takes dedicated time to practice paying attention to yourself. No matter how busy we are, there must be a time when we have a wake-up call that something needs to shift. Some things need to change. An illness, a loss, a move elsewhere, a new position, a baby. We're busy, but when we have an internal alarm, and we ignore it, we go deeper into sleep mode until the minds of our body and soul will push us again. She could pay attention this time. Let's see.

This process is not malicious. We often feel resentment toward our bodies for experiencing pain. We end up identifying with our condition or that of our ancestors. Someone came to my studio once for healing sessions and KiGong training. As she introduced herself, she must have said, *I have Hashimoto,* I'm not exaggerating, about 12 times in the short five-minute conversation. Maybe she was hanging on to this condition very strongly for a reason, even though I was showing her my interest and was completely paying attention. She thought this was how it was supposed to be. *I am this thing, I've resigned from changing my vibration, this is who I am now.*

Our cells will do what we tell them to do. We can help, though, and determine who is talking to the cells and what we are actually saying. Let's be honest with ourselves. Let's really look at what we're saying, whether internal dialogue or externalizing our thoughts.

I always envisioned our new cells doing one of these scenarios: ok, so let's say we're in the liver. New cells form, and the old cells that are there wear these hideous bandanas. They are loud and obnoxious, they spit, smoke cigars that really stink, and they're really, really bossy. A new cell comes into this environment, and these old cells come to greet her, but it's more like a bullying situation. The new cell is surrounded by these other cells, and they yell at her, ok dude, this is how it is here. You've gotta make sure you adapt, and you behave just like us. We're pissed, I mean really pissed. We can't even remember why, but this is our MO. You're gonna be alright just as long as you become like us. Nobody else matters. If a spleen cell comes to you to check in and asks your opinion or wants to collaborate, you shove it back to where it came from, turn around, and return to your area. That's it. Got it?

Shocked and under such intimidation, the new cell absorbs this vibration and these messages. It's instantly perpetuating the same sound, or should I say noise... bandana, attitude, and all.

We know now, from the amazing work of Dr. Bruce Lipton, that our environment can change our cells. Yes, we have DNA, and yes, our ancestors gave us a bunch of information we hold in our body and in our energy fields, but our environment influences the expression of our genes. Internal environment and external environment. Moving to a new house or a new city can change things. I certainly know that type of change well. But changing the internal environment is the key to accessing our true, unique form of expression. Isn't it amazing? Isn't this where our entire focus should be?

The internal world echoes in the many, many layers of our energy fields. It's not this miniature space inside our body, instead, it's actually incredibly vast. I call them energy fields because as I see them, they are not just the energy body, astral body, or ethereal body, but also include the many layers of our spiritual bodies, so for simplifying, I just use the terms energy fields. Still, it's a much more complex system than what the words imply.

Going within and exploring the internal realms allows our minds to come together, collaborate, commune, and exchange. As a result, we expand and can hold more of our light; in this sense, we include our three fires - minds.

Going through this process by *thinking* about the spiritual realms is incomplete. Focusing only on our heart is not complete either. Being fully absorbed in our body is definitely incomplete work.

We are simply used to processing in categories, separating everything, even language creates this phenomenon. When we speak of inclusion, oneness, union, it implies the opposite, which is refined movement, pertaining to a reality that includes both polarity-vibrations - that is the alignment and mind-dimension intended in the work of upgrading. We become that quality of vibration along with Earth.

Reverence & Honor Toward the Work of Becoming

The *Wab* or *Uab* is one of my favorite hieroglyphs. *Uab* is the temple priestess and priest. This temple figure must be completely pure in order to handle temple affairs and to do the work of the god. The hieroglyph depicting the *Uab* is a leg with a vase tilting forward, pouring water, later adopted as the symbol of Aquarius. The meaning is that of purification. Prepare to enter the temple. Prepare for sacred work. When I see the *Uab*, it not only reminds me of the enormous importance of purifying our minds to do higher quality vibration-destined work, the work of our aligned self, but it also reminds me of bowing practice, which I learned as I began my training.

Bowing involves folding the upper body forward. In a half bow, we greet others and recognize our own divinity is reflected in the other; we are made of the same essence. As a full bow, we bring our forehead, chest, and palms to the Earth; we then rise, reconnecting to the skies, creating a full circle, a rhythmic motion emptying our minds, bridging the entire universe within and around our physical bodies. Through bowing practice, we also fully open our energy meridians and our internal chakra system as well as activate all of our joints, tendons, and muscles. It is such a beautiful practice, referred to as *sincerity training*. It is still the one type of training I will do before meeting with clients, as I prepare for sessions, and when I want to begin any kind of sacred work. I will also practice sincerity training when I'm struggling, tired, confused, and unsettled. This practice always allows me to return to spaciousness, presence, and neutrality, where I feel fully balanced and grounded. It's one practice that helps me show up and take care of myself, informing the minds that I am here and want to go deeper.

We used to do a half bow as we entered the main training room at the studio where I started my training. Since all the other more senior students did it, following the instructors of course, all the newbies would too. I really resonated with this simple act, even if so brief and apparently meaningless. It created an atmosphere of reverence. We're about to take care of our minds through our bodies, as we focus on our breathing, on all of the areas where our body and minds feel any kind of pain. We will ask to release the tension, stress, and anxiety we are feeling. This is special, and having a sense of devotion toward this work made me feel like I found something that really worked for me. It was a joyful and light atmosphere, but it was held in a container of reverence and devotion toward ourselves as the healers. The teachers could only guide us, we were the ones who had to do the work. Yes, this was definitely for me.

About three years later, when managing my own business, I felt the same sense of reverence when I gathered people in the studio. To me, the training room was alive; it literally was her own being. I would spend time cleaning and cleansing, not just ensuring it was super clean but also creating rituals for purification and transformation of energy. Any type of experience, whether a group class or individual session, was unique, and it was my responsibility to serve in my highest state. I think this aspect of myself was something I've always had since my hotel days. Of course, this is because I learned from the best, a five-diamond resort with the highest standards of service and products. I wanted people to focus on themselves deeply, so the external environment was also important. Cleanliness, lighting, sound, color, my vibration, and state of mind. This work was a new way of life, and although I didn't know where it would lead me, I had to do my best and move forward.

3

COMMUNICATION

Expression

Every few years, my dad would send my mom, my sister, and I to Oregon to visit mom's side of the family. We would usually stay a few months or all summer long. It was so great. I loved watching regular TV. The commercials were the best. Italian TV was so hideous to me. American television was way more interesting, I thought. My grandpa used to record the *Funniest Home Videos* show, dozens of episodes, also *The Guiding Light* for my mom, and some other shows. I remember we bought a small US TV and VCR to bring back to Italy. We used to receive these packages from my grandpa with several VHS tapes. It was so exciting. Mom was so happy every time we received a large package from grandpa. This was a way of connecting to her home, to her culture. From my view, it was my culture too. I felt a powerful connection with my mom in ways I could not understand then. Her desire to *go home* had always been so strong, and this homesickness was constantly present.

So, we would spend the summer at my grandparents' house in town and my aunt's property up in the mountains. It was like the wild west for me since we lived in the city. I was so intimidated by the woods, and extremely scared of the dark. Sometimes bears would come close to the house. My aunt would make comments such as, oh, that's bear poop on the front porch, watch out. I was like, really? We're probably gonna die tonight! My aunt had horses, and mom was raised to ride and care for horses since she was a little girl. Mom learned to ride on Walter Brennan's ranch and always yearned to have this part of the US back home in Italy.

Eventually, she did achieve her dream of importing quarter horses to Italy when my parents decided to buy a piece of land and build a house years later. The land is what mom wanted. Some piece of property to have horses, to train and take care of them, not just our own but to help others train and take care of their horses too. It was hard work, but she finally brought more of her own *home feeling* to the life in Italy.

Going back to the States to hang out with my American side of the family was wonderful, but strange at the same time. Like all families, there are deep wounds, lots of unsaid things, and hurtful experiences that nobody likes to talk about unless it's behind doors, while the sense of gossip and misunderstanding fills the air.

Many years later, when my dad could retire early from working on the ships, my parents decided to move to Oregon. Dad recalls that mom always said, when you retire, we can go to the States, right? So they did. They spent about 4 years there. She went first right when Grandpa was dying, and the plan was to just stay until dad could complete the retirement process, then get a small house and settle down. One thing became clear to my mom during this time more than ever. She belonged in Italy. Oregon was her home, and she missed it dearly, but she realized she had a better life in Italy. Some time passed, and she made the best of it, and so did my dad, who thoroughly enjoyed his time there, and even worked in a carpentry shop doing beautiful woodwork. They soon prepared to return to Italy.

I didn't know until much later that I had carried mom's yearning for home my entire life. As far as I can remember, I wanted to move to the States. It didn't matter what I would do or where I would be. I didn't care. I just had to go. On July 19th, 1994, I had my final Liceo exams, and was on a flight from Rome to Portland the next day. This was the first time I had left home.

Going back to the summer trips when I was a child. Upon our return to Italy in late August or September, I would have to start school right away. It was a nightmare. I hated it. I literally made myself sick with anxiety. Why? Because they made us read out loud in the classroom. I always had the same problem. Especially in the first month, or three. The hardest time in school for me was reading out loud. I had a difficult time switching back to Italian. When visiting Oregon in the summer, I communicated in English well enough but not like I did after moving there in 1994 and having a fully immersive experience.

I would talk to mom in Italian all the time. It was just unnatural to speak to her in English. Mom always spoke English to us, but we would respond in Italian. That's how it was. The trips to the grocery store were always quite interesting until they got to know mom and treated her like a *local*. At first, though, we always got strange looks. Mom would ask me what type of ham or bread I wanted, and I would respond in Italian. People were like, what is happening here? And it was the same even when we visited my Oregon family in the States.

With my cousins, we would always communicate effortlessly, but I can't remember how good my English was. I always felt so embarrassed when speaking out loud. Something else shut down in me. Another way to communicate was shut down by my observation of the outer world. I was continuously haunted by what others were saying about me, and the biggest dagger to my heart was my sister's compulsive repulsion toward me since I was born. These are strong words, but that is what it was like. Complete rejection for just being. Kids were mean, and so were my teachers for being impatient. I felt inadequate and small all the time.

And so, I kept operating this way. Each time I experienced feeling small and inadequate, to any degree, I would create stronger and thicker armors, compensating with other qualities like humor or being quick to think on my feet. Although I became a good communicator in later years, out of necessity for my profession, I always had severe anxiety about how I was expressing myself. This overwhelming wave of thought-emotion distortion was also caused by the strong sense of receiving too much information.

I would be leading a department meeting, or a simple staff meeting and kept being bombarded by what others were thinking and their expectations, modifying my talking points to address all of this input. At that time, I had no clue what an empath was or what in the world was happening. I simply avoided understanding completely and labeled it as extreme anxiety and an overly active mind. So, I would say to myself something like this, I should just have another coffee and a smoke, I will be just fine. I'll go to the gym again and come back to work, it'll be fine. *I'm fine* became my motto.

Returning to the notion of sharing, this aspect has been challenging for me since childhood, throughout my school years and professional career. I certainly managed to overcome these obstacles, driven by my determination to achieve success and lead exceptional teams, ensuring their needs were met. However, deep within, I had an overwhelming sense of not quite fitting in, leaving me feeling lost and frustrated. Whatever I tried to express was never quite right. Often, I blamed this struggle on the fact that I grew up in Italy and primarily studied in Italian, and I usually thought in Italian before thinking in another language.

Additionally, I strongly believed that my incomplete university education severely limited my vocabulary, causing me to doubt myself and feel inadequate. However, I now realize that these insecurities were not only rooted in my language skills or educational background. They were projections imposed upon me by others, influenced by the environment I was raised in, meaning my family, cultural history, and later my professional background. Despite appearing outwardly confident and capable, I harbored a deep-seated belief in my inadequacy - a conflict between pretending to be Wonder Woman and not knowing who I really was.

I was in Mexico, working for one of my all-time favorite properties. I will always remember this team as the best in the world. This was my first time seeing a team so focused on quality. The standards were incredibly high, and the team members were hardworking individuals and sincerely interested in helping each other succeed. Of course, there were occasional difficulties with some people, but overall, everyone was genuinely dedicated and aimed to excel in their work. I absolutely loved it. High standards, happy people, and support, this is my world. I experienced great success within that team, feeling like a rock star. Spanish, being my third language, was something I worked hard to master and communicate naturally in. I learned by listening and drawing connections between Latin, Italian, and Spanish. All I needed was a book of verbs. I wrote, spoke, and did my best to improve each day. It was far from easy, and there were moments when I felt so uncomfortable, but I was determined. I knew I could do it, even if I made mistakes here and there, people could still understand me. I was simply myself, even making jokes when I stumbled, and eventually, I became very comfortable with my communication style. Sure, it was tough work, but it remains the most fulfilling period of my career while speaking a third language. My communication challenges were not solely about language, but I would wear that difficulty like a tailored black suit that I never took off.

When I started learning and teaching mindfulness techniques to change one's energy, such as KiGong, and helping people see for themselves how they can improve the quality of their minds, I found myself increasingly drawn to a different form of communication. While someone can use words very effectively and be quite articulate in expressing themselves, alternatively, I realized I could receive such deep wisdom from my teacher, a lovely, petite Korean woman whose English is definitely not perfect. Along with other teachers I've encountered, she could transmit powerful energy and high-quality vibration while delivering profound messages through very simple language.

Words are powerful and should be used mindfully, and simple words can create a profound impact. Simplify. Throughout these years of intense personal growth, I received this consistent message: simplify. Simplify your mind, simplify your message. Consider what you convey to your minds, body, soul, and spirit. Contemplate the essence of your communication with others, which is how you communicate with yourself.

Light language allowed me to open up to another dimension of expression where communication with our minds, ancestors, guides, and companions can be more powerful and direct. Energy knows how and where to operate; it doesn't need the brain's thought processes to interfere. Such vibration levels lead to uncovering more of who we are, unveiling deeper layers of our true essence, and this ding process continues to shape and develop my path.

I've strongly wanted to share my story for so many years. I've shared this lengthy background to bring us to this point and understand what has been happening. My unique way of circulating energy is expressing myself in this manner, which feels like the perfect way for me right now. By sharing my story, I want to honor the part of me that has always supported and cherished me like a precious gem. They, my guides, and higher self, have shown me that this is something I've done before and will continue to do in the future.

This isn't just about me as an individual in this time and space; it's about the important process of becoming. My logical and protective side may be hesitant and judgmental, but my spirit and soul are ready to step up and out. They say *it's no longer a time to hide in a cave; it's time to face the world and embrace the doubts and fears, to enjoy everything with all of your rays.*

I have spent the past 47 years consciously and subconsciously seeking balance and alignment. I have been dedicated to sharing my experiences of change and helping others navigate and embrace change in their own lives. My ultimate goal is to live a life that supports the Earth and the people around me as we embark on the next phase of evolution.

There are various versions of ourselves, each representing a new awakening and a unique vibration quality. I receive messages from my guides, who encourage me to embrace the wisdom I gain and share it with others. This act of sharing is the essence of my work.

I am continuing to move through the limitations of the small mind, as they're not so loud and obnoxious anymore. Instead, I find myself guided by a lighter and brighter purpose, which resonates with a more profound and delightful sound.

Here are some words from the guides - *the current that moves the oceans is the mission. Create the ripple effects. The vibration of your Earth-Soul name holds the path. We hold you.*

Meditating with Seshet and Thoth

Reordering - declutter mind and space - outline the heart wants - align with higher will - merge fire energies - hold that fire within, this is YIN Fire, feminine divine leader, compassionate warrior technology, storing this energy deep within, using it for the soul and spirit merging into one and able to direct and lead it for the service of higher planes.

Follow the laws of the universe for darkness, light, space, and time. Be like the cosmic waters. Activate the Ren and Sekhem bodies—the vibration and will, the highest powers that hold your signature song.

The exploration is in the visionary world - dreamtime. Not a search to conquer, an exploration to reveal a journey of becoming. Access and journey to all bodies and planes of life. The skills and abilities you hold have been accumulating throughout the ages. See the guidance that is being recalled. Ask, and it's here to be given.

Purification to solidify the foundation. New ordering, foundation of communication, and energy lines are made brighter. Share as you learn/teach-teach/learn. Take one step forward, and the way is shown. If there is no movement, no path can be visible. Make your minds empty. The seed appears. It needs pure sunlight and air to grow. It knows and will recognize the vibrations, keep going. Now, the heart is the only thing that you can manage.

Letting the Heart-Mind Lead

The evolution of our becoming goes through the steps of a spiral staircase. We can't jump steps, we can try, but it would make one leg a bit unstable with the risk of falling. Sometimes this happens, and that is all perfectly designed, pain and all.

This process is natural law, universal law. As outlined in the sacred texts of the Chun Bu Kyung and the Hermetic teachings, our becoming is a sequence of transformations from one state to another.

The energy bodies are multi-layered, linked to the versions of our higher minds, higher as in faster vibration, different light spectrums, always linked and connected to Oneness - thus higher - receiving and transmitting information constantly. Whether the boundaries between each layer are ripped, bumpy, broken, or smooth, there is still a constant exchange. We reach the level of soul-mind when we feel like the superficial is no longer fulfilling. This is when we feel like we are in a t-shirt that's too tight, it simply doesn't fit. Nothing is good or bad, it just doesn't work anymore. We become discordant when we prolong the lingering in this mindset, which is a box, one container of one version of who we are. Things start to be more chaotic; we become sick and think things are unfortunate incidents, this fall or that sprain, the car accident, or the illness, but it's all part of that voice exchange between all the layers of our minds. When the conversation doesn't have cleansed and polished pathways - visualize a sponge absorbing streams of light instead of a path - the inevitable experience on the plane of matter is pain. A parallel experience occurs in the emotional plane. On the mental plane the unavoidable experience becomes confusion, such as heavy brain fog - a form of pain. The brain is the instrument for our spirit to connect to our soul. This is why we have two sides of the brain. Left-ego led, right-soul led. Spirit can access the center-zero-point when our head-brain is balanced. This phenomenon creates a lightning-like spark that ignites a different level of energy line connection between the three portals of the minds, the three dahnjons (dantiens), located in the lower abdomen, the center of the chest, and the center of the brain.

The opening to living in a version of ourselves led by the heart-mind is a challenging big step up the spiral staircase - the spiral structure being the ascension journey. Courage must be cultivated. Holding the vibration of courage allows us to maintain the level of consciousness that our bodies need to proceed forward. There is no going back; the mantra becomes *keep going, no matter what,* standing up tall with a bright face and sparkle in the eyes.

The risk is dis-ease. Another more considerable risk to be aware of is not living joyfully and being too serious. Why is this bigger than the dis-ease? Because the lack of joy and lightness causes all levels of dis-ease.

So much internal conflict arises when we experience this phenomenon. Suppose we could use a *translator* in the energy bodies; this conflict is always connected to an argument between our first levels of mind and our upgraded versions of mind. We use the terms *higher minds* because they *know better,* being closely resonant with Oneness. The translator would show dis-concert-ment, highlighting a mismatch of vibrations. We're basically making some serious noise, some awful sounds. Who wants to listen to disturbing music? You can find all the remarkable studies and research about the impact of vibration on water and matter. We are music. We are vibration.

I want to live a life where I choose to create a lovely melody that makes me joyful while maintaining courage, helping me to stand up tall, lifting my face up toward the sky, and fully receiving the sun rays. Raising my arms to the sides, feeling my spine arch back, exposing my throat, chest and belly to the Earth, nature, and universe, embracing infinity, merging with the universe. I want to *be* like the tree and all of nature, deeply interwoven, connected to each particle, the ecosystem itself. Experiencing my whole self, not just the little bits and pieces concerned with superficial minds.

Yes, I am the dreamer. Aren't we all supposed to be dreamers? Break free from the box. The box is the small self - you can linger there longer, no problem. It's a choice and our right to decide what journey we want to walk.

I want to flow, not walk. I want to break through all the boxes, to live surrounded by light reflections of my mind, opening to more of who I am now. Heart-Mind is the mission.

Dream Visions of Earth

Expansion of consciousness would be incomplete if we cannot fully merge with the Earth-Soul.

Earth has worked hard to provide us with alive intelligence running through our bodies. You must root at the gateway in the center of the Earth. Make room for conversations with Earth.

Insight From the Study Hall

Rewrite the story. This is a gift. Clearing the path as we shine light into your own study hall - your library.

I see my guides making adjustments to my manuscripts of life. We are in my study hall, and they're rearranging the order of some of my books. Moving some of them from one part of a shelf to another, dusting some other areas. Lots is happening in my study hall; they are so busy. The group is so loving and bright. They are showing me an upgraded version of light. I am surrounded by this light layer as if it was an elaborate gown, while I am being prepared to have a formal meeting. In the dream, I know it is a veil of a distinct light frequency. I am alone with them now. We are starting this big meeting; it is literally like a department meeting. I have a sense of reverence and respect. We are ready to be with each other. We are all here for one shared mission, each having the same caliber of responsibility. They are so very pleasant, and I am reassured that everything is as it should; to go and shine bright. I am on the new, brighter time-space continuum and moving beyond those old versions of my story. They communicate.

This next phase is about connecting with the wisdom and messages of the Earth. Earth will share what you need to know at the right time over-passing fear, doubt, and confusion. The light beings send Earth messages tuned to your sound. She will guide you step by step. Trust and follow, knowing we are with you through the Earth. She is the great transfer device of information, which is precisely what you are, too.

Our light spectrum vibrations connect with you through the Earth's grids and points. You must root at the gateway in the center of the Earth. There you find the source of everything you need. Step by step, she will show you. The ancient gifts, the shields of protection, can transform into higher forms of love expression. The heart of the source of all that is constantly breathing with you. This is the wisdom you receive through the rhythm and breath of the Earth. You are this

30

light frequency. Maintain groundedness and centeredness in order to expand more.

You are allowing your light to move past your self-imposed limits, and you are moving beyond them. Step out and forward. The pain is a reflection of the patterns. Fears and strings from this and other lives that created inner conflict are lifting. This is the awakening into trust. As you receive energy, you will see the way. We hold you and support you.

When You Heal, The Earth Heals

Earth is releasing information through packets of data - significant bits of information that contain ancient technology - using intention and nonphysical eyes, ears, and movement to master the purification of energy. There are streams of light rising from places within the Earth, strings vibrating faster and faster. You can barely detect this fast movement - it looks like one line, a stream. It's a myriad of beads of light linked all together forming lines. They are of different lengths.

The Earth's breaths and these strings hum, pulsating in brighter light, moving in rhythm. Some get longer, then shorter. They are alive. These streams of light look like a series of lighthouses shining their light upward toward the sky. The Earth turned them on recently, circa 2010, and they've been delivering more info packets. More and more are visible and perceptible now. From a distance, the entire Earth looks like a sparkling ball with light beams moving outward. People feel some effects, actually feel a lot of impacts, but don't recognize fully what this is.

The Earth is gradually sending or emanating this quality information - energy - so we can adjust slowly. It's so gracefully cautious about how we adapt. The energy holds all the information on ancient Earth. It contains all our influences from the universe. Many people might experience the low vibration of what needs to be resolved. The circulation of physical actions moves and purges the low quality of contraction energy, to be connected with the assimilation of pure energy. A quality of energy that we have not experienced before. This is why it takes us humans time to adjust and integrate.

31

We are seeing more, hearing more, and calibrating to this energy. The Earth needs resilience to support her as a whole in this next phase. When you heal, the Earth heals. She waits for us. She is providing us with all the information to go through this process. A more extensive creation process is happening, and we are absorbing this communication.

Refrain from concerning yourself with the small-self-tasks for you to mean something or stand out. Others in humanity are silently experiencing these visions of light and listening to messages from Earth herself. Make room for this type of conversation.

Earth Preparing Us for Clarity

I find myself in a daze, a feeling of being surrounded by a cloudy substance. As I move around, it's moving with me. There is an opening and reverence to what I can only describe as seeing my life like a series of activations and bits of code packets being presented to me. Moving into the space of composition, I can now put them together.

Looking through the memory reflection pools, I found myself drawn to specific teachings in many instances, but now, more than before, I see they are all connected to the same wisdom teachers. The story of my life in this time-space is in a bubble of activated wisdom as the journey to what's to come. I am in awe of this overview and expansive feeling. The true essence, guided to one corner of the world, then the next, and the next, has facilitated my discovery of this state of awareness. Something has turned on, yet it's just a small, minute glimpse into the most illumined parts of the journey. This cocoon I find myself in seems like a protective field and, simultaneously, an activation body. I am guided once again to the ancient mysteries and texts, and I am seeing the opening of a new way of perceiving the laws, a more expanded, clear view of how to be. I am overwhelmed by the work ahead, yet I also know I will find the words, the connections, and the frequencies. Now is a time when the Earth has prepared humanity for clarity. It is through the Earth that humanity can find the sound-vibration-light of Soul.

Many wisdom teachings of ancient times have activated a level of light vibration unique to this era, such as light, sound, vibration of a different category and quality. Sources of knowledge as we know this word in the mental body are calibrated to their original coding. There is a deep opening to the original code transmitted to Earth-Humanity. We have lost our original mind in scattered pieces, experiencing portions of ourselves, stopping at one or few versions of one tune, neglecting to seek the entire composition. At no fault of our own, out of pure innocent small-mind seeking to return home. Tools and beautiful words express many ways and principles of how to return home while creating even deeper gaps, creating attachments, and confusion.

The original code shared with the purest quality of love is available to everyone. Earth has worked hard to provide us with alive intelligence running through our bodies. The cosmos recognizes this refinement and matches its delivery codes to this unique emergence. What draws into our hearts is a vast convergence that calls for a new version of us and the Earth. The ancient ones lead us to freedom by awakening us to these different qualities of light, sound, and vibration spectrums available always yet perceivable only now.

4

HEALING

Ongoing Process

Healing work is an ongoing process, and I've come to understand and appreciate this truth. We often hear a lot about healing, and people are drawn to anything associated with the word healing and willing to do whatever it takes. However, healing occurs even without our conscious presence. It's a natural phenomenon that is constantly flowing, much like our breath or the circulation of blood in our veins, as well as the energy coursing through our meridians and inner and outer energy centers.

It's always happening. This is not a one-time event where something miraculous occurs, like taking a powerful Earth medicine or embarking on past life journeys to uncover blocks, attending a couple of training classes or retreats, and then it's done. Healing has no distinct beginning or end; it follows universal law. However, the Earth's resources, enjoying soul journeys to view some of the wisdom we've accumulated throughout other lifetimes, and taking care of our inner world through the powerful container of a retreat are enlightening and can provide us profound direction and structure - a needed doorway to continue on our journey.

Through these events, we literally become *lighter* in brightness, and that is the key to powerful healing. This process, though, happens regardless. When we become a little more aware of who we are, what we want to create, what we are ready to face, accept, and then follow the steps to literally be there for our own selves as the most precious friend you could ever have, that is when healing magic occurs. It results from alignment to our higher will, alignment with the original signature of our Soul. This level of opening is what the ancient people in East Asia called the elixir, sourced from the lower dahnjon (dantien) energy complex. Once revived, then how can we *be* and what can we *do* with this innate healing power?

When I explored the sacred words of power within the Chun Bu Kyung, I focused on the eternal principle of one mind continuously evolving. Although there seems to be a starting point, there is no true beginning or end. It all originates and culminates in unity.

I dedicated myself to studying these characters, which are light codes, light language, comprising 81 characters that hold multidimensional wisdom passed down through ancient teachers who evolved by sharing a particular quality of vibration. Similar sharing and transmission occurred in the ancient times of Lemuria and then Atlantis. The sacred words of the Chun Bu Kyung resonate with and resemble the ancient Hermetic principles. I am continuously expanding my exploration of this work, and although I won't extensively dive into it here, I continue to receive guidance with sincere openness, which will enable me to offer further insights and details regarding this topic in the future - including how the vibration of these symbols and principles are embedded in our physical form and energy bodies.

And so, healing is ongoing. I came across Light Language through a talented and bright healing artist who had developed her own method of expansion. Intrigued, I felt guided to learn more.

Light Language is a form of advanced technology, and most people are awakening to this primordial natural form of communication. Opening myself to it felt like a reawakening - a familiar essence returning to me. A safe passage was being created for me to navigate through the protective barriers I had constructed, breaking through those layers with powerful bursts of energizing lightning. Reflecting back, I had no idea of the significance of those experiences. I had undergone numerous *initiations* through my personal training journey in ancient SunDo KiGong practices, creating a deep connection with my true self. However, through Light Language, my guidance system, including my highest self and guides, would communicate more directly with the inner teacher and healer. I felt as if I was entering a deep cycle within a giant washing machine, setting things up for a new evolution - a revolution of the spiral.

During this process, forgotten qualities of vibrations within me began to resurface. I experienced different aches and pains, swirling emotions and thoughts, new energy sensations, and other sense perceptions that became normal to me as the physical senses. My Soul, Spirit, and guides supported me as I connected through active dreaming, inspired journeys, music, writing, and movement.

The most remarkable aspect was the beauty and elevated quality of vibration transmitted through this form of communication. Previously, I had experienced inspired movement, practicing it daily through KiGong. I had also witnessed others transmitting Light Language during healing sessions. However, when I surrendered to this natural flow of technology within and without, embracing my voice frequency and the intelligence of my body, it was truly magical.

There is no right or wrong way to embrace Light Language. While one might resonate with certain expressions and not with others, the true essence of the message lies in the vibrational transmission, delivered in different forms through us acting as a transfer device. Consider singing, for example. A singer may create amazing sounds using their vocal cords, which is a gift. However, those who don't possess such a gift can offer powerful uplifting and bright quality of energy that may sound like a different form of song, creating, and transmitting a unique sound through energy words. The same principle applies to conveying energy through writing, drawing, or movement - it is all art, wouldn't you agree? We are all artists, each carrying a unique signature vibration. We all hold a beautiful Soul song. If we can open up to this knowing more and more, the benefits to humanity and Earth would be monumental.

Everyone should consider themselves an artist, and any creation emerging from a pure, expansive state through deep presence is inherently beautiful and impactful.

Since my introduction to Light Language, my focus on the diligent practice of emptying my mind, expanding my inner spaciousness, and amplifying my *other* senses was greatly enhanced.

I can fully accept my role as a transfer device, allowing more aspects of myself to flow through and deliver what I feel in each moment, whether working with an individual or a group.

Dreams ~ Visions ~ Journeys

Psychic Attack

I'm in a large bedroom. It's someone's house. I'm entering as the healer, approaching a client lying on the bed. She is clothed but has some exposed skin. At first, I thought it was someone I knew, but then I realized I did not recognize this person. She's older, fragile. I begin rocking her gently, but she's so weak she's uncomfortable and begins to complain. She rolls to her left side, gets up, and starts putting some more layers on, seeming disappointed and a little upset. I pause and notice. Suddenly another woman appears in front of me. An assistant. She's a younger woman with long black hair pulled back slightly. I can see her face clearly, stunning, large piercing eyes. She's wearing what seems like a long lilac summer dress. She's suddenly in front of me, sitting and laying out two stacks of square napkins. Asks for my hands to come forth. The napkins are upside down, and I notice the inseam faces up. I extend my arms, palms up. The woman is smiling slightly, like a Monalisa smile. She begins wrapping my left hand with a purple napkin; her energy is powerful and almost forceful. I'm pulled in. She then asks for my right hand, puts one napkin over my middle two fingers, then another over my whole hand. As she does this, she is also chanting, singing, and humming... a sound-vibration is coming from her.

I am just observing, recognizing I'm in some trance and starting to feel unwell. She looks at me and says 'smile'...so I do, then keeps telling me to smile, smile, smile. Stronger and more potent are the magnetic sensations all around. I feel my arms and hands being pulled toward her with force. I keep smiling but now feel downright uncomfortable. In an instant, a massive wave of energy comes from her that pushes me away. It's like I was hit and flown across the room. I see myself lying flat on the floor, with an intense sensation on my neck, chest, and solar plexus. As if she was pushing down on my neck and chest, although she never moved from that chair folding the napkins. With such immense pressure, I can't breathe at all. As soon as I feel this wave and am pushed away with suffocating pressure, I hear her question through telepathy; she says, "What did you say to us?" ... I feel such pressure; it is hard to breathe, and I think, what did I just think and project to them?

Now I just focus on my lack of breath, feeling my panic and heartbeat growing. I try to scream, hearing my physical body try to scream. In a flash, another part of me steps forward. Focusing on my light within, I let go of fear and see it expanding outward as a protection capsule, trying to push this force away from my space, saying to my brain, I don't want this! with conviction and powerful intention. Immediately the pressure is off of me entirely. As I open my eyes and catch my breath, I realize this really happened, and it was an attack. Closing my eyes, I'm back in the scene, opening my eyes, I'm catching my breath here in my room.

My mind first went to recover my light, to expand it brighter and wider for fear that I would return to being attacked.

I lied quietly while focusing on downloading pure cosmic energy for protection, calling my guides and higher consciousness beings, along with my companions, my mom, and my higher self, for protection and reassurance that I would be safe. I slept the rest of the night and do not recall any other encounters since then.

Companions

Two white Tigers, one big and one smaller. Just sitting, looking at me, sending messages.

Then an image of me floating in the ocean. A little unsettled at first, but then I knew to call the giant Whale to support me. She gently came up from the deep, approaching me so softly. I felt the nudge behind and trusted she would know how to support me. I let go and didn't fuss, noticing her eyes were carefully watching me. She was lifting and carrying me through the ocean. I had no worries at all.

Light at the Bottom of the Ocean

I see these kitties in front of me. It seems like I'm in a bright cave. Bright because light emanates from the cave's floor, underwater, not from above. I'm in the ocean.

The cats are sitting in water, breathing comfortably and the top of their backs are out of the water; it's shallow. I'm standing behind them, feet in the water up to my shins, and they're waiting for me to keep going. There is someone else around me. I can't tell who it is. Someone watching after me. I feel comfortable following the cats, so I continue.

I'm walking further into the water. The area is lit up; it's bright, so vast as I keep going. In the dream, I hear myself, maybe this is not water; perhaps I'll be breathing some kind of plasma or liquid that won't make me drown, then I see that I clearly don't care, it's irrelevant in this realm, and I just go in. The cats are just walking on the bottom of the ocean floor, not floating up to the surface.

I briefly wake up, finding myself in the sleep-awake state. Requesting to reenter, let's go back there; what is this place? Once again, the water world appears in my mind screen. Floating, I see above the water massive cliffs similar to the Grand Canyon but more rounded, old rocks towering over me. Looking below, there is light all around coming from the bottom of the ocean. The water is really deep, and the area right below me goes so far in the deep canyons. I can now clearly see a huge city down there, noticing my location so far up, looking through the depths of the water, and hearing myself speak my intention to go down there, thinking, seems pretty lonely up here. There is a sky, but it's not like the Earth's. I didn't notice anything else, except I see the cats, who guided me here, and they telepathically tell me to come down.

I'm mesmerized and so enthusiastic as I swim without any breathing restrictions. Within the dream, I ask to turn around to see myself floating in the ocean, heading toward this city. I have large, bright

40

eyes and a huge smile on my face. I am a giant being, and I feel so at home. As I swim around, I am drawn to go deeper and deeper. I know I'm supposed to go there. This is so wonderful. I know this place.

We Accompany You

Smile, for you are light.
Clear in your eyes.
Power through your words.
Love within and through your heart.
Do not shrivel or lose the way. You-we are light.
I am here. "I" is us. And us is the All.
My-your light keeps opening to All where your-our knowing is, lives, breaths.
There is no time. All is now. Inside you-us. Trust light. Guide others in light. There is nothing else but light.
We accompany you. We feel you rigid in the need to know. However, knowing is already there.
Step back and see with your-All-senses. Beyond what you already know are limits of your physical senses. All is within. We are the All. Rest in All-knowing. In All-light.
Keep the pouring from the eyes of light itself. The throat of expression. The heart of connection.
We are you. We are All.

Atia

Vision after light language transmission and request to connect with the guides.

In the distant now, you revered the creator through its ambassador order in Atia. So grateful to channel this glorious energy as oracle, for bringing healing to your people was the mission. Only a few really knew and understood. Many were your enemies. Many sought to destroy you and everything you held. You ran and ran. You were protected but kept running until old age. Others continued to seek your counsel and energy. They could see. You healed Earth and many of her creatures. Small and large creatures with so much love for you, the healer. Trees were your home. Ocean, your protector. The gods kept you safe. Alone in the journey of healing.

While in active dream state, I recorded and then asked the following questions:

Where is this?
- *This is in the area now known as Anatolia, in Turkey.*

What do I look like?
- *A woman of specific order and rank. Tall, strong, and defined features, big shoulders, squarish jaw. Piercing, dark, shining eyes, full lips, glowing dark skin. Barefoot. Long gown, open to the sides. Legs exposed. Jewels, bracelets on arms, and a headdress. Feathers attached to the shoulder cover. Weapon-type devices as hair decorations and belt components.*

When?
- *2500-2300 BCE*

Healing Journey - A Reminder of Love
White disc of brilliant light moving outward from the center of 6th chakra portal - blue outer light.

Pink wave of energy - a warm summer wind - straightening the energy line. Who are you? I ask. We are here to provide support - to help guide you to the next phase. Observing struggle, we invite you to let go of everything, for we surround you in pink waves and sheets of beauty and grace - emerge from confusion.

Yellow triangle opening in front of me. I am in the triangle. A sphere hovers inside. I can see through its outer core - vastness of space within. I hear light language sounds-vibration. Multiple beings sharing messages. Feeling grateful, loved, supported. Can I stay here and learn more? I ask. You are here with us now and all-time. Focus on being here, and you can open up more. A being comes from the distance behind the others. Immediately I know it's mom - such bright, blue eyes. She is showing me something familiar, the eyes, for me to recognize this energy. Please stay connected, they say, as I receive a warm, nurturing, caring touch.

I receive something in my hand. It's something I can wear or carry. I can see it's a little heart pendant mom wore long ago. I have it, it's on my table. Use this to connect with us. Stay pure. We love you. Back through the triangle - the 6th center portal. I close my eyes, and I'm there. I open my eyes, and I'm here. Thank you.

Let Go, Be Free

Clarity may be painful as you shed and detox your mind. Clear and bring harmony to everything. Become the light you are. Do not rest in dust. Allow transformation and change to cleanse inner and outer environments. You are protected. You are the teacher-learner. Go forth with open chest to give, for you will much receive. To expand and create means unknown becomes known. Learning-teaching continues and creates new ways for transformation and sharing. Let go. Be free.

Another Dimension Self

I am somewhere else, another world. As my eyes open, the vivid colors mesmerize me. There is such bright green grass and trees infused with the brilliant orange rays of sunlight. I feel the warmth of the sun's rays. Everything is alive. There is a deep sense of joy and wonder as I look around, noticing my body feeling so light. As I slowly stand up, my feet barely touch the ground. I am not really sinking in the dirt or grass. My skin looks luminous, and my hair is flowing gracefully in the wind. My whole body is actually floating. An insect-like animal slowly approaches me, but I am not scared.

In the distance, there is a being waving at me, then keeps walking forward, as if they have just seen a friend, waving hello. A fox is coming out curious about me being there; then it goes on to wherever it is going. From behind, something is approaching, I look back, and it's a giant cat. She meows, then comes by me and brushes her head on my body to say hello. I feel such warm and loving energy from this beautiful cat. She is here to help me and guide me. Her role is instantly clear to me. I am walking toward the trees. My body is so light; there is space, I get close to the tree, and then I become the tree itself. My eyes and my smile appear on the tree bark; there are others like me becoming trees, then I decide to move higher. As I look up, a tree branch lifts me to reach a higher branch. My view expands, and in the distance, there is a large body of water, it looks like there is a beach. Thinking, I want to go there, I am immediately brought to the shore. It's sandy, but my feet are not sinking in the sand. The cat being is near me, strolling, catlike; she's so smooth. A giant turtle makes its way to me to greet me; she's so cute.

Then I see a little tiny being, he's white, on my index finger. It is literally the size of half my finger, if that. He's so small and joyful. He's greeting me too, looking so excited. I can now fully see my face in this world. My eyes are bigger and different; there is an extra tiny pupil. I have two pupils. The color is blue-gray and sparkling. My smile is so beautiful, and I'm glowing. My hair seems a bit longer than it is now, it's floating in the air, and it is so soft, lots of white and gray. I notice my body feels so good. I love the way I look. The clothing I have on makes me feel so good and comfortable.

Then in the distance, over the water, I see something that looks like a structure coming from under the water. There are many spikes that look like the top of a skyscraper, beautiful and shiny, and look like jelly-like liquid substance, shimmering blues-white-green-purple. Wow, I have to go there. The big cat telepathically tells me to follow. I think in my mind, how do I walk underwater if I can't stay on the ground so well? I might float. She responds right away; all I have to do is intend to walk underwater to reach the structure.

So, I immediately see myself walking in the water. I become heavier and proceed with the cat, the turtle, and the little being on my finger. We approach the structure, which is actually many, all connected. I am mesmerized by the colors in the water; the cat is at the bottom of the ocean floor, walking smoothly; I am floating, playing in the water, swimming, and am extremely joyful. Then I see this structure as we get a bit closer. It is massive. I didn't realize it was so big. On one side, I see millions of these little, tiny beings, just like the white one that came to greet me on my finger before. They are all looking toward me, and they get so excited. Everyone is welcoming me. They have different colors.

Wow! All communication is instant and happens telepathically. I ask a few that approach why they're of different colors. I see pink, these are healers. The darker green are teachers. White ones, these are ambassadors. I see gray ones, and they seem hard at work, they are like nurses and surgeons of the group, and they care for the sick. All these little pink and gray ones start climbing up my body, and some just float over. They are on my arm, taking a closer look. Some come to my face and give me little kisses, touching my cheeks with their tiny hands. There is brightness in their faces; they glow. I am so excited to see this. I know I'm in the right place.

While swimming and floating over here, I could see various ocean-like beings, a strange-looking dolphin, and different types of rays. Now in the distance, I see a super-giant being. It is slender, and the body is sort of bluish-white and shimmering. It wears some sort of flowy gown, a long piece of clothing. She welcomes me and talks in the 'we' person. We want you to connect and remember these aspects of yourself. How you see this world and what lives in it is here for you to connect with more. I have lots happening in my mind, many questions, and comments, and I really feel like I can't keep up. She says a few times that this is all for now, patience, you will be relearning more, you will see more. Bring back some of these aspects of yourself. We are here for you and your growth.

I have the sense that my time here is short. The tiny pink beings start coming to my left clavicle and insert a few of what seem like tiny stones or crystals, maybe 3 or 4, on my chest; then others, the green ones, put some other series of stones along the right side of my back, from my shoulder blade down. My arms are open to the sides. I know they are administering some sort of healing technology. Then the giant being puts a small stone on top of my head, which merges with my body, sinking in my brain. The stone is a pinkish crystal, not so big. I'm fading. Then I feel like I'm moving back, being pulled back, away from this area I'm in.

Now, I look toward my cat, and she's starting to move back with me; she was instructed to help me walk back. I turn toward her and ask her name... I hear the letters SI or SSI, I try different sounds, and then land on ESSIA. I am fading. Everything starts to be fuzzy. I ask what my name is... it's blurry. Some of the tiny beings come with. I am leaving and suddenly feel an incredible amount of love in my heart and simultaneously a sense of sadness. I do not want to leave. The giant being reassures me that they are here for me and that I will be back.

I feel myself back here, breathing, feeling my heartbeat. My eyes stay closed a bit longer, lingering in the beautiful sense of this world, in the images my mind holds. I am mesmerized.

Running Alone

I'm in my early thirties, a woman, wearing lots of layers. It seems very cold. It's northern Europe, a long time ago. There is a conflict, and I'm alone carrying a heavy bag, all of my belongings, what is left at least, walking alone, away from where I'm from. I am shown I am a teacher, and have cared for many children. There is some form of attack, and I have to get the children to safety. I kill a few of the perpetrators and attackers, then have to flee, leaving the kids and some other caretakers alone, but they are safe, hidden away. I run alone; the aggressors will come after me eventually, and I absolutely must leave. I then approach this forest, feeling hesitant, but walk in anyway. There is a group of women, strong women. They are doubtful of me at first but soon welcome me in. I immediately connect with one in particular. I spend some time there and have an intimate friendship with this woman. It's a tough life, but the community feels like home. We are all very independent, with high ideals.

Then, there is a time when I have to flee again; somehow, a few of these women come along with me, and we run together. We hold several weapons. There is a flash, and I see myself fall. There are rocks, and a horse stomps over me. I die. When I ask my guides why I am seeing this particular life experience, they respond that I have to keep the high ideals and that it is a valuable life to live. The determination to restore this ideal is the purpose.

I'm grateful to see the ease of connecting and receiving this information. I trust that this life is shown to make me more confident and that the qualities in that strong woman are in me now.

Contact - Crafts and Way Station

I'm on what seems like a deck on a boat, from my memories of being *on the ships with my dad. There are several people. I'm off to the side on a bench next to another person but don't know who it is. Then in the distance, we all see three, maybe four, crafts approaching. At first, I can't tell what it is besides the thought of them being weird planes. Then as they come closer to the ship, flying by, I can see they are white and look like a big Tic Tac, but they have some extension on the side. There is one that's closer to the ship, coming from the left side and moving slowly, then it sort of quickly turns around and comes back moving even closer. The other Tic Tac crafts are waiting in the distance.*

I'm able to detect so many details. It looks like a big white pill. From the sides, it has what looks like extensions. One side has a longer one, which moves up to the top of the craft. It's like lifting its arm. I can describe this arm-extension as a cylinder with a lens on the outer tip with rounded, smooth edges. This extension is passing close by and scanning all the people. I say scanning because a beam shining a laser scan emanates from the apparatus. The entire thing looks shiny, then it moves in front of where I am standing, pauses, and comes closer. It moves so that the front of the Tic Tac shape is facing me. In the dream vision, I know this is probably the front. Then I see it change, becoming a huge spotlight, beaming like a giant flashlight. It isn't blinding but extremely bright to look at directly. It's flashing, and seems like it's taking pictures. The impression is like a camera when it takes a series of photos, and the light keeps flashing very rapidly. I can sense the warmth of this light on my face, not feeling scared. It's targeting me. I also recognize these flashes of light and their rhythm; it makes me think of morse-code messages, as some form of information exchange.

Then a big puff shoots out, it's quite strong as it moves my whole body, again not feeling frightened. It feels like a gush of sudden strong wind, like when you get an eye exam, and they check the pressure by blowing a puff of air in the eye. It feels exactly like that but on a total body scale, then the light goes out. My body is being scanned up and down a few times by a laser or transparent light of some sort. There is a humming sound. In my mind, I ask who this is. A thought and sound come in right away. Zetas, they answer.

The craft then backs up a little, moves in its position toward the other vessels, and then they all suddenly leave. Physical sensations are so real; my face is smiling, and I'm flooded with a sense of wonder and excitement, wanting to know more.

Shortly after, I have an image of being in a large hall, like a mall area, with many people; it looks like a gathering place. It literally feels like an extremely large mall, with a food court area, several store-like venues, and sitting areas. In the dream, I think we are off the boat in a holding area, like a terminal of some sort, then I actually realize we're in an enormous way station - this is another dimensional craft station. I then see Jason come to meet me from a distance. We embrace, and I'm so excited to see him. I tell him about the experience of seeing the Tic Tac crafts and the scanning, the light, the puff of air. Besides what I remember and describe above, I'm also telling him other stories. Some are so emotional, I feel like I haven't seen him in a while, and that what I went through was intense. Talking and being together brings tears to my eyes, feeling like I'm safe now and can finally relax. Within the dream, I can see myself recognize so much that has happened, and begin to remember. This place looks very modern, bright, beautiful, and clean. People are greeted by their families and friends. It seems like a very happy and safe place. It feels so comfortable. This is a place where we could all recover from the long journey we just experienced.

Upon waking, I knew I was somewhere else. I am feeling grateful that I could return with these memories, but also know so much has been blocked out. Was this a recall of a parallel life? I know this experience actually happened.

Meeting the Guides

I connect the energy line and adjust my posture, observing the feeling of going higher, but also deeper within, an intense inward motion.

A being appears in the forefront, then a few others. I have the impression there are many at a distance. I feel a big wave motion, a strong wind. Suddenly a face comes forth. It's a tall being, coming down toward me as if she's kneeling. She wears a light-colored silky scarf over her head, the face shaped like a heart, cat-like, very sweet.

She comes closer to me; her hands reach forward caressing my face with such loving eyes. I feel my heart swell, and tears roll down. I can now see these other beings. One that steps forward a bit more is a shorter, elderly being with a cane. All the other tall beings around him look like floating clusters of light. I can almost see figures, but they're very subtle, almost blurry, there is mostly light. A big cat stands up, comes behind me, and stays close to me. I'm encouraged to ask for my guide to come forth. As soon as I ask for a guide to come forward, one being steps right out of the circle toward me, walking in confidence. I can suddenly see his body more clearly.

Through the light a glowing body forms. I can see more of his outline. The energy feels feminine and motherly, very nurturing, although he appears as a male figure to me. He's a beautiful, tall being, moving smoothly like a martial artist. He is wearing a long robe over other clothing. It's flowing as he walks toward me. He then sits down in front of me with his legs crossed, and immediately makes a connection with the heart. There is a bright, sparkling string of light that he pulls from my heart and connects to his. He begins to maneuver it around my throat and head, then around my waist and connects it to his body. It looks like he's connecting my energy centers to his. He proceeds with making some gestures with his right hand, it's a light code, light language. He works on the top of my forehead, drawing a shape, and continues to transmit light signs in the air. I can clearly see codes of light moving in a straight line across my heart, then in 4 directions, resembling lines crossing, then stemming from my heart outward horizontally, expanding even further, creating a spinning wheel - a series of lines shooting out from my heart. In the next moment, there is a vertical line connecting to this wheel. I recognize this ancient language code - the whole thing, the wheel, the light strings moving in all directions, the vertical line - a whole packet of information. Experiencing intense sensations in my heart, with tears streaming down my face, I feel at home, accepted, and understood, being nurtured in loving hands.

I then lift my head to look into his eyes. They are big, warm eyes that make me cry even more. They have a smaller pupil next to a normal size one. Two circles, one larger than the other. I know this feature. He communicates silently, remember all your experiences. I suddenly have a strong inward motion sensation on my forehead, eyes begin to *flutter, light flashes, and like a fast film strip is being shown to me, scanning quickly, I detect a few images, scenes of me, many lives, experiences, and roles.*

An instant realization. This guide IS me. I am this person. Are we the same? There is an immediate response with a loving nod. He then holds me as I cry. It is time, he says. I ask if he will be working with me, he has always worked with me, and yes, he will be helping me forward. What do I need to do, he responds, you're already doing it, we will help you refine it. The big cat comes forward during his energy work. She has such loving energy, comes close to me, purring, brushing against my body. Both the guide and the big cat are very ancient beings and have always partnered together in their journeys. They work very closely with one another. In the background, I can see the slender, tall, heart-shaped face, cat-like-featured woman with the head covering. She is delighted and expresses an energy of love toward me and this encounter.

Also, the words spoken are not human language but light language. I am also speaking light language and trying to express with my throat the sound I am hearing. The tall guide then gets up, time to let this absorb and digest, he says, backing up slowly, step by step. Bright and loving energy emanates from his entire being. He reaches the circle. As I look up, I can now see I am surrounded by all these beings. To his left is the loyal cat, and to his right is the shorter, elderly being. They created a light circle all around me, and beyond this circle of brilliant light, I can see there are many tall light beings.

I feel a sense of reverence. I can't wait to see them again.

Description. The hands and feet are very slender, and the whole body is tall, muscular, and thin. Light-bluish skin. His eyes are beautiful, almond-shaped, large with two pupils. The hair is very long, a light color, white and gray. He wears a long sleeve flowy suit with an interesting necklace, which seems to be part of the clothing, a V-neck chest piece with an intricate pattern. He also wears a headpiece. There is no speaking, I only hear sounds and see hand movements. It's a different kind of communication. He looks young, but I learn he's over 4 thousand years old. We have been together since the beginning.

In subsequent connections, I ask the guides where they come from. Sirius is where the big cat and tall blue skin being come from. Hyades is the home of the female cat face shaped like a heart. The being who appears as a short, elderly person, is from the Pleiades but doesn't specify where in the cluster.

The guides know it's just curiosity on my part, so they are inclined to convey this information. They are all part of a group I also belong to. We've all lived together for a very long time, moving together, traveling.

Healing on a Lightship

I see the beautiful cat-faced being with the veil over her head; she is standing behind my back, supporting me, in a position as when someone is about to catch you if you fall back. The little elderly being is quite a distance from me, projecting a beam of light connecting to my heart. This is a protection beam creating an invisible Shen circle around me. Through the energy line, I am breathing in my heart, and begin to feel heaviness on top of my head as I am shown a lightship. My mind immediately knows that I'm about to experience a form of healing.

A white-blue light bubble encapsulates me; it's blurry, but when my sight suddenly adjusts, everything becomes clear. There are little beings everywhere. One of the tiny beings becomes a little bigger; he can change his size, proportionate, just slightly bigger. This is very clear to me; it's not like he's coming closer, which is why he looks bigger; no, he simply expanded in size. He holds my hand as we walk into this room; it seems like an ancient chamber. The tiny being floats as he escorts me to this place. They make high pitch sounds; their voices are almost like a chipmunk or bird. There are many of these beings around and in the distance. Although I'm not usually fond of high-pitch sounds, they all sound so pleasant. A very joyful and peaceful feeling washes over me. Arriving at the chamber, I am told to remain very still. I lie down, feeling very comfortable. The area is empty, but I see and feel metal tools penetrate my head, reaching my brain. On my forehead are two prongs, another one in the high occipital lobe, creating pressure in the temples.

There is a jelly-like blue substance that is being injected into my brain. The forebrain is being encapsulated with a blueish jelly cap that is now all over the space behind my forehead and eyes. It expands toward the top of my head into the remaining parts of the brain. The left side feels some pressure, as I notice a neon light-blue and white laser beam coming in to clean it out. The blue substance continues to expand. Words resounding in my mind, enough for now - the effects are spreading and will continue for a while. After being escorted to what looks like a platform, I find myself standing with feet shoulder-width apart. A cone-shaped light from my feet with the apex at my heart appears through this platform - just like a hologram.

Thinking I have to kneel for the apex to reach the top of my head, the little beings, smiling, gently guide me to stand tall. The apex is supposed to be at the level of my heart.

After standing in this cone of light, the being holding my hand guides me forward into another space. He places something over my head and temples. It looks like a head decoration; it's beautiful and feels alive and very natural, as if it was part of the body, like hair or fingers. I am then presented with something else, which suddenly appears around my waist. It's a belt. I touch it to adjust it. It is a wide waistband belt, 10-12 cm. One part reflects a shimmering mix of colors, depending on how the light hits it, hues of blue-gray-white-greenish color.

I instantly know this is a seal, the closure that brings together the ending and beginning, where nothing and everything come together. These beings are communicating the entire time. I am receiving healing tools embedded into my body to assist me in moving forward. There is complete trust in this process.

Held by the hand, we walk toward an enormous oval structure, but then I notice it has a pointed top, so it's not exactly like an egg. Shapes create the outer shell. Once closer, I can see it as a domed cone. A bright, yellow-golden light surrounds it. Finding myself on the inside now, it appears the entire surface creates light. It is so bright, but not blinding. Recognizing and smiling with a sense of wonder, I hear myself say, this is a cosmic being I can interact with. Then I go *through a smaller opening and am lifted on an elevated platform - still inside this domed cone, but in a different area. The outside is suddenly clear, revealing beautiful ocean-like water. There are many islands and land masses in the distance, an archipelago with several floating light bubbles, carrying entire cities and communities. Although it's a little blurry, I see buildings and movement inside these spheres of light. Floating vehicles, islands with facilities, structures, water, and many types of beings. So big and spacious, bright colors, and a sense of peaceful joy filling the air.*

The guides advise this is good for now - a little at a time, they say. Feeling a movement of being gently pulled back, my body begins to wake up, noticing the unexpected heartbeat speeding up, and the sudden heaviness in my chair.

I feel so grateful for this experience, and ask my guides if they can show me or make me feel their presence. When I connect with them or when one comes through, how do I know? The cat face being with the veil comes in front of me. She will show herself by making my left temple sensitive and holding my left hand. The little elderly being will connect with my heart's energy from a distance. The big cat will connect with me through my eyes. I see her sitting, purring loudly, staring at me. The male Syrian guide will come through with pressure on my right temple. *Trust visual images, and let's go from here, they say.*

Wrapped in Light Threads

I am pulling out my thoughts, setting them aside to the outer left of my body. Sitting on the chair, feeling my body, I begin breathing energy from my feet, moving up my whole body and expanding energy outward. I kept pulling thoughts out into their time-out zone, far left away from my body. Energy is expanding more and more.

Reaching the still, quiet space, my higher self comes closer - the movement detected is inward, light language echoing all around. A vortex axis of light cleanses my aura, shooting out to the sides and some areas below and above, clearing stickiness in my fields. The image of a wheel appears, lines of light from my heart going outward, then moving up and down. It is a disc scanning my body, moving quickly, emanating bright, yellow light. I know what's happening; this is a laser-like cleanse. Light language continues as the physical body's systems absorb direct messages. Then I start seeing bright blue-turquoise-greenish light threads creating patterns on my body, weaving a protection-like armor. From in front of me, this stream of light, blue-green bright light, comes in next to my nose, on the right side, over my right eyebrow, and the side of my head. It continues behind my head, then moves downward across the shoulder, around my chest, making an intricate design. Continuing around my waist, down the legs, splitting along my calves, then up again the legs, then to my shoulders along my arms, after my elbows, it wraps around the arms, toward the top of my hand and middle finger, then thumb, and the threads of light reach my index and middle fingertips.

Three of my fingers - thumb, index, and middle – have an implant of light. I can draw with them in the air, and light appears wherever I make a paintbrush-like motion. Seeing myself with all these beautifully colored threads of light over my whole body, I recognize this as a beautiful enhancement to my body, not only an armor of protection, but it's also an outfit belonging to an order, more like a uniform. My face is confident, peaceful, and wise. This entire time, I can hear the light language being delivered into my whole being as I'm being wrapped with light threads. I then fully return to my body's feelings, breathing.

Codes of Light - Wall Writing

With a massive headache, I sit quietly to absorb all the information coming through, still in a deep theta state - awake, but not fully here, receiving downloads-uploads and clarity. Over two hours go by while I am processing everything, in silence.

The first images and impressions are that I am underwater. Everything has a bluish look, iridescent light with a blue-turquoise tint, this is a water world. I see the top of my body; my head has a sort of crest, little spikes from the top of my forehead going back through my upper back, they move, they're not so rigid. My face has large eyes and a beautiful smile. I am a very large being with long arms and large hands, and my body is very lengthy. There are legs, but I am floating. My whole body moves very fluidly. I am a water

54

being. In the distance, I see giant whales - I'm so happy to see them. They are like my cousins or sisters; we are the same even if we don't have the same appearance. I also see a big manta-type being, just floating in the waves, greeting me from a distance. They know who I am, as they see me and recognize me. Then I see other beings just like me, and feel such warmth and a sense of expansion within my heart. Like a deep breath of fresh air, I'm so happy to be here. We do not speak with words, but I know they tell me, so good to see you.

I am being shown a giant structure, but I can only see a portion of it. I am in front of what looks like a wall. My hand reaches out, touching it, then hovers over some beautiful large symbols. They are codes; I don't immediately recognize them but hear, oh yes, I know this. I know our people did this; this is where we come to receive.

The symbols on the wall are alive, the entire structure is a being, it is breathing. The characters glow and move as if breathing light and sound. There is a frequency, a sound, I can hear it. The sound frequency of each part of the symbols holds specific information. At first, I can only see a very small portion of this structure. This is a library - a repository of information. The data is a collection of imprints of experiences from various parts of the universe and multiple civilizations. Our people built this structure, collected the information, and encoded it into sound and frequencies, which last forever. There is no time where these codes and sounds began nor an expiration date. Our people are the holders and store this knowledge so others can learn.

The structure, an actual being of pure intelligence, is the holder, the protector, where our people encoded the collection of knowledge. There is such a sense of reverence, of humbleness in front of such infinite power of light, of what seems to embrace All that is. The structure interacts with the purest frequency of the heart. A person is placed on a platform at the very top of this structure. The purpose is to receive the most suitable information needed for an assignment. The physical-energetic-spiritual network of a being may be easily overloaded by the powerful information transmission, its frequency, and the manner in which this information may come through. Therefore, it is calibrated to the frequency and level of the being who is receiving. The platform has a glow, it has a shape and structure, *but it is not really physical in nature. There is a beam of light that comes from the very top, the apex of the structure. This is a sacred chamber to receive the information one needs to accomplish the assignment, whatever the assignment is.*

I am shown standing on this platform, receiving a beam of light through my energy line, there is a strong vibration, and I am fully accepting and receiving. I do not know my assignment yet; the structure itself is calibrating what that will be and allowing my whole being to become one with the sound and frequency of what I am to know and do. There needs to be a full match in vibration for the person to receive their assignment fully.

I can now clearly see up to the top. This entire structure has a pyramid shape, with a smaller base and an extremely tall body up toward the apex. It's more like an obelisk. The apex is where the receiving chamber is located and appears above the waters, meeting with the cosmos. It has many layers within and without. It looks like an actual physical structure, but it's not made of matter. The outside of it glows with these magnificent symbols that emanate a breath of frequency, and one immediately feels the power and great respect for their messages. This is a place of magnificent power. The receiver is to commune with the transmissions received and rapidly move out of the chamber. The transference is brief. I am soon to be released and allowed to rest and integrate.

The information stored within the structure belongs to all beings of all-time, and of all universes. Our people facilitate a university-type setting. There is an open exchange of experiences where others can learn the best practices and share in the excitement and all aspects of one's experience during an assignment. We are all dressed the same; it looks like some form of uniform, very functional. A sort of gear around the neck comes down toward the solar plexus. I recognize it as a type of technology. Not heavy, but mechanical. It's so beautiful, almost resembling jewelry, with various layers braided into one piece. There are indents or casings where one can insert devices. It is practically attached to the clothing layer but can be removed. There is a technology that allows us to absorb the frequency, decipher the sound and codes given to us, and we just know there will come a time for us to understand what needs to be done. The assignments are revealed as a series of guidance programs. We help guide other groups throughout the journey of their growth. What we receive is specific to their development needs and their culture. This allows us to facilitate the program and interact with them as a family.

I am now being pulled toward what seems like a flat structure, a platform; this is a big gathering place. The floor is made of a liquid, shiny metal with beautiful geometric shapes on its surface. I can see through it, although made of solid matter. This large space I am in is very much like a massive plaza with many levels. Beings are everywhere, gathered in small and larger groups. There is a sense of harmony, very light and bright. This is our time to study through sharing.

As I enter this space, I am greeted by tiny white little beings that look like Casper the Ghost. They are so cute, and they make some high pitch sounds. I, somehow, totally understand them, then suddenly realize I know them. I've seen them before in a recent healing vision, but now I can see they actually work here. They smile at my realization, hold my fingers, and pull my wrists, leading me to an area where I am to be scanned or checked out. There is a smaller chamber where I stand on a platform. It's almost like an airport scan. To my right, I see a thin blue beam of light that starts scanning my entire body, beginning with my right temple, going through the side of my body. They say something is happening with my nervous system, and this blue beam will help. Something needs to be corrected in my left brain, which is affecting the right side of the spine. I stand here while they're just doing their thing. The little beings become a bit larger. So weird, I hear myself say, they can change shape and size; floating to hover at shoulder height, their size grows to 2 ft. They are very friendly and just tell me to stand still, please don't move, almost done. As they clear impurities, I am being prepared before going to the larger plaza area to be with my people.

After I'm done here, they let me off this platform and lead me by holding my fingers and hand. I'm directed toward the plaza, and I'm ready to gather with the others.

In a grand circle, I see some more senior beings; they provide explanations and sort of an update on various happenings. This is just like a full line-up. It looks like a scene from ancient times in Alexandria, where philosophers gathered to discuss mysteries, sharing theories, truths, and wisdom. I am invited to speak of my experiences, and I am happy to share. We are all friends here; there is such love and compassion, and we have such high respect for one another and our value within the universe.

Moments later, I am shown floating in space. Enjoying being one of everything, I feel so free and part of infinite intelligence. I am loving this as if I were a tourist admiring the sites. Oh, here is this constellation; there, I see beautiful planets and their wonderful colors; there is an asteroid in the distance; wow, so immense and peaceful. Such beautiful sounds are coming from the aliveness of the universe. I can sense things from extreme distances, then notice particles floating around me, just being in my space as I am in theirs. All of a sudden, I realize I'm not just floating as energy, but I am in an actual vehicle. It is simply invisible. The outside of this capsule I find myself in is clear so that I can see everything. The magical universe becomes a welcome home message. Seeing this so clearly makes me feel extremely grateful. I then recognize the structure I'm in. It is quite a large ship. I am greeted by the lovely, bright face of the guide, whom I've seen before. She is the beautiful being with the cat-like face and a veil over her head. I am so happy to see her. She caresses my face with such a soft, gentle touch. She really knows me.

This being shares with me I can now look down to notice what I look like. Wow... I understand better now... the blue being I experienced about a month ago with the big cat companion is me. This being is my primary guide now. In my prior experience, the blue Sirian being came forth as my higher self in this form to administer healing energy and integration between this aspect of myself and my physical self as Enrica. The body has blue skin, a muscular build, long grayish hair, long ears, large, beautiful eyes, so brilliant, there is actual light in the eyes, my eyes. I now realize I am there and here at the same time.

Turning toward the cat-face being, instantly responding to my inquiry, she tells me I can call her TIA-KA. She wears a veil extending into a long silk robe, which is very light, almost see-through, over her head. Her face is shaped like a heart, with beautiful features. A very fair complexion, skin like a pearl. The robe she is wearing is part of some kind of order; it symbolizes a title, a leadership role, a level she achieved - some type of responsibility. Her body is very large and lengthy; under the veil, she wears a beautiful gown that covers her whole body. She is very graceful in her movements and holds tremendous knowledge. We have such respect for one another. We love each other; there is a deep level of care. She shows me that we traveled together as a team to help many people in the past. In one assignment, we went to help a civilization integrate their energies with the energies of their earth and soil. There is a technology they could access to become one with their earth so they can facilitate growing food and become totally independent. We were so loved, and the people were so grateful for us being there. Our stay lasted for quite some time, facilitating, and helping in the role of leaders but more like teachers.

She touches my forehead, my chest then my upper back. This is like a code of some sort that I recognize – a greeting and farewell - and tells me to enjoy everything, stop worrying, overthink, and just be. Things will simply come to me. I don't need to know how, I don't need to accumulate more knowledge, I already have it, and it will come to me as I need to access the information.

There is a mission in this life to teach, to show people what their light is. I have the assignment to gather and lead. It doesn't matter the way. To show people how to go beyond the intricate smallness of our human thinking, to help people see their formless part.

Mussia

I'm restless but not fully awake. It's 3:30 am. In the sleep-awake state, I feel there is a lot going on, and ask my guides to come help me. I immediately see Lynx Mussia on my mind screen. She's there to help me relax, massaging my back and pushing on my body. Communicating with her, I ask her to help me sleep and to allow me to see any messages during dreamtime. Then I am lifted to another space, and I am shown these images.

I see myself in the studio but also in the house, in both environments, simultaneously, surrounded by stuff, tall furniture, and boxes. There is hardly room to move. This makes me feel very overwhelmed and say to myself, take everything out! There isn't anywhere to move in here. In addition, I'm getting ready to receive my clients for class, and there is all this stuff everywhere. I desperately try to move things out of the way, it's so stressful. Then I notice all this luggage and backpacks, and I can't tell if it's in the house or the studio. In the dream, I hear myself saying, there is a lot you need to get rid of and clean out of your inner space. I become very emotional when I hear this message. There needs to be a deeper level of cleaning and letting go.

I then see myself in what looks like an airport or a large hotel lobby with many people and an atmosphere of relief upon arriving in this space. Wow, we're here, what a long ride. There is a room similar to a hospitality suite I can use to shower and get cleaned up. Someone lets me in, and I get ready to relax. As I begin to undress before the shower, I realize I don't have anything. Where is my suitcase? I put my dirty clothes back on and the guest robe, walk out, then see someone I recognize and say, I don't have my bag. Do you know where it is? Maybe in the baggage claim or landing area; why don't you see if it's there? So, I wander through hallways with lots of people, it looks like I'm walking in an airport terminal. But now the weird thing is that I'm walking as if underwater. There is so much resistance as if walking against the current, or a very strong wind. I'm so tired, almost there but can barely move. Trying to continue forward feels impossible as I'm being pushed back. Feeling anxiety about going against the current, I ask myself, why so much struggle? Going after something I think I need, like new clothes to change into after showering. There is a need to let go of old stuff that feels heavy, in my way – a distraction, and clutters my space making me anxious. So much resistance. I'm struggling, feeling so overwhelmed.

I wake up tormented by these images, but I know in my heart, I needed to see this, and I'm grateful they showed me in this way. I feel like crying, breaking down, shedding. There is so much tension built up. I am exhausted.

Lynx is a close companion. Mussia is her name. When I asked her name in deep meditation, the sounds were so clear and familiar. The SSIA sound brought me back to the large cat guardian I encountered in a vision months earlier.

When this companion came to me, I was lucid and completely clear on all the details of her beautiful ears, eyes, spots, and features on her entire body. It is a Lynx. In the past, I just saw her as a giant cat, unable to focus my inner sight. The sound MU and the previous sound I heard, EH before the SSIA sounds, are codes representing a form of identification. Identification may not be the correct term. The distinction is simply a way to differentiate the quality of energy that my mind could perceive in these encounters. Eh and Mu are sound codes corresponding to the role at that particular time - the quality of vibration transmitted - what my energy-spiritual bodies resonate with. She now comes to me as Mussia.

5

PROCESSING

Resistance

I've had this lower back pain for what seems like forever. When I had my studio and I was teaching between 15 to 18 classes a week, I hardly had any issues. When I practice KiGong with such frequency, I never experience this level of discomfort. I finally decided to go see a medical professional. I wanted to get an X-ray or, even better, an MRI. However, the medical system is broken, especially since I had signed up for some form of discount healthcare system after resigning from my company and becoming self-employed. I don't even want to begin with how ridiculous health care systems are *worldwide*. I never complained about it when I worked for a corporate giant since I had amazing coverage. Sure, I paid a premium for it, which I could afford back then, but my company paid high fees too. Why does healthcare have to cost so much, especially in the United States!? I honestly didn't care. The era of the current health care systems of what we call the *first world countries* needs to dissolve completely and rebuild. There is too much inequality and suffering.

So now, I'm a self-employed small business owner, and what do I get? No, we can only do an X-ray. You must do 6 or more months of physical therapy before we can do an MRI.

I get the x-ray. My S1 is not fused with the rest of my sacrum, so I have 6 lumbar vertebrae instead of 5. I thought this was really interesting. I have a unique genetic condition, which I then learned is actually quite common, and that is it, at least I know what's happening physiologically. With my inner senses, I could feel and see something like this going on during my practice.

Another big *change* was about to occur. A break from this path. Turning away from conforming to this company, just like a corporate employee would, or perhaps moving to another location, working for someone else. My spirit and my soul knew the answer. No, there is something of your own you need to be doing, teaching, and sharing.

My lower back tormented me, and it was becoming worse.

As I closed my business and began to plan the big move back to Italy, I felt like the pain was simply because I wasn't training enough. I just needed to do training, I thought.

The big jump occurred, with all of what comes with an international move on my shoulders. Feeling fully responsible for my partner's experience, as well as our dog Charlie.

In addition, here we go... a huge wave of energy coming from the depths of the Earth. Old information stored here, in my homeland, waiting for me to come back, to physically touch the ground and activate floods of transmissions. Not only was I fully stepping into what was the hurricane of distortions involving my process of armoring back when I was so little, but I was also flushing out the spikes of sorrow my mom experienced throughout all the years she lived as a wife and mother, sister-in-law, the rejected daughter-in-law, a Mormon in a predominantly Catholic culture, the American in town, the horse lady. None of this processing - or simply accepting and nurturing my lost pieces - was fully possible during my yearly visits; no, I was *on vacation* then and only consumed myself with enjoying sites, food, and experiences, never mind the unsaid, the deep entrenched ideas and stories we all crafted so carefully years prior, not just my family, myself too.

Upon entering this side of the world, I was frazzled and had difficulties caring for my mind as I was overwhelmed with too much happening. My sense of order, balance, and high standards clashed with the aspect of reality that is all about *the old*.

I've lived my life on waves of change. There were times when I experienced change as an escape from the current situation, but then I also experienced change as an evolution and always learned so much along the way.

Sometimes people use this concept of change too easily, or it's simply misinterpreted, often misused. Change is our natural state. We may not realize that we constantly resist change, which is merely a mechanism to remain in one specific state, as if we unknowingly choose to stay in one container; this inner process always creates tension. Staying in one state, one version of reality, saying things like *this is life*, is OK for a short while. However, when we do nothing about the innate force of adapting to the waves of change, we generate tension, and in turn, tension creates our world.

If there is resistance and some form of mental, emotional, or physical stress - tension - it means something needs to change. Eventually, we need to proceed toward change consciously. When we stubbornly choose the idea that change is not good, change chooses us all the same.

Change and consciousness are the same thing. All is movement - a wave. Once again, change is our natural state because it is of the same substance as our own consciousness.

We always constantly change, that never stops, but as we grow into adults, adaptability, flexibility, and resilience, which are innate qualities, become dormant, rusty, cement-like blocks. Most of us can't even recognize the distorted vibration, which inevitably reflects in the development of our surroundings as well. Inside and outside.

Change was happening, but I saw resistance to change all around me. I was changing, but the outer world was pushing me around, and, at times, violently.

I want to share a short example of how *the old* no longer works, no matter the circumstance. It's stagnant. It doesn't hold purpose anymore.

In Italy, if one wants to get married, the registry office in the town where you have residency has to *announce* your wedding day publicly in a formal manner. This is an actual procedure; there are forms to complete, legal documents with signatures, and stamps, and it's all super official. They post this notice of marriage for 10 to 14 days, working days, then you can have your wedding. This idea made complete sense a gazillion years ago... maybe.... Actually, it didn't make sense back in the day either, but so is our history. Long ago, when it took time to circulate information, the townspeople learned about events like weddings, for example, by relying on the announcements made by the city council-type bodies, whoever that was. If someone was to oppose the union, they could step forth and object. It took some time for this to happen. They really had to give people the opportunity to speak up. Let's leave that alone. Hence the ritualistic sentence *speak now or forever hold your peace* came about, which is still used today as the priest performs the wedding.

Nowadays, is this necessary? Yes, I sound sarcastic because I am totally being sarcastic! This outdated procedure costs so much effort that it's no longer relevant. Everyone actually agrees, from the public figures working in these government offices to everyday people. However, the mindset behind this type of bureaucracy infuses all aspects of life. Modern life holds all these bindings of old, outdated, completely irrelevant small-minded traditions with tremendous low vibration, making people lazy, tired, and mistrusting.

That's just this one example of how *the old* perpetuates. The unfortunate thing is that most things are like this. Getting your driver's license, your permanent visa, a vet appointment, a bank account, your cell phone, whatever. It has been a very challenging experience. Yes, I was complaining a little bit. Thanks for your patience.

I do want to also add that I am absolutely in love with *Tradition* - with a capital T. Traditions are magical; they infuse the spirit of the ancient people, of the land, of myths, stories, and legends.

Traditions are exceptional. I still only focus any extra time I have on the study and review of ancient traditions. Today's society takes such a small percentage of valuable symbolism and initial intent and misuses it to *keep us in line* in that one constrictive state, one container for all.

As many have seen in recent decades, people are waking up to their inner intelligence and compass. Is this my idea or someone else's? We start to really wonder what's happening.

Lastly, I just want to be 100% clear that I'm not insinuating that it was better in the USA, no, not at all. There are severe distortions in all levels of systems, and that is all over the world, I mean *all over*! Some things, though, feel like a kick in the teeth, which allows us to practice *true-seeing* our internal flow between dark and light, resistance and surrender, contraction and release, over and over.

I kept reminding myself - wow, there is going to be a good swing the other way because I'm feeling it. So much contraction, I felt like a wet rag being squeezed to death. Incredible!

My lower back pain worsened, and I started feeling extremely sharp burning sensations in my right shoulder blade and trapezius muscle. Occasionally, my shoulder blade would blow up with lightning-sharp pain. I saw a doctor here in Italy, and they immediately ordered an MRI. They said I should have received one instead of the X-ray long ago. We learned I have herniated discs and a bulging disc. I became a little worried, but I knew better. I really need to focus on my training so I can take care of myself. As I grounded and allowed my head-brain to rest, I could see ways to relax, restore my nervous system, open my heart, and hear her say, nothing physical is happening here, your pain is energetic realignment. You're fine, but you need to focus. This is expansion through recalibration. Remember your training to take care of your symptoms. You can do everything on your own.

Yet, I sought assistance from a few external sources including acupuncture to help me relieve some stress and calm my back. It did help me for a while. I kept being nudged toward what I already knew. Again, reminders of my own training. I can do this. What's happening is just a realignment. *It's been going on for a while. We have been at a critical phase for you to be fully open. Trust.*

Surfacing clarifications on why I've experienced pain and blockages along my spine became clearer. The suspicion is that the cause is more than just isolated to the first few energy centers in the body. Not feeling rooted, going through another big move, and needing a place to call *home* or a permanent residence. These are old ideas, superficial concepts of belonging. I always belonged everywhere and nowhere, never feeling like this was a heavy burden. There are people who do feel they don't belong anywhere and wish they were on some other planet. I honestly never felt that way. On the contrary, the more experiences in various places in the world, the better. Creating a *home* anywhere is how I function, while feeling completely insane at the same time. This sense of inadequacy is now recognized as a projection from others - society, culture, immediate environments.

In the past, throughout all the different places I moved to due to my work, I always felt like I belonged and began to feel comfortable. As most of us do, I soon started to identify with my roles, the relationships, who I was trying to be to this and that person. It's not about *having a home* as in location, but about who you are.

I've dreamed of this type of lifestyle since I could remember; wanting to live there for a while, experience as much as possible, then go over there and do the same. Seeing a place for a week, a month or so, is not enough; I don't want to be a tourist. There is a strong desire to fully savor life and become abundant with experiences, not possessions. Hear the music, smell the food, and enjoy the deliciousness of everything. Dance in the water, live in the sun. This is still how I want to live. There are many preconceptions about this lifestyle, and that is OK, but this is *my* dream. What happens, though. We get distracted with stuff, I mean literally *things*, as well as this concept of home. A house is a good investment and security. If you don't have a residence, you are basically a failure; you can't understand how the world works; you don't have anything; you're worth nothing. These are genuine convictions of many, including my family. I rebel against this notion that my value is linked to material things, and this point doesn't imply financial distress. Sure, having things to create a beautiful and appealing environment is important to our well-being in many aspects, but things do not make us whole.

I love many of my own belongings, as they represent something deeply meaningful to me. I enjoy the beach sunset tapestry and several scrolls on my walls. Some of my favorites are the rising phoenix, the nine koi fish, and the sacred words of ancient texts. I cherish some of my healing tools, crystals, instruments, and books. I store mom's Mormon scriptures as they have her name engraved on them. Her vibration is linked to these books. She made notes in them; she held them dearly. I keep them as they make me feel closer to her.

OK, so all I'm saying is that it's nice to have *some* things and enjoy them. It's another thing to think of possessions as a way to value a person or completely identify ourselves with our stuff.

There was a time when I had thirteen black suits amongst all the other suits in the closet. They were all different, of course. The pants were of varying lengths, and that is because I had shoes with different heel heights. Anyone who appreciates a really nice, tailored suit and great quality shoes understands what I'm saying. When I worked for this particular brand of properties, there was a clothing etiquette for the leadership team. We could wear colored blouses and modest jewelry, but dark-colored suits were preferred. I loved rules. It created more order in the chaotic world of hotel operations. I absolutely enjoyed structure, order, organization, and high standards.

Nevertheless, I was always deeply disturbed when a person was judged and put into a box if their particular way of wearing their hair, the quality of shoes and clothing were sub-par, and sub-par according to who? So frustrating. We each have our own scale of what's acceptable. As human beings, we can't turn that off, right? Actually, we can; it's just like being a moderator of our own thoughts and emotions. We can absolutely turn that off, that low-quality judgment vibration. When we're so disconnected from our true nature, we tend to see the other as better or worse than us, and we're constantly creating some form of opinion about this or that person and thing. Everything around us shows a standard scale. If we can meet the standards on the higher scale, we're worth more. Does this mindset still fit?

Now, I want to be clear that professional appearance is very important, especially in the environment I worked in. I was the first to send team members back to the heart of the house to shower, shave, and get a fresh uniform if they decided to show up looking like they had just rolled out of bed. I'm not talking about this, and by professional appearance I mean clean, awake, ready to serve.

Timing Yourself to Change Vibration Practice

Let's go back to the feeling of *home*. I was shown that these feelings in my body are related to other aspects of myself beyond the nurturing sense of home. My guides have been so gentle and patient with me. Showing me through my body in multiple ways. The neck and trapezius muscle inflammation has revealed more clarity to what I did not fully see, clouded by feeling sorry for myself, not always, but yes, definitely feeling a bit small.

I usually time myself and share this in my sessions. We absolutely must snap out of our victim mentality, so *timing yourself* is a good practice. What does that mean? We must feel whatever we're feeling, stay with it, and allow it to move through our bodies. Really paying attention. It's no longer the time to push it down, avoid it, put *the guest-face* back on, and move on to the next thing. We must see it.

In the past ten years, I learned the immense value of seeing through superficial resistance. I sit quietly for a while. I just let my body do what it needs to. Sometimes I will be guided to move; others, I will just sit and pick up a stone, a book, or oracle cards. I ask my quiet, still heart to show me where this feeling is in my body and help me understand the authentic message. I may not receive clarity right away, but the insight definitely shows up; it's a practice of paying attention. Sometimes, I see myself as a hurt being that needs attention. I sit quietly even when I think and feel that I really screwed up and am mean to myself. After a while of being present with myself as if I was sitting with the dearest friend I love so much, things tend to soften, loosen up, and become spacious. There is something beyond the initial resistance, whether that is physical pain, a triggered emotion, or loop-like thinking.

I am fascinated by the symbols, and looking through the shapes, the colors, and what they represent is exactly like language to me. Everything surrounding us is a symbol, a message for us to receive. When these symbols catch our attention, it is an indication from our inner teacher-healer that we are connected to something much larger than what we perceive. We contract as we feel resistance and have difficulty seeing the bigger picture. Unlike when I handled inner conflict with band-aids years ago, I now stop everything, sit quietly, and try my best to listen. I time myself if I want to wine for a bit while I sit, then I inevitably have to do something to shake things up, to move my energy, to create circulation, whether I think it's stupid at the moment or thoughts such as, I don't want to, this doesn't help, or whatever the self-pity party has me momentarily believe. This is a continuous practice. I am quite disciplined, and I feel we need to have this approach to our well-being. Disciplined in taking care of your own mind.

If sitting quietly is nerve-wracking, then using the body to move energy is a beautiful practice. We use the body to calm the heart-mind, the nervous system, and vice versa. There are myriad practices, and it doesn't matter what one does; just the intention is enough. But this intention of offering time for yourself and no one else is imperative. We must become used to honoring ourselves completely no matter what we see, feel, or think. That is the discipline. How can we show our Soul-Spirit complex that we are paying attention? Maybe that's not your goal, and that's perfectly fine, then this reading is not for you. Perhaps I want more, and I just don't know what it is, but I generally feel unsettled and restless. Then, this reading may be for you.

It's not complicated; it's actually quite simple. Connecting with our higher self is so natural. We, as human beings in this era possessed by the illusion that accumulation of knowledge equals intelligence, tend to make things very confusing, complicated, and distorted by our thinking alone. Thought processes and the function of the head brain are not the guiding principles of Soul inspiration.

So, sometimes we feel sorry for ourselves, we feel like we've made mistakes, we say things like, I can't believe this person did this to me, I was passed on this promotion, my mother-in-law hates me, my sibling is jealous and thinks I'm an idiot, my parents abandoned me. Nobody cares about me; why should I?

Yea, so what? We may think.

Well, *timing myself* – as a process of feeling and paying attention, then changing energy – is what works for me, and it's a continuous practice of refining my own thoughts and emotions to see beyond them and interpret what is really going on. The more I honor this side of life, the more refinement occurs, the clearer the filters, the brighter the road.

A beautiful practice is to literally talk yourself out of it. You must hear your inner, encouraging, true voice to help you through whatever heaviness you're experiencing. Someone else's words may be extremely helpful, and there are times where that is needed; there is value in a dear friend, a counselor, or even a stranger. It is more profound to become aware of our own true voice listening and providing words of wisdom with a stretched-out arm and a strong hand to help us up and out of the heaviness.

This is not wishful thinking or telling yourself words you don't really believe in. You must treat your hurt self just as if it was the dearest person to you; maybe it's your child, your spouse or parent, your best friend, or perhaps you don't have anyone in your life that feels like the dearest person to your heart, and so this is utterly the most important thing you can do. Make *you,* your true self, your most special precious friend. One that knows way more than you *think* you do. The friend who's been with you throughout all of life's events. Not only that, even the ones you can't remember in this life and all previous incarnations. How amazing is this true self? So wise and beautiful. I can't wait to connect to her daily. It's like visiting the brightest version of me because she actually is. Her role is to help me sift through some garbage and clutter. She shows me feathers when I walk the dog; the shapes and images in things I have around my room, translating the deeper meaning of the energy vibration I've surrounded myself in. While busy figuring things out, I recognize how she operates through the wisdom and mind of the body, reminding me that my body is way smarter than I think, so not to worry so much, don't be so serious, I sometimes hear. There are times to push forward, and there are times to stop everything. The wake-up call to stop everything and pay attention may not be so pleasant; it's usually a bit of a mess, a situation where your mind is blowing up, your body is in pain, and often both. Stop and pay attention; I'm here and I'm the only one who can truly help you.

In the past, there have been many moments when I was so overwhelmed that I didn't know how to handle anything. Occasionally, I would hang on until I could take a vacation, literally holding it together up to the three-day weekend or actual week-long trip. A few times, I instinctively decided to just stop everything and simplify life.

This concept has always been a go-to, no matter the circumstance. Now, it's the automatic response. I'm overwhelmed, it doesn't matter why, so I stop, simplify, sit, and watch myself. When I say simplify, I mean literally decluttering. It may mean eliminating some things from daily routines and eliminating outside sources of distractions, even if they are apparently good for me. To simplify means cleaning my diet for that day or week, wearing comfortable, simple clothes, and cleaning my house again! Those who know me know I love to clean, as it's just like meditating for me. It helps me become quiet inside. I also feel really good about making my main source of input - what I see (visual input), less busy and less *dusty*. What I'm practicing is purely a mental cleanse process. I may move furniture around, rearrange my things, refresh the organization of sacred objects, etc. It's difficult, sometimes impossible, to watch myself objectively and be as neutral as possible. Still, inside of me, I know this reset mechanism is happening without me even being conscious.

Years later, after I learned about the map of consciousness and the work of Dr. Hawkins, I recognized states of neutrality as the basis and the vibration of courage as the threshold emotion. When I go up and down the scale, no matter how many times a day or week, I absolutely have to get myself back up to courage. It's like being on your tippy toes looking over the fence, like Mr. Wilson, the helpful neighbor greeting you from the other side. Only part of the big picture is accessible. I have to get on my tippy toes and reach the level of courage in order to see more. There is no other way.

The practice of timing myself to feel, then shake things up to move energy, talk myself into a higher state of vibration, find that memory or sensation of courage, and rise to that unique vibration, elevates the mind to a higher photon production from the body's cell. What do we do after that? Keep moving forward with patience, extreme kindness, and love for yourself.

This whole process happens daily, sometimes multiple times a day, sometimes I neglect myself for a bit, then I'm back. And so it goes on. One reaches a point where you can recognize a significant shift. When things would take days and weeks to *get over* - or process, whatever that was, now it may take a few hours, maybe a day or two, sure, but most of the time, when we slow down, stop, and pay attention, we can shift and have a wider perspective within a very short time. It's not a pill or fast acting agent. It's continuous work that takes diligent practice, however it can absolutely be a nanosecond of a recalibration phenomenon, once we fully awaken to our innate power.

The efforts to connect with our inner teacher and healer may seem like too much work - that's only one point of view. Again, a reminder that this is our natural, most aligned state, to have this constant flow and exchange with our true nature, but there are times when we need to do a bit more to remember, and with focus and a diligent, sincere mind, doors open, allowing us to feel the rewards, retrieve gifts and treasures we were born with, making us feel more whole and complete. The benefits reach all levels of your energy-spiritual bodies, and transformation continues. There is no external force more powerful than your own inner fire purified, shining the brilliance of your own heart-mind to reveal more aspects of yourself, more tools for you to use. This is the most interesting and engaging work.

If we feel a low-vibration emotion, that's fine; we need to feel it but also manage it. Maybe you're not ready to fully experience grief, anger, or whatever. Today in a small dose, that's fine; just as long as you don't avoid or shove it back down as it will inevitably sink in deeper. Think of something like psoriasis; you can put medicine on it, a cream to help this manifestation of discordant energy on the skin, but then it will go further into the body and travel to another area so it can be seen and heard.

All emotions must be honored. It's like dismissing yourself. I have value, the anger says. Listen to me. So do all other emotions. Our role is to be good managers and leaders. Who's in charge here? We should ask.

I see thoughts and emotions as one entity, one continuously moving energy structure. Sometimes, the vibration-color-sound of emotions may be stronger, and at other times thoughts rule. Still, there is a constant flow exchange, like a moving blob that hovers in and around our physical form.

Thinking and emotions are linked like twin brothers-sisters; they walk around together, interlocked in their arms. Let's ask ourselves: how long can I be in this vibrational state until I change something? Why? Because we must return to our tippy toes to see more light and emit more light. That alone will assist us in feeling stronger and more resilient in processing the deeper versions of those lower vibratory states. I feel angry for a bit, maybe it turns into pity and then sadness, but really, it's all grief. A part of me is so deeply hurt it's dying. Ok, how long? 3hrs, 3 days, 15min? Whatever. Then do something to shake it up. Change your energy. Move! Laziness is no longer an option. There will always be something you can do to shake things up. Options involve any kind of movement, food, a chat with your friend or doctor, holding your pet, holding your babies, going out in nature, watching your favorite movie or series, reading a book, listening to music.

During fall and winter in Seattle, I would often put on Lord of the Rings and just doze off after coming home from work. I was so mentally tired that I had to take refuge in my favorite story ever, and this process helped me fully rest my mind. Whatever works.

There is not one way, there can't be, we're all different. We each have a unique smile, therefore, we each have something different that works for us. And each moment of each day is different.

Coming back to Italy after spending 28 years away stirred up a complex mix of emotions within me. There was a lingering feeling of resentment, as if I had been forgotten or left behind. I felt frustrated, angry, and hurt by the sense of separation and abandonment I experienced. It seemed like nobody cared about what was happening in my life. Whenever I tried to speak up, I was constantly interrupted, dismissed, and made to feel insignificant. Being treated like a foreigner in my homeland was disheartening, I think mainly because my English proficiency was better than my Italian - but that's just the story I made up. There were moments when I struggled to understand or articulate my thoughts, and I wished desperately for the words to flow effortlessly. Anxiety overwhelmed me as I weighed how to communicate with my family and what to say. Should I remain quiet and simply enjoy their company? After all, that's why I'm here, or should I share my experiences, my life, who I really am? This internal conflict tormented me as my voice was repeatedly silenced and overshadowed. It didn't feel authentic. However, amidst this frustration, I realized that the guides had presented this experience as an opportunity for growth and healing. Despite my ability to lead meetings, conduct training, and organize various events, I found myself shrinking in the presence of certain individuals, particularly my family. The frustration and inner conflict manifested physically as increased inflammation, demanding acknowledgment, and expression.

More than ever, I felt such appreciation for how life gives us the opportunity to love deeper. *You can't go back, only forward - yes, vulnerable with walls crumbling down, doorways opening. You must truly see the bigger picture, finding pieces of your own puzzle map.*

Our Bodies Are So Intelligent

The inner vitality, accumulated and stored in the lower dahnjon (dantien), the lower belly area, allows us to adapt more gracefully to the healing process, whatever that is.

Our other filters such as our heart, our communication - how we express our thoughts and emotions, the processes of everyday interactions, and thinking will be supported with more energy. Our bodies will have more power, allowing the energy to mature. It will transform into a different quality of vibration. We have lots of energy in our hearts, but it's continuously moving and flowing, coming in and out; that's what it needs to do as it holds a specific quality of energy. In the lower dahnjon, located below the belly button, there is an actual storage unit. We can practice accumulation and refinement processes, including visualization journeys or as simple as bringing the hands to the lower belly, to simply inform the mind of the body that more energy is needed *here* in the ocean of energy storage. When we are depleted with too much energy consumed by the upper energy centers, we quickly become disconnected from the rest of the body's and the Earth's intelligence. The practice of centering is to bring more focus to the lower abdomen. If the head-brain is depleted by over-thinking, we can't replenish our head by filling it with more energy; it just isn't safe to hold energy in the head. The brain is an instrument. The brain *supports refueling*, but it doesn't actually *lead* this phenomenon. When it does, transforming energy is incomplete. However, focusing on the lower dahnjon gives this energy the true power of transformation. It refines the sources of input, and we need refinement as distortions are absorbed into our cells and our energy-spiritual bodies, just like we drink the sun when we walk outside. Refinement is the purpose. We want purified energy clearing through the clutter, recalibrating, realigning, and bringing more order and harmonious sounds within and around our bodies.

Visualization is a powerful tool to help us hold the energy in the center of our body, our lower abdomen, so we can draw from it when needed, just like a battery.

Energy is not one-dimensional; we hold different qualities of energy. When we eat fresh fruit and vegetables and drink water, we replenish our bodies with this specific energy. This is one way for our body to help our energy systems return to a level that allows us to sustain another task, another interaction, etc.

However, we have a baseline, like a threshold indicating the energy level we hold. You probably know someone who always speaks about being tired and exhausted. Who hasn't felt this way recently? This is the age of being bombarded with information; we are drained by our technology and the speed of things around us. It's draining. Everyone is fatigued. We don't sleep the right amount; we've become tired people. Humanity is tired and experiences many distortions in the minds because of it. We need to work in a different way to restore that natural vitality through the lower abdomen, which acts as our own special reservoir. This type of resource can't live in the heart, head, or hands; the most suitable place for this energy is in the center of the body.

We are trying to manage the world with our brains, and with our thinking, we are transported by unbalanced and unchecked emotions. We become depleted in our energy-spiritual bodies, and our physical body suffers. And when we are tired, energetically tired, we start to develop physical modifications due to posture and misalignment, not only on a physical level; this is energy misalignment. Then we hear things like, my posture has caused this or that discomfort, but maybe it's because 40-50+ years of thinking has caused the body to adapt, to redistribute the energy in the best way it knows how.

Practices such as visualization, breathing, holding postures, and movement help us bring energy to the lower energy complex, where it can safely be accumulated and stored, giving us immense power to distribute it where and when we need it. Can you think about keeping energy in the head? It's just like when we have a fever or a migraine. There is too much stored up there, that's not its function, plus it's just not safe. That fire energy needs to move, and it needs to move down to the belly. Our energy system flow is literally upside down. We've become accustomed to operating this way. This upside-down energy flow is the root cause of most forms of distortions.

These are laws of nature, and our bodies, including the physical body, follow the laws of nature. When we're upside down, we are consumed with lower vibration energies, we feel heavy in our minds, and our filters are polluted. Make the belly like a volcano and the head like the clear blue sky. There is no such thing as holding fire energy in the lower abdomen and simultaneously in the head or heart. It just does not happen; this goes against the laws of nature. We can temporarily feel our entire body *on fire* during extremely traumatic events. However, it will eventually return to a flow of yin-yang energy exchange. This flow may become used to moving in the direction that perpetuates the state of unrest or it can return to the direction that promotes healing. We may not even consciously know it's happening. We also hold *fire* energy in the solar plexus and heart. I will delve into the different qualities of fire energy a bit later.

If we *store* fire energy in the solar plexus, there is a risk of the fiery emotions becoming distressed even more and an even higher risk for the flow of energy to move upwards to the heart, the throat, and into the brain. This results in a disruptive way of processing information, including how and what we communicate. Mostly disruptive to ourselves. The head brain doesn't know what to do with this impure information, so it tends to go back to what it knows, memories, patterns, and old ways.

The reverse flow of energy, rising through the spine, through the back of the body, coming over the head, and down the front of our body, is most beneficial as the fire and water purification energy complex transforms. We elevate the power of fire and water energies used by our internal and external chakras and our meridian channels.

Once we have strong, stable energy in our belly and can use it for a higher purpose, then what happens? Well, we do need to continuously work on it. It's like a tree. We have to take care of it. What are we going to do with it? Nurture it. The practice of renewing, restoring, recharging, and refining is our bodies' natural innate healing process. This goes for everyone. Even people without knowledge or understanding about energy or spiritual concepts have this phenomenon happening inside and around them. This is how our system is built. Once we have this information, even if only intellectually, we may become more aware of the inner medicine, this wisdom becomes more available.

I am 100% convinced that all people know how to uncover this healing power. It's a gift of the Soul. We already know how to process things in a way that makes us feel good, knowing that we have this energy to do everything, that we have amazing healing powers, and that we don't need anything outside ourselves. But we don't know that this *is* the truth, that there is this other dimension to our true essence, or maybe we know it, but then we doubt and dismiss our abilities.

Think of this. I notice my skin feeling a bit scaly and rough, then days later, it's back to a smooth texture and natural glow. The body is amazing; how does it know to do this? Or something bigger, a deeper scar, or going through other major changes, hormones, for example. The body accepts herself and loves herself already; we, with our thinking-emotional processes, are the ones who form all kinds of opinions about her - the body.

The body has an incredible amount of power. She says it's ok, we got this, it may take a bit for this one, but we got it. The feeling of making a mistake, doubtful, worried, lost, and frustrated simply gets in the way of the body's processing. How about this other way of talking to the minds, as an invitation. How about, considering that the body already knows what it's supposed to be doing. You may then think or say to yourself, I just don't know enough about what's happening, my body has all this information, and I'm just being bossy and controlling, wanting to get in there and micromanage. This quality can be directed toward the other energy bodies, such as thought processes, the quality of thinking, and emotions. We must recognize or remember, repeatedly, with sincere reverence toward the immense wisdom swirling inside our bodies and all around us, but often we just can't see it. Instead of wanting to figure out what's wrong – why is it that something must be wrong in the first place – and maintaining a tendency to control, we should be in awe. More relaxed about the changes that are happening, more curious and compassionate, without being attached to any expectations.

Frequently, we misunderstand strong emotions and are overrun by them. With a neutral point of view, more allowing and humbler, we can see that those feelings began by the impure filters in the brain.

It's all a ripple effect of the vibration of thinking. *I like, or I don't like this* is a thought, an opinion, and an evaluation. If the opinion makes us feel down, then it's not of good quality. We shouldn't blindly listen to these opinions or fully trust them.

My body is exactly like my teacher. Even when I didn't like what my teacher would say, it wasn't my place to say something. I have the same sense toward my body's mind and energy systems. Sometimes all we need to do with energy is let it be. We can release any form of expectation and opinions and allow the process to be what it needs to be; it's too much on our part to interfere. We can allow, flow, and relax a bit more. Where am I holding tension in my body? I would ask. Focus there and try to release it, but then get out of the way. Then bring that energy into the center of the body to store it there - cultivate the center so it can recalibrate healing power and redistribute where it's needed. The head brain can't know this - so thinking may derail healing. Hands on the belly, just visualizing the center of the body, for example. My neck hurts, then focus on your lower belly and release the tension from the neck, without too much-fueling thoughts of why this is happening, I did this or that; push all that away and bring the focus to your zero-point, no matter if at the grocery store or waiting at the doctor's office or presenting in a meeting.

This process of maintaining a cool, clear, and neutral stance behind our thought-emotion processes and a strong, stable, resilient, grounded sense of belonging is the ancient KiGong or QiGong practice of the shamanic microcosmic orbit. More on this later.

6

CALIBRATION

Path Of Light ~ Vertical Alignment

I was led to move to the area inland from the coast of upper Lazio. I moved in the middle of Spring when nature expressed itself beautifully in all the deep shades of green. The land is surrounded by a series of rolling hills, mountains, deep valleys, streams, and lakes. I found a nice place in a newer construction, spacious, comfortable, and clean. The space allows for a peaceful flow and creative expression. My meditations and guidance remind me daily that Earth continuously transmits energy through us. Just a short while ago, I was led to learn about one of the main roads just a few hundred meters away from my house. It is the ancient road called Via Amerina, which was built around 240 BCE, and known as "Il Cammino della Luce" which literally means "The Path of Light."

As I read these words, my whole body felt that electric-buzzing sensation I've become used to feeling, a deep vibration that is a signal of turning inward-then outward, a sign of the presence of my higher mind guiding me. It's the feeling of spaciousness I experience when I connect with my guides. I knew I had to learn more. It was called the path of light because the ancient believers would conduct pilgrimages to and from Rome. This road connected to the old town of Ameria, today known as Amelia, in the beautiful region of Umbria. It went through the vital commercial hub of Hortae, today known as Orte, where I currently live.

How perfect, I thought, that I am on the path of light. I'm following a different light, that of the internal lighthouse, not an external force, institution, organization, or man-made construct. It is the light inside. Earth constantly transmits her wisdom whether we pay attention or not.

This ancient road is built of basaltic rocks, igneous, fiery, magmatic volcanic rock. It holds Earth's magnetic field, and when the volcanic rock cools and becomes solid, it contains the magnetic fields that the Earth expressed millions of years ago. The Earth pulls us in this direction, then in the other to help us regenerate. A new fire energy and transformation phase is developing that facilitates new creation.

When looking at this road on a map, it is a straight line from North-East Rome upwards to the bordering region of Umbria. In later times, this road extended east toward the Adriatic Sea, but it was initially a vertical line across the latitudinal Y axis, symbolizing one dimension of alignment.

In this spacetime, fully align to a new fire that burns to reveal a new creation. It is regeneration, rebirth, beauty, and joy. The Earth holds you and you must find her pulse within your body. Trusting. Creating. Circulating. Sharing. There is no other task that is more important.

When I first moved back to Italy, besides initially landing at my family's house, I soon moved to the countryside just west of Siena, a truly extraordinary town in Toscana. It was a difficult time, but I was surrounded by beauty. The landscape is magical, and nature supported my transition back to my homeland. After being there for a while, I learned I was living on the St. Michael/Apollo Ley line. Then too, I could feel that strong vibration through my body as if something had turned on, signaling that I was in the right place. This ley line is a semi-diagonal line that begins in Ireland, aligning sacred sites through the UK, France, Italy, Greece, Cyprus, and Israel. Another symbol of alignment. From right to left. If my head is toward the North Pole and my feet are toward the South Pole, this line leans from right to left. Looking at a map, this made perfect sense for me. I studied the numbers, the cipher corresponding to latitude and longitude. It does matter where we physically are on the Earth.

I've struggled with inflammation and intense, debilitating symptoms on my entire right side of the body. I began to understand the reasons and observed my patterns, having a clear impression that I only see a fraction of the entire picture, the real alignment process. Realignment from overly Yang force, depending on self-reliance, now pushed toward the left, a more Yin approach to thinking, processing, and leading.

I took a short drive to the old Abbazia di San Galgano one day. In most sacred places across Europe, the church-institution adopted some of these sites by erecting buildings for worship, imposed some flowery additions to the ancient myths, and claimed these sites as their own by renaming them or modifying their original symbolism. That occurs all over the world. In my journey, I was guided to these places to gain healing, collect, and absorb Earth transmissions at the right time.

The energies of St. Michael and Apollo embody protection and a heightened quality of fire energy that can cut through perceived limitations. Behind the scenes, adjustments were taking place - a preparation - for opening and allowing me to reclaim the lost pieces of myself. It felt like a culmination of everything that had been buried deep within was now being processed, rising to the surface with an intense burning desire to be acknowledged, felt, seen, and heard. Alongside this transformative fire energy, the path of light guided me toward true seeing.

As I integrated these healing energies within my heart and voice, they became radiant beacons illuminating the way forward. I found relief and strength in the nurturing embrace of the Earth, harnessing both the Yin power of Fire and the Yang power of Water to balance and support my journey. In our understanding of Yin as Water and Yang as Fire, we often overlook that *each element contains both energies*, much like the various aspects of our own microcosm. We each possess a unique vibration that operates in the background, acting as the strategist on the bridge of a ship. This underlying force governs our chosen patterns of thought, the personas we identify with, and how we express our emotions.

However, there are moments when this force can become a weak leader, easily swayed, or exert excessive control, becoming overbearing or even tyrannical. During such times, finding harmony may involve inviting more of the opposite energy to influence our physical, energetic, and spiritual systems, allowing us to reconnect to a balanced and harmonious flow.

Pillar of Light: Yin ~ Yang ~ Balancing Beam

Realignment and calibration of frequency is like tuning an instrument. Yang Earth energy. Fiery ancient wisdom transmissions from times passed. Earth recognizes your vibration and activates the encoding. Yin Sky energy. Divine light upgrade - it's a renewed light spectrum. Gently, effortlessly flowing from above. Infusing a soft flow through the above minds into the brain. Balance is a process manifesting in the physical, already present in the cosmic mind.

Find it in the lower dahnjon (dantien). Meet the energies here. Higher frequency expands from here. See the more extensive role of the cosmic orbit. The pillar of light is one dimension. You are in the circular *Shen* process. The multi-dimensional circulation and becoming aware of the drops of wisdom all around. As you perceive more of your own capacity, you can hold more, allowing more to be presented.

Vision of circular structures of energy fields creating shapes and colors like a dream catcher represents entering a new reality, holding potentials. Alignment will present the exchange in and out of the bodies. Manifesting in this reality using the six senses, experiencing learning. Receiving well is giving well. What do we do with the beads of light we can receive into the physical structure-complex? It is not ours. It is a gift to embody, absorb, from it craft something with your own vibration, then continue the movement of flow outward, in and out, in and out, in and out. This is the law. Allow it to reach the other in the continuous flow. This is a genuine exchange with a grateful and sincere mind.

Earth center - the aspect representing fire and heat of transformation. The three lower-dimensional sphere structures of body-heart-brain are held in the Shen, which is vast and pure. The circle is the beginning and the end, that which has no beginning nor an end. It is the sacred sound *IL*, the One, in the sacred Chun Bu Kyung text, where the three spheres are generated and merged into the one.

The completion of our essence is navigating through the structures of our spiritual bodies, experiencing, and embracing more of our true selves. Walking in these worlds simultaneously, using the life we participate in the earthly realm with our six senses as a tool for becoming. Expanding our focus to hold a bigger perspective. Live with the sight of the great birds, zooming out, far out. Choosing where our focus should be and why. Embracing our own unique song-vibration. Continuously purifying ourselves and flowing in and out of our communities, revealing the light and beauty that we are.

Lower dahnjon (dantien) - Earth palace - is the master alchemical mind with the capacity to hold the entire universe and in-form (send-receive) frequencies to the rest of the bodies - the minds. Earth palace in an ancient tradition is symbolized by a volcano, and from this volcano rises a dragon. It reminds me of Wadjet, the feminine fiery dragon energy, which is such a powerful, transformative, regenerative force. She is the great teacher. The fiery magnetic codes from Earth activate a process of transformation - another initiation into being.

In Chinese medicine, we know the yang meridian channels flow energy downwards from the top of the head along the back of our body toward the heels, and yin energy rises from the bottom of the feet along the front of the body toward the top of the head. If we reach for the sky with our arms and think of ourselves as a tree, yin energy rises through the front, and yang energy descends through the back.

However, internal alchemy occurs when we create the microcosmic orbit, which refers to the circulation between the governing vessel and the conception meridian. These both begin in the area of the first chakra and rise, enveloping the front and back of our torso.

Healing happens when energy rises through the back and descends through the front of our physical body. This pattern of circulation creates the vesica symbol, holding us in the place of creation.

By creating circulation that matches the laws of the universe in our body, we can begin the process of internal alchemy. In my experience and inspired vision, inner alchemy involves many layers. Studying the hermetic principles and the nine levels of *change and transformation* resonates with what the ancient Taoist shamans and wisdom teachers were transmitting.

Hundreds of centuries ago, the wisdom from ancient times was held secret and disclosed to those who could honor its sacredness. I don't claim to fully embrace all teachings, but I continue learning through experience.

The Taoists teachings speak of the nine levels on the path of enlightenment, nine energy accumulation postures of *becoming*. We have the nine phases of transformation as per the teachings of Thoth. The ancient Egyptians knew the wisdom of the nine sacred bodies with their own unique purpose, density, and dimension, such as the nine gods on Ra's solar barque. In the beautiful sacred text Chun Bu Kyung, I see the multi-dimensional teachings that mirror those of the ancient people before the land of Khem was established. Codes of light, language of light, are transmitted to be embedded within humanity and Earth for us to interact with in spacetime realities. As our physical, dense body is governed by the invisible pull toward Earth, our other bodies interact with these codes of light, collaborating, coordinating, and manifesting on various levels.

We tend to keep ourselves so busy all the time - needing outside stimuli to identify with and believe it's the source of *functioning*, yet we often feel so heavy with our everyday lives, with our dense bodies and minds. We are shut out from the other aspects of ourselves.

One doorway to communion, integration, and further expansion of our minds is through the portal of the lower dahnjon energy complex. It is often referred to as the second chakra, but it's actually only one dimension of this beautiful sacred space. The lower dahnjon includes the second chakra, but that's not what it is. It consists of the lower energy centers in the internal chakra system and expands to the outer energy centers around the body. This is why I am using the term *complex*.

Imagine a ring around your lower waist, a donut-like shape. A toroidal energy field emanating from the center most point of the lower dahnjon. For those unfamiliar, the lower dahnjon has an entry point called the ocean of energy, located a few inches below the belly button. If you travel inward toward the lower back and sacrum area, about halfway, you will find the zero-point of this energy center complex. The hieroglyph image of Ra, the sun god, is a big circle with a dot in the middle. The dot is the central point and the zero-point field creates a specific quality of pure energy with a unique vibrational signature. Imagine holding the sun's energy in your lower belly, breathing with the entire universe from this zero-point, brightening as you become one with the rhythm of the universe, then expanding this energy outward in all directions.

We are so linked to the Earth. This energy center is the one that can be closely related to the fiery core of the Earth. It is home to profound alchemy, transformation, healing, and awakening. To create the natural force of the universe within and around us and to complement universal laws, we must create the transformative flow of creation that is the medicine of our planet and the cosmos.

In creating the microcosmic orbit, we begin by harnessing fire in the belly. Allow the fire to burn enough to create steam. Water energy from the kidneys rises through the spine; once it reaches the top of the head, it transforms into a higher purification water energy which clears the brain, refines the heart as it descends, and aligns the wills (plural to align with multi-minds Will), reconnecting with the fire for more profound levels of regeneration.

This process is never-ending. In KiGong practice, it is something to be experienced not just physically but relaxing our minds enough to allow the feelings to arise and for the energy and spiritual senses to awaken. As we focus inward with a relaxed mind but keen focus, we automatically expand to greater edges of our true essence. It's so peaceful and bright out there - but out there is actually right here, now.

Properly developing the lower energy center complex is a significant part of transformation. An indication that we are beginning to achieve a level of mastery is to observe how big the pendulum swings are. The law of rhythm appears in our lives on all levels, and its significance is so deep, as a glowing bead of light in our brain. If we react to something with a big swing, the pendulum will inevitably swing in the other direction. There is no such thing as preventing this phenomenon from happening.

Even experiencing exciting positive feelings may not be so good after all. Neutrality is key. Strong opinions about anything indicate that we need to balance some aspects of our minds. I catch myself having strong opinions about things and situations all the time. For example, rude people. I simply can't understand why people are cruel and mean. No smiling? It's probably because of my years in hospitality, walking around smiling, and creating positive experiences for my guests and team members. Why can't people smile? So many people are suffering; why are we adding to that by not being kind? That's a big trigger for me. It's totally ok, of course, we're people, and we need to feel all our emotions. Nobody can tell you what you should or shouldn't do, but I do observe this in people as I walk through town, in the grocery store, at the post office and so on.

The laws of the universe give us pointers and instructions; they act as a hint to pay attention. Can I maintain a true level of neutrality not masked by avoidance, shoving it down deeper just like I did in the past? Can I create space in my body for my heart and thought processes so that I can listen? The Earth's energy provides us that key.

Our bodies are so amazing. We just can't grasp how extraordinary everything about us is. Through training, our physical, energy, and spiritual bodies can come back online in a more resilient manner. What I mean is that once we can activate the lower dahnjon fully, the natural healing power within works at a deeper level. It's always online working hard for us, however external sources tend to get in our way, such as this recommended medicinal treatment, the message in this book, the suggestions of friends or family, this strange idea that is not our own, this fear and doubt we've carried for too long - all forms of disconnection from the vibration of love toward ourselves. We are in sleep mode, and the lights are out, acting as if we're completely dormant, but something is still happening in the background.

Countless times I've seen people recover from surgeries, injuries, and emotional roller coasters in a smoother and faster manner, gaining more resilience because they have learned how to manage their energy systems. This phenomenon is our natural state. When consumed with the mental world, we are completely disconnected from the rest of who we are - and I don't mean simply our physical body. When we can awaken this innate power closely linked to the Earth's vibration, we can source the specific type of strength we need at any given time.

There is the strength for handling a job interview, the strength you need for listening to your children, managing your relationships, and handling a loss, whether big or small. Any form of loss means parts of ourselves leave along with the thing, person, or situation that is passing away. Each time we are deeply hurt, we lose golden coins from our giant light reservoir, which is *the holy grail*. If we can learn to reactivate our source of power, in-gather our lost or stolen beads of light, we can come back to center, zero-point, true balance, and order. The swing is less, things happen, but we can handle it without so much effort. Some good stress, some good pain, some good joy, and some good sadness, they all represent balance. Dark and light, space, and time. Not only gravity but other forces interact with us. We are to be the best *surfers* we know. We must absolutely become the leader of our groupie fan base. When did we start losing trust in ourselves? Hug yourself right now. Rub your hands, and feel the power of your palms. Place your palms on your heart and breathe with a spacious mind. Rub your whole body, sweeping, caressing your entire body from the face, your hair and head, your neck, shoulders, and arms. Sweep down along the front of your body and the back along the legs.

Say out loud, I love myself, thank you, my body, soul, and spirit for working hard for me and with me. I will pay more attention. And in reading these words, you may feel like ... ok, whatever, I can't say that. I look hideous, I've gained weight, I'm going through menopause, I hate my job, and my kids drive me crazy, my husband thinks I'm ugly, I can't remember a day where I had time for myself, etc., etc.

I encourage you to simply place your hands on your chest anyway and pay attention to your breathing. Notice and say quietly in your mind, everything I feel and see around me is not really who I am, it's mine to manage. When we are ready, in moments of surrender, with a spacious mind, we must be brave enough to ask, who am I and what do I want? over and over until you receive a simple, clear, honest answer. It is a practice which takes devotion and patience, watching yourself honestly, honoring all experiences of the past and all unknowns of the future.

Who's in charge here? Whoever is in charge is not a good leader if she/he makes me feel small, powerless, and ugly. Have a department meeting with your *people* - your groupies, gather them all, and organize a strike, a coup, a full-on insurrection. Burn it all away and rebuild with a strong foundation. Get a new leader - this is *Choice*. You're the only one that can do that. No one can ever tell you 100% what is right for you. If this or that teacher, method, book, music, or location resonates with you, even if just for a while, then it's right for you. When something doesn't, it's done with you, and you are done with it. Change the leader - meaning allowing the true leader, who is your higher mind, to complete her/his mission. We are all creators. We just shut down several parts of our innate healing technology into deep sleep mode.

The work is connecting. To what? I want the answer. Well, it's connecting to a million aspects of ourselves. As we practice paying attention, grounding, feeling like we belong on and to Earth, and practicing neutrality, we can retrieve more wisdom and connect to more and more of our essence. This is the work. Just as we each have a unique vibration, there are myriads of paths. You are the new leader who gets to decide this way now, then that way for a while. I will step forward. I'm scared, but I also feel trust. Higher frequency is exponentially stronger than lower frequency. Feeling shame is heavy, yes, absolutely. But if I can counter that level of lux with the vibration of courage and neutrality, the brightness of frequency can raise me up so I can see above and beyond that fence. It's not so bad now. I can see more; there is way more.

I will keep going. It's not wishful thinking. Wishing is a very superficial, and limited aspect of the sense of purpose. Choose and then do it. I will keep going. Not, I hope things will be ok.

Enjoy everything because when something heavy comes, it's an excellent opportunity to focus on the lower Earth palace within the center of our center. Something light will come soon. That is the law of the universe, and I am part of that same universal intelligence. I will be ok.

7

DESIRE FOR FREEDOM & ADVENTURE

A Mission of Self-Reliance

Leaving Italy at 19 years old, with acceptance to BYU (Brigham Young University) in Utah, was an exciting time. The chance to finally move to the USA had arrived, giving me the opportunity to meet people from the church community and begin this new chapter. Departure on July 19th followed the intense Liceo Classico final exams. My mini theses focused on the subjects of ancient Greek and Physics, preparing the five-year program as the final graduation project. This was a unique situation, as no one had ever presented final exams on two topics so far apart. Being a Sun-Libra and Moon-Sagittarius, this made complete sense to me later on, explaining a lot about so many layers of my personality. We are truly given breadcrumbs throughout our entire life, with no such thing as a coincidence or mistake. Why not philosophy and history, or Greek and philosophy? These were all subjects that the Ministry of Education selected as possible mini-theses options for the final exams, but no - I had to be different.

I went to Oregon first to meet my grandparents, who drove me down to Utah. It was great. We listened to the Gipsy Kings in the car during the entire trip. I loved my grandpa. He was always positive. Sometimes he would be strict and rigid, reprimanding us kids for misbehaving, but he always went back to being a joyful, optimistic, let's enjoy each moment type of person. I admired him so much. My grandma, on the other hand, was a strange person, and since my mother had some severe traumatic stories about this woman, I didn't completely trust her. I remember I would observe her very carefully. There was something very sinister behind the fragile outside layer. I was feeling overly protective of my mom, of course, and didn't want her to experience any more pain.

So here I am in Utah. The intensity of university life and, more than anything, the English language overwhelmed me, feeling unintelligent and inadequate as I had never studied in English before. There was a strong feeling of wanting to run and give up right away. Something inside of me, deep inside, said, no, this is not good for you - you just have to get out. Mom sent a returned missionary, who I really trusted, to come visit me. He lived in Salt Lake City. Not knowing any of this, when Brian came to my dorm, which was the same dorm he stayed in when he attended BYU years prior, I was thrilled and in disbelief. Brian tried to convince me to stay and give it some time, but my mind was made up. Now I know what that is, but back then, I just didn't care, going along with my feelings without overthinking. The over-explanation and excuses were only for others, not for me. This whole situation just didn't make any sense to others. Looking back, I was acting like a stubborn kid, upset and annoyed, without realizing that I was directing all that negativity toward myself. The first words to my dad when I picked up the phone were, I'm coming home, the school advisor confirmed they can provide a full refund. It's ok, my dad said. He was just happy to have me come back.

I returned home and was back to whatever normal life was supposed to be like. Ignoring what happened, going to church with mom, figuring out if attending Archeology in Viterbo University would be the right choice. Three months later, I met a missionary who was about to finish his mission. He told me he would be back for me and was in love. Fast forward to that following winter, I'm flying to Rhode Island to soon marry this boy. I thought this was my path. I was following the same path as my mom, leaving her home long ago to meet my dad in Italy. That was it! It was a new life. It felt right. I trusted the feeling that I gained through diligently praying daily. Years later, as I recalled these moments and feelings, I couldn't really tell *who* was talking in my head and heart.

There are no regrets as I look back at my life experiences. Still, I can see now that whatever I felt as a guiding system was distorted and masked by my inner natural sense of adventure, freedom, and seeking my value without any help. The self-reliant mission was beginning to take a new form of expression.

In spite of everything, I really enjoyed Rhode Island, the beaches, and the people who spoke with a cool New England accent. I learned about the peculiar conflict between Boston and New York City, and also traveled to amazing places in New Hampshire and Maine. Such incredible beauty. If it wasn't so terribly cold in the winter, I would move to a small village on the coast where I could live in a lighthouse.

I started working in a nursing home in Warwick. Someone from the church got me a job in the activities department. My manager was pleasant at first until I realized she was having an affair with the general manager. He was very handsome, and she behaved in such odd, inappropriate ways around him. I was shocked about this whole situation as he was married, and she acted as if I was totally blind. I think this was a time when I understood people didn't realize how observant and intuitive I was. It was a bit shocking as I didn't know how to process this realization, feeling like I had to create this outer shield - *I don't know anything* - so others wouldn't feel uncomfortable or see right through me. Years later, I always used to say I could probably train to work for the CIA because *with this face, nobody would know what I know.*

Working with seniors who had severe conditions was challenging. I would often cry my eyes out in the elevator or the stairways. My parents or I could end up this way. The time will come when someone I know will not have mastery over their minds anymore and will regress to being cared for as a child. My job was to spend time with them, to make them laugh and play fun games. My mom would come to visit and volunteer there during her stay, and that was a really meaningful time for both of us.

Shortly after my marriage started, I knew it was the wrong path for me. I couldn't explain it. I just kept going along. My mind kept saying, you heard the call of the holy spirit, and this is the life for you, but I soon started doubting this feeling I had back in Italy when I was praying and asking if this was the right decision. Since I had no idea what to do, I enrolled in a year-long travel and tourism program, which I loved. One thing I can confidently say about the Italian or European school systems is that I really learned what studying means. I've always had an excellent memory, so memorizing all those airport codes was like a game. I met a few great individuals who had a significant influence on my life. My marriage was dying; I was hanging on, but then I soon realized that it was meaningless to continue like that. Unable to process my frustration, feeling like a little kid, I would yell at myself, nobody should get married so young - why would anyone allow this? I didn't know anything back then. How does anyone know who they are at that age? Deep down, these questions came up over and over: are you free? Are you alive? I was so depressed and had a few dark moments of true desperation where, in one instance, I knew I was divinely guided off the highway to safety by helping angels in what seemed like a certain point of no return.

The school program included an incentive trip to Cancun toward the end of the education schedule. I was still Mormon, so all the drinking and madness in these spring break places didn't affect me at all, unlike all my classmates. The experience was remarkable, and for the first time in my life, I saw what seemed like home. The crystal turquoise waters of the Caribbean Sea. I mean, water that color is a dream. I didn't care about the rest of it, the crazy party town and hotel congestion, just the blue water. That felt like returning home; such a beautiful, rejuvenating energy came over me.

Upon my return to Rhode Island, I successfully completed the travel program, graduated, and began the divorce process. By that time, I had moved out. My friend from school really helped me see what was happening. She spoke to me honestly, like a good friend and mother. I moved out and found a small place to rent with my cat, Micio. I really liked this place. It was an old house with lots of windows. I felt so alive - alone and free. Through a hiring agency, I started working at a bolt and screw company. This was office work, entering data from invoices and plugging in hours for payroll. The office ladies were the best. It was such a pleasant, positive environment. I learned how to type faster and faster. Here I am, moved into a house, alone, working an office job I found on my own. After my trial period, they hired me directly and even gave me a raise. On weekends, I would meet with friends and go dancing. For the first time in my life, I experienced feeling girly and having fun as all young people should.

After what seemed like about three or four months, I decided it was probably time to tell my parents. That day is unforgettable. Sitting at my kitchen table, I called my dad and told him about the separation and filing for divorce. He was quiet as tears of release started streaming down my face. There was so much I was holding, wanting to keep it together. My mom was there too. She got on the other phone in the house. It's ok honey, it's gonna be alright. Are you sure this is what you want? Can we call the missionaries? You could talk to them.

I'm sure they were extremely worried about me after we hung up. I was so far away, alone. Before, I was with this other family, at least. Mom thought the girl missionaries could help me, but really? What do they know about anything to do with me? Will they care? There was a strong, overwhelming sense of doing the right thing, but for who? What about what's right for me, I asked. So, what happens? My mom was sent to be with me. By then, my lease and the school program were ending. Mom was heading to Oregon because Grandpa was dying. His 23 years of heart conditions trapped his body into this cycle of open-heart surgeries. He was tired. She came to Rhode Island as I was finishing up some things, and the plan was that I would go with her to Oregon. When mom arrived, we moved into this long-term motel. It was such low quality. I would go dancing at night, meet friends, and do immature things while mom was stuck in the motel, with the roaches and my cat, watching TV. I felt so bad later in years looking back at how much mom was there for me, always, no matter what, even when I was kind of mean or thoughtless toward her sometimes.

We were finally headed to Oregon. The Pacific Northwest is the best! Except for the gray weather, I love this region. If I could move to Cannon Beach and have a house on a cliff, I would, although the need for sun is definitely a priority - something I learned much later.

I was still part of the Mormon church and would go to the youth sessions on Sundays. I met many interesting individuals and felt part of a community, which was very important for me. Before too long, I fell for this boy who was quite a rebel. We used to go dancing and hang out late into the night. His story was certainly interesting. A few years before we met, he withdrew from his mission, then married and divorced a short time afterward. His sense of creativity was strong, and he would soon become an architect. His brother was the golden child, who had recently gotten married, bought a house, and began a great career, building the perfect life. There was an underlying conflict with this whole family. They treated my friend like the black sheep of the family, which is what I felt like, so we had much in common. Our conversations were truly some of the most meaningful in this challenging period.

This time, transitioning from living in Rhode Island, not knowing what would happen, to trying to establish something in Oregon, was quite an adjustment. I struggled with expectations versus what I really wanted.

I Have a Gift – Hotel Life

With my diploma from the travel program, I got hired on the spot by this prominent hotel in downtown Portland. Hotel life was incredible, and I learned fairly quickly this would be my future. The people who trained me were so amazing and we soon became friends. Learning guests' names, realizing that I had a natural talent for dealing with people, and being a quick learner made me recognize I had a gift. As the natural planner that I am, I soon started thinking about what this type of work could mean for me. I want to work for the best hotels of the highest quality; for the best companies; for the best places. How do I do that? We had the internet back then and some cell phones, but not like it is today. I mean, nobody I knew had a computer at home and I only had a beeper, remember those? And my first cell phone was this grossly clumsy Motorola which I had to carry in a backpack. It wasn't as easy as it is today, but I did a lot of research on locations and got help from my managers at the hotel to understand hotel categories and tiers.

I started applying for the highest category hotels in Cancun, four and five AAA Diamond ratings. Having been there the year before, I knew that if I got stuck, I could just speak English, and most people would understand me. Why not? This will be the best way to learn a third language. I always felt like Spanish was so beautiful, but I didn't want to learn it in school.

I decided to apply and see what would happen. At the same time, I also applied to be a flight attendant for American Airlines. The goal was to travel and be of service, so why not on an airplane? Never mind the fact that I hate flying, and even though I do, of course, and since then I have traveled a lot, I get severe anxiety, and for the life of me, I cannot understand why in the world there is turbulence and why doesn't the pilot control that, oh my gosh, why is this happening, I mean how irresponsible is this, don't they care about people, on and on about this while sitting in my seat, sweating, with my heart in my throat; on every single flight, it's over the top. Totally irrational.

A month later, I was interviewed by this amazing property in Cancun. Feeling really confident in the interview, I did well, and was waiting for the final offer from human resources. They told me it would take a bit of time since some individuals on the leadership team were on vacation. In the same time frame, I received a call from American Airlines. That interview went well too, and I was to go to Dallas to do a medical test at their hub. Based on the results, I would be assigned to a city, likely Boston, working on international flights. A dream-come true, I thought. It was an exciting time although I felt intimidated. Would the fact that I was nervous about flying be a problem? I smile now with this look as if I was reprimanding a little girl; c'mon, this is probably not a good idea; how are you supposed to help people if you will need help first.

This was a waiting period. Uncertain about moving to Cancun or Boston, I took the opportunity to return to Italy for about a month since I hadn't gone home yet after the Rhode Island Telenovelas years.

Soon after, I received info from the Airlines. They were prepared to hire me, however since test results showed high levels of anemia, I would have to be grounded for 6 months, and undergo iron therapy. The plan was to have me work as a ground agent until I would be cleared to fly regularly. They asked when I could start. Within a few days of the airline offer, I finally got a call from the hotel in Cancun. When can you come, they asked.

It was an easy decision, I instantly knew. No airline - what was I thinking? Hotel on the beach - yes, that's for me. So here I go, all excited, flying to Cancun. The goal was to spend about 3-6 months learning Spanish while working and then return to the States.

Initially, I would only communicate in English, facing learner's block. Although Spanish wasn't hard to learn, speaking presented some challenges. I finally decided to buy a verb book to learn conjugations, which allowed me to see how to construct meaningful sentences. For the most part, I would really listen, understand how things needed to be said, and copy the tones and sounds I heard. It was about three months until I could speak fairly well, and my coworkers would step in when I needed help at work. Most of the guests came from the States, and everyone was listening to me more than me listening to them.

I became romantically involved with one of the doormen. The second story began. I loved life in Mexico, but in the more typical neighborhoods, not the hotel zone, solely catering to the party lifestyle and tourism. It was so crowded most of the time. This lifestyle becomes normal for hotel people. Tourism was impressive in those days, and for that reason, working in a 4 or 5 diamond resort provided a privileged lifestyle, a truly remarkable adventure.

This experience lasted exactly one year. I was able to transfer back to my first hotel in Portland, since it was part of the same company, and they really valued my short time in Cancun. It was certainly the best school as far as hotel standards go. Although I loved Oregon, I felt miserable. I couldn't bear the distance to my doorman. The feelings of going back were strong. Mistakenly, I believed it to be love once again, and at that point, nothing else mattered. All I yearned for was to return - and I did. Another cycle, and this time, the transfer was to another property. It was a much better experience for me. I loved this hotel so much that 9 years later, I returned to the position my current manager held. It was an exceptional experience with wonderful friends, and so many meaningful moments. My managers and directors were the finest leaders I could have asked for. I learned so much from them. As I watched them deal with the team and guests, it was always mesmerizing to witness their gifts - they truly had superpowers. They made dreams come true, not just for guests but for all of us employees. They could create experiences of a lifetime, and lead the team through challenges, as well as great moments of success. I was in awe, feeling so lucky to be part of this. This was the life I must pursue, I thought. I want to be just like them. Working on creating a beautiful experience for guests who come here and for the teams that make it all happen. I wanted to hold it all in my arms, feeling encouraged and supported. So, a more structured path in this field began. This was the property and experience that propelled me to seriously pursue the leadership training path.

Over a year later, the most favorable next step was to move back to the US to go after leadership positions since growth opportunities were more prevalent. I realized it would have been more challenging to move up if I had stayed in Cancun at that one property, understanding the potential of transferring from one property to another to gain valuable experience. This path would allow me to return to Cancun if it worked out in the future, which is exactly what happened.

In the year 2000, I transferred back to that same hotel in Portland and married the doorman I met two years before. This hotel was also very important in my formation. I learned a great deal by living through everything that I could ever imagine, including a bomb threat shortly after 9/11, with the FBI and bomb squad in the lobby, power outages, cyclical staff changes, ice storms, and various types of events. Here too, I experienced influential leaders and created beautiful friendships.

By this time, my parents were ready to go back to Italy. After so many years, mom realized that her family was, and is, a bit strange, and things just didn't fit. She felt homesick for Italy now, not the other way around. I'm sure it was excruciating for her. So many years of wanting to come *back home* to then recognize her life in Italy was much more fulfilling. My parents moved back, shipped a large container with a purple Ford Ranger pickup truck for my dad, and were on their way. The addition to the family house in Italy was finished, and they would have their own apartment while my sister fully took over the main house and the entire property. I ended up staying in Oregon, buying my parent's house, and remaining for a few more years until the transfer to Seattle.

My hotel career was the only thing that mattered to me then. After a year, I became a supervisor, then was offered a leadership position as department head at the smaller sister property a few blocks away in Portland. I took it, and soon became part of a task force team to open a hotel right outside of Seattle. While the hotel was still preparing to open, I was offered a position as department head there. It was an awkward situation since they already had a person in that role, but the assistant general manager was adamant that she wanted me to help lead her teams. This was a wonderful opportunity to move to a new city, so I sold my house and moved a month after receiving the offer. I felt it would be a good fit, although I ignored that she was a bit of a nervous wreck and would eventually cause me extreme stress reactions in my body, such as explosive hives episodes, including several trips to the ER, due to the level of stress. I knew this situation couldn't continue much longer - resignation was on the horizon. One day after my one-year anniversary at this property, I formally resigned. Waiting for a transfer to another location was not an option, the circumstances were extreme, driving me to a complete severing. Leaving the company was an extremely painful decision, as this company was all that mattered to me, but I was at my wit's end. The decision was settled months prior but waiting for the one-year mark was important in order to avoid repaying the relocation benefits. It was brutal. I was so sick.

In those last three months, I had learned a property in Rome was about to open, and I applied without thinking. It was a franchise property, and I didn't need to go through the corporate HR channels. How wonderful, I thought - being able to go back home and work for this company? What? That's incredible. It was all very exciting. Since my resume was impressive and I am an Italian citizen, the leadership team called me right away - of course they were interested, and hired me immediately. I didn't even get a proper interview, which should have been a red flag, but I jumped...again...

It was a wonderful experience at the beginning, but also a nightmare. A three-month opening project took nine months. I was dying. My dad even told me, you should probably return to the States or Mexico. My standards were too high, I was told. They're not too high - people like to cut-corners, and if you want the company's name on your building, these are some basics you need to have nailed down - it's that simple. I would hear requests like these all the time: you have to hire this girl; she's the councilman's cousin's daughter; or, you have to hire this other person; she's the sister of the mayor's brother; the chief of police needs his son to get a job at the Concierge desk; you need to make it happen. And, of course, I would rebel each time. I will interview anybody but will consider people based on their experience, motivations, and how they fit with the rest of the team, and each time I was warned - I should say threatened - not to cross the big bosses and just do what you're told. A rebellious fire would explode in my belly, and I just couldn't keep quiet. Very professional, as always, but can't *just do what I'm told* if it's not fair. So, I became a *problem* for the big bosses - the American doesn't want to keep in her lane, I would often hear. When the corporate office sent the regional European team to review the opening processes and their status, I just wanted to hug them and cry. I know they knew of some shady business and weren't too happy about this property, but they were also being very professional - or political - smoothing out some compromises. Except, I simply couldn't. How about integrity and ethics?

I realized then that I would never, ever, in the world ever, without a doubt, ever, ever work for an Italian company ever again. I said *ever* way too many times, but that's how passionate I was and still am.

My family completely understood and supported me when I finally told them it was time to resign, that I simply couldn't stay. The next day, as I informed my director and HR, they strongly encouraged me to leave right away instead of finishing the month. It was hard, thinking, how rude! I hired and helped train all your people. They were a very good team.

I had reached out to my ex-managers from the property in Cancun, asking them if there were any leadership opportunities for me. They responded right away and said, yes, of course Enriquita, claro que si, regresa! (translation: yes, of course, come back!) They gave me two options to choose from, both a step down from my current role, but it was ok for me, I didn't care. I was just so grateful that I could go back there. It felt like home.

So here I am, 9 years later, back in Cancun at my beloved resort. The same people who trained me, the same loyal bellmen who took care of everything, the same leaders responsible for the executive team. I was so happy and relieved - back to high standards and people knowing what service really means. Of course, there were lots of new faces too. I was placed in the Front Desk manager role. My direct supervisor was my night manager nine years prior, and his wife, my best manager ever, worked at the new resort next door.

I went back right as the hotels were reopening after a nine-month closure due to the terrible destruction of Hurricane Wilma, and because of the severe impact of this natural disaster affecting the staff, the properties, and community, being there at that time was a huge deal and particularly special. My team was incredible. Strong connections were made, especially with a few individuals who created such powerful experiences for us as a team and the guests we were serving. As always, there was much to learn. I became an even more confident and strong leader with loving team members and colleagues, grasping the Spanish language well and growing to be an influential contributor. I wouldn't have left if it wasn't for the desire to expand and experience change. A persistent feeling of growing stagnant and bored became obvious after three years, going through every possible big curve, including hurricanes, staff changes, exclusive events, thefts, betrayal, drama, you name it.

It was about 4 years later when I started looking for other opportunities, including a beautiful desert resort in southern Arizona. After applying and interviewing, they hired me with little effort. They flew me there for an in-person interview right before the Christmas holiday, and I fell in love with this strange environment. The unique, beautiful, and peaceful Southwest landscape captured my heart.

I had been to the desert before. While living in Portland years prior, I attended a training class in Palm Springs. It was August, and although I was dying of heat and thought I would pass out in my black suit and nylons, I discovered an absolute love for dry, hot weather. That's when I put out there the thought, I will make this happen one day. I must live in this type of climate. There was just so much sky in the desert, and I had never seen a clear blue sky like this in my life.

When the opportunity presented itself to move to Arizona, I took it. They really valued international experience, and they provided me with a significant raise. The lovely golf resort has great views from the top of a hill and is surrounded by desert plants, such as the great saguaros, truly magnificent.

The move took a lot of work. When is it ever easy to move internationally, even with a relocation package? I also had my little dog Tito with me, he was so brave.

Back in Seattle, he traveled across the skies to Italy and nine months later across the skies again to Mexico, followed by a move to southern Arizona. Never again, I said. It's too stressful. From Seattle to Rome, I also brought my two cats. Wow, that's just not right. I couldn't leave them with anyone; they were my children, so they came with me. My family has land and lots of space, so when I returned to Mexico, I left the two cats with my mom, who loved and cared for them. It's too traumatic for cats and dogs, but the little Tito - no, I just couldn't leave him; he had to come with me. I miss that little guy. He was the best. My companion and friend.

I'm in Tucson now. It's January. Why is it so cold in the desert? I soon adjusted to my new surroundings and began to feel really comfortable. I adapted pretty well for someone who adores the ocean, the sea, anything blue, the wind, and the waves. Sure, I missed the water, especially since I had just moved from Cancun, but the strange environment with the magical Saguaro cacti and beautiful smells of the desert plants also made me feel very much at home. I enjoyed where I lived, and my work colleagues became my friends, as usually occurs, for hotel people at least. My dearest friend Beth was an angel. She taught me a lot, and we shared many important moments, especially the transition through a difficult decision and two life-changing events.

I had been distant from my husband for a while. During this time in Arizona, I recognized it had been happening since the beginning, sensing things weren't working out and wouldn't work out at all. Avoiding these thoughts and feelings and shoving them deep down wasn't useful anymore. Overworking myself became a refuge since I felt a great sense of responsibility toward my career. Although apparently caring for the relationship, there was more focus on creating a life in my bubble, thinking, we must focus on *my* career; I'm the manager here, so my job is more important; who's gonna pay the bills, with all the money you send home to your family who's taking advantage of your being in the US? Tormenting resentment was strongly felt. The options were few. I had to make things happen, if not who's going to take care of anything? Thoughts such as, it would be so nice to have someone take care of me for once. My drive has always been so strong, determined to make it happen and to be successful. My company, its values, and what it represented, were very crucial to me as they provided independence and opportunities, even amounting to be somewhat like a cult. Discipline, high standards, training, managing people, ensuring everyone is happy, sacrifice, *watch this-I'll fix it* scenarios, influencing and affecting people positively. The underlying drive was making a positive impact. I had found it - this was my calling. Recognizing my affinity and connection to this lifestyle, pushing forward no matter what; continue to grow, experience a bigger hotel, a different location, another team, and a different environment. Determination and manifestation. Never mind the fact that my insides were dying. The crumbling had started then, but I didn't realize it. It manifested as the ending of my relationship at first.

Mom came to visit me in the summer of 2009. She went to Oregon to visit her family, then spent a whole month with me in Tucson. We had wonderful moments, even though I was so stressed during that time. Looking back, there were instances when I was a bit mean to her, lashing out carelessly about anyone's feelings. Taking care of others was my gift, but when it came to people close to me, they were on the receiving end of all that stress. I felt so burned out, not just of work but also of my marriage, knowing something had to change rapidly. The inability to manage the frustration was overwhelming. Decisions were made, although I was stalling, scared of the consequences, always needing to please people. Mom was so patient. Oh my goodness, so many times I saw this scenario of meanness come out of me, and she was always so supportive and sweet. Like that time in Mexico when we went to visit Chichen Itza, the pyramid complex that so resonated with me. I was snappish, in a negative mood, and couldn't enjoy anything, unable to fully absorb the magnificence of this sacred site because I was too busy worrying about my hideous attitude toward my husband and my extreme unhappiness and feeling inadequate, frustrated, and holding so much heaviness on my shoulders, buried under a constant state of annoyance.

So here we are in Tucson. I'm behaving the same way. I was ignoring it - as much as I could. However, we did share some great times. We spent time at the spa, visited friends in Apache Junction, and enjoyed the desert, shopping, and cooking.

Mom was traveling back to Italy at the end of August. I had already planned a trip to visit my family in September, so I would see her again after a month. So, after this visit to Arizona, here I am, spending more time with mom but back home. It was still so warm when I visited that we could go to the beach together. My favorite thing in the world was to sit in the sun like lizards, walk on the beach, swim, and be salty and joyful. I still have these awesome selfies of us. Mom driving, and I'm in the passenger seat, all tan, salty, and oily. In these pictures, we were headed to see my Zia (aunt) Anna, who rented a vacation home in the Argentario peninsula in Tuscany. I remember we drove there two days in a row since the beach was so pleasant. It was like a mini vacation. I loved it. Just the two of us. We would drive this road, which became very familiar to me as I rented a home on that same road for about eight months in the fall of the year I moved back from the US. You could see this little town on top of a tall hill from the highway. Look at that - how neat, we should go see it one day, she would say. It was the little town of Capalbio.

My September trip back home was a good visit. Trying to unplug, I was contemplating what to do next. Some major change was happening in the background - my mind was adjusting. I didn't have the guts to tell my family yet. I'm gonna get another divorce; how do you feel about that?

Only years later, I realized these were the last moments I would spend with my mom in this vibrant, joyful condition. The fun pictures I took of us were posted on my wall for the longest time. Every day, I could see her smiling face and bright eyes, and hear her voice and laugh in my mind. It was all so well-crafted for me to enjoy those moments. Just us two, nobody else.

I returned to Arizona, working like a crazy woman. About a week or two afterward, my husband said he needed a break in our relationship, knowing in my heart that I had driven him to say those words. I needed him to leave me, not wanting to disappoint anyone, even though we should have parted ways years earlier. It was going to be nine years together. We separated. He found his own place within days. I filed the divorce paperwork at City Hall, and it was done.

8

CATALYST ~ MOM

When Everything Became Meaningless

Mom's birthday is around Thanksgiving. Soon after the holiday and her birthday, I got the call. Mom had a series of doctor's visits. They detected cancer, and they were about to operate on her. My dad was very matter of fact about it. Mom was minimizing, saying I'll be alright, you'll see - something like that. I remember in those days, no matter how awake and caffeinated I was, every time I spoke with my family, it was like being in a water tunnel, having difficulty hearing or understanding anything. I was in a daze, in a state of shock, defeated by a sense of loss and extreme anxiety. My sister and I hadn't spoken in 10 years, making it impossible to communicate with her to see what was really happening. I just had my dad and mom to talk with on the phone.

Feeling isolated and adrift, I shoved it deep down and worked hard even more. Back then, I didn't know what was really happening, but my nervous system was so heightened that I would shake as if I had several espressos and smoked a whole pack of cigarettes daily. I was constantly trembling. The only way to function was to suck it up, put on my best guest-face and keep working. My good armor would help me survive. Just make sure nobody sees your hands shaking like they do, and keep your foot at a normal speed of swinging back and forth when your legs are crossed. I'm fine, I'll be fine.

I was able to return to Italy to spend time with mom a few months after we learned about the cancer. She had gone through surgery and was receiving chemotherapy. I remember going to the hospital. There was a large room, one other very young lady who had lost her hair was also receiving chemotherapy. Mom seemed very sleepy and had to sit there for a while. The attendants allowed me to stay with her, but would then sit outside so I could let her rest. Why wouldn't I shut up? I kept talking while she needed rest.

While sitting in this terrible hospital hallway, checking back in here and there, I realized my whole world was so upside down, not knowing how to handle anything, shoving every emotion of panic down. I was trying to be light and breezy - everything is going to be alright, you got this. After learning of the news in early December, all I could do was research as much as I could to get my mind around something. Through the American Cancer Society's website, I ordered two really nice real hair wigs for my mom, and to compliment them, I also bought several colorful scarves that she could use around her head - green, pink, and one that was black with huge irises - she really liked those.

Looking back, I was so blind. I can just picture her sitting in this disgusting chemo room; her body began feeling so weak. A few days later, she would feel stronger, and it seemed ok to go out. We went downtown for a walk. I wanted to buy something, so we parked under the 'Portici' (name of an avenue) and walked a bit. But it was too far for her to walk. We had to pause and slow down, and she was simply too weak. It was so terrible. I was trying to hold it together, sitting on a bench and just resting. Inside, I was kicking myself, and all I wanted to do was pick her up and take her back home, but I didn't want her to see I was freaking out inside. She was trying to be strong for me so I could think of something else, but she couldn't. My heart wept and is weeping now.

It was time for me to go back to Tucson. It was a time when I felt like I was in a movie. As I returned to work, I dove in deeper. Working and covering up the deep sorrow, loss, and anger. I started practicing indoor cycling, and it soon became an obsession - a new addiction. It made me feel so good. This was my routine - working out early in the morning, going to work, working extremely late, then on my way home, I would go to Thunder Canyon Brewery and have an amber draft beer and a pretzel. Sometimes, I would have a cobbler too, and smoke at the outside bar while having my beer. This was my processing system.

I was so lucky to have an amazing role model and leader at this property in Tucson. He was so supportive and really listened to me. There was never a time when he made me feel bad about asking for time off to go see mom during this time.

In retrospect, I should have just quit and spent all the time I could with her, helping and supporting her, instead of being stuck in this hideous idea that work is the most important thing in the world. Meanwhile, my marriage was falling apart, I had started therapy to help me navigate through the process, and was on the verge of exploding or imploding; either way, I knew it wouldn't be pretty. Sleeping stopped altogether. The stress level was so high that I was worried I would flip out at work and be completely inappropriate in meetings and other interactions. There was a strong feeling of isolation from my family, under the impression that they didn't care about me except my mom. When I moved back to the States in Arizona after living in Mexico for the previous 4 years, there was no credit history. Of course, I opened a bank account but didn't have any credit to apply for a credit card. Although my salary was high, it was too soon to request a bank credit card, and this forced me to request another advance from work, but unfortunately, it wasn't approved. Finally, my dad paid for me to go back. It was early May, and nobody knew what to expect.

My relationship with my sister was overly concerning, and her bond with our mom was troublesome for many years. When it came to taking care of mom, my sister had everything on her shoulders. Interesting, I thought. After treating her so poorly your entire life, you are now the one to help her with this illness simply because I'm not there. My heart was crushed. I should have been there, as I was closer to mom. We shared so much. No one had the bond we shared. There was a spiritual connection that is still persistent today as she continues to guide and watch over me. Whispers in my mind, caressing my hair and kissing me on my forehead. My sister had strong connections with mom, especially later in life, but in a completely different way. Why am I not there!? I was so angry at this situation and resentful that it had to be this way. Feeling so trapped because I had to work. Nobody would help me financially if I didn't work. My husband had to send most of his income to his ridiculous family in Mexico. I was spread thin, and now I couldn't fully be near my mom, suffering in a hospital bed.

My dad and sister tried to take mom to a specialist between my first and second trips back home. A terrible road trip up to northern Italy. I couldn't believe it. This was something that was shared with me after the fact, never mind telling me what was happening or what decisions were made. I was exploding inside also because it was too late to bring her to the States. In my mind, they would know how to care for her properly. Of course, this is not true, but I blamed the entire world for what was happening. How is it possible that people still die of cancer? Because it's good business, that's why. Nobody gives a shit. My heart became so hard.

I was able to help her cleanse her face, put on lotion, do her makeup sometimes, and change clothes. It was terrible to see my sister bring her to the shower, barely holding it together. She had lost weight and looked tired. I was there, holding her hand, checking my phone, keeping my mind busy with whatever was on my blackberry. When I told mom I was getting a divorce, she was understanding and convinced me to stay in Arizona, even though I had the opportunity to move. Stay there, you need to stay there, she would say.

The sense of living in a dream or movie was because I saw the situation and kept my hopes high, but was also fully aware that mom was dying and there was nothing anyone could do. We were just waiting. The doctors told us that they were trying to make her comfortable. I remember running outside in the parking lot of this dreadful hospital. I started smoking again out of despair. How do I process this? Mom is dying, and I can't change it.

I said goodbye while she was sleeping, full of morphine and not entirely conscious. Heartbroken and crushed, I hated the world. Everything was meaningless and dim.

About a week later, I received a phone call on a road trip in California. My sister was on the line, it was hard not to panic, while driving on the 101 from LA back to San Diego. I tried to pull over; there was a small rest area where I could park and get out of the car. My sister says mom is awake, she wants to say hi. Sounding so aware with a lot of energy, like a brand-new person. Whatcha doing? She says, with her perky voice. I could sense the smile on her face while stopped on the side of the highway. I'm actually looking at the Pacific Ocean. How perfect is this? I'm coming back mà, coming soon to see you again. She says, oh honey, don't worry, you don't need to make the trip, it's ok. I love you. *Ti voglio bene mamma*, I said, and I was crying but couldn't let her hear that through my voice. I was looking at the ocean and saying goodbye. So that was it. I had this feeling of completion; something was coming to an end.

After the call, I stood there for a bit, then went back in the car and drove back down toward San Diego. Mom died on May 23rd, 2010, a day and a half after that phone call. She had a spritz of energy to say goodbye. Her body was tired - it was time. The call came while I was at home in Tucson. I looked up at the skylight windows, said these words out loud - *Grazie mamma per essere sempre stata lì per me, ti voglio bene, ora non soffri piu', sei libera e sai dove andare. Mi dispiace per tutto. Ti voglio cosi' bene (translation: thank you mom for always being there for me, I love you, you're no longer suffering, you are free and know where to go. I am sorry for everything. I love you so much).*

Shattered and disoriented, I briefly talked with my sister. During my last visit, mom asked us to speak again and reconnect. She held our hands as we sat on each of her sides, and we agreed we would.

Many hours after receiving the call about mom's death, I spoke to my dad. He was very matter of fact, hiding the tremendous loss and sadness he suffered. He probably felt so powerless, and helpless in this situation. Could he have done more? Did she suffer more than she should have? I can't even bear the thought of what he must have gone through. He loved her. Yes, he was often mean to her, and mom would get offended more times than I should remember, but he loved her, and she loved him.

That evening, I went to a gathering, focused on the next thing, shoved it down deeply, and worked to exhaustion, trying to carry on with my life. Putting on the guest-face and moving on, unable to manage taking care of my heart. I couldn't handle anything actually, plus I wasn't sleeping, feeling terribly miserable inside.

For the longest time, I couldn't feel mom. My heart was too broken, and another armor came over the protective shields already present.

Years later, I could dream about her and sense her presence daily. She appears as a bright platinum glowing bead surrounded by a deep cobalt blue light. In different scenarios, she comes as a guide, as part of a team, or alone. She always tells me, you can do it, Ri.

Mindfulness – The Opening to a New Way of Life

Although I was seeing a psychotherapist, I decided it was time to see another specialist. It took all the courage I had to ask for help. My primary care physician was a younger, lovely woman who seemed to care about helping as she spent more than four minutes with me and was genuinely observant. I remember telling her - I can't sleep, feeling overly anxious, worried about blowing up at work, unable to control my extreme restlessness, and feeling like I'm having a heart attack all day long. I don't know how to handle anything inside. My mom is no longer here, and I pretty much hate everyone. If I had a million dollars, I would run away and hide somewhere on the beach where nobody knows me, stop everything, just be and rest. The world is stupid, everything is broken, and moving forward like this is unacceptable. I know this is not really me. I'm a trainer, a leader, and manage people - hearing my words, who is this person speaking right now? This is a complete breakdown. Do you see it?

She was pregnant at the time, and would smile with a loving motherly look. I almost cried but held it together, although my gut and chest were so contracted that I was getting severe cramps. Are you kidding me? I'm like Wonder Woman - I mean, I am her, so everything will be fine. Having high tolerance is my talent. I can take it all on. My doctor prescribed an antidepressant, anti-anxiety, anti-everything. Not really sure what these medications were; a series of trial-and-error *anti finding the root cause medicine*. This therapy helped somewhat as I began to sleep, but I still had severe difficulties.

In the meantime, my job facilitated a smooth transfer to Scottsdale, finally landing another dream role at my dream property. I established care with another doctor, and we started different types of medications for depression, stress, and anxiety. My attitude those days was careless - give me whatever, just make it stop. I began having severe panic attacks to the extent that paramedics came to the hotel to take care of me multiple times. That was so unsettling and embarrassing, I thought. What is happening? This is such weak human malfunctioning. I was disintegrating inside and out. The fact that I went spinning early each morning, was over-caffeinated, sometimes smoked through the day, only focused on work, and neglected my mind completely didn't help - and I didn't know any better. Why aren't we taught to think about the inner worlds? No - that's woo-woo, right?

As usually happens, serendipity brought me to meet another specialist whom I resonated with immediately. She invited me to participate in a mindfulness-based stress reduction (MBSR) program that went on for several weeks, after many psychiatry sessions. What is that? Mindfulness? Sharing my concerns about not knowing what I was supposed to do - utterly clueless. However, I trusted her completely and felt very strongly that this was the answer. You want me to just pay attention with no opinions of any kind? If it's challenging, I want to do it! Let's see what happens.

Mindfulness literally changed the course of my life as I discovered a new sense of curiosity about the invisible worlds, slowly opening up to another part of myself. Years later, I recognized I was led here by angels, and mom, coming to assist me in finding my way back to myself.

While in Scottsdale, my father decided to visit and bring my mom's ashes since she wanted to be placed next to Grandpa at the cemetery in Forest Grove, Oregon. It was something to look forward to, anticipating dad's arrival, and taking a road trip with my little blue Ford Focus up to the great Northwest. I was very happy to show my dad the remarkably beautiful landscape of Arizona, the wonderful hotel where I worked, and have time to process our loss together during our road trip. The problem was that he decided to bring one of his ex-coworkers from the ship, a man I couldn't stand. He was inappropriate and intrusive. He just decided to invite himself to a trip to the US. My dad has always been so generous, simply couldn't say no, and thought it was a fantastic idea to have his friend come along too. In hindsight, it was good for my dad to accompany him, otherwise, he would have been alone on his return trip back to Arizona.

On our drive toward Oregon, we stayed in hotels along the way, but we had planned for me to fly back to Phoenix instead of driving together. There were only so many days I could take off of work, and I didn't want to push it. My dad and his friend drove my car back, stopping along the way to the great national parks and other sites. Looking back, I really wished I had taken extra time off work to be with my dad, even if this other guy was there. It was my first month at this new property, the worry of misperception consumed me, and it didn't seem appropriate for me to take so many vacation days. Undoubtedly, it was a mistake. I felt guilty as my dad was driving using the GPS in English and perhaps getting lost, not really enjoying himself.

The road trip to Oregon wasn't so pleasant, finding myself drowning in tears, venting about the fact that we couldn't really talk about the immense loss. Why can't we talk about it? Why is this guy here? Being quite mean about it. Dad recognized my pain and was so gracious to let me vent like a little kid, but he didn't say anything. He was so hurt inside, too, and I was being selfish, telling him, I'm hurt, and never got a chance to say goodbye and get closure at the funeral. You didn't help me come back home for me to be present in those moments. There was a service at the church. I was the Mormon one, needing to be there, to see her in her temple gown, to hold hands with our dear friends, sharing the same prayers and thoughts of her spirit. We had a connection nobody had. I wasn't there. It's your fault. Recognizing these words were harsh and knowing my dad was suffering probably more than me, I wanted him to know my difficulty in processing. He was the only person I could talk to that I thought could help me, but there was nothing. No reaction. Pure grief.

The cemetery event was alright. Mom's side of the family came. They were so kind and gracious toward my dad. That side of the family felt very distant and strange to me. I did not want to connect with them. I thought they were the reason mom suffered a lot and had many issues she wasn't able to navigate through completely.

Portland has a special place in my heart. We stayed at my old property. I was able to see my dear friend who then took me to the airport the day after the cemetery event. I was extremely anxious about leaving my dad with my car back, but got on that plane anyway.

My dad is truly incredible. So patient and lovable toward me. I was so hard on him, and it wasn't fair. Everyone manages pain in different ways. There is no right or wrong way to manage pain, and of course, I regret how I handled myself.

Back to work, immersing myself in what I knew best.

Time passed, and I found myself heading to another dream hotel, in San Diego this time. It was the biggest property I had ever experienced, jumping at the opportunity, thinking it was exactly what I had envisioned in my growth path.

That year was amazing. I won a prestigious performance award from Headquarters, getting noticed at the corporate office. I attended events, other advanced training programs, and met influential corporate trainers. The San Diego experience represented the final stepping stone to the pinnacle of my career. I love the ocean and was so happy to be there while continuing to learn. It was a difficult team, having the perception that some individuals secretly despised me, which is perfectly fine. I can't remember the last time I encountered such push back and adversity in adapting to change. Although there were many young people, the majority had a very old fashion mindset and way of doing things. Expressions such as *but we've always done it this way* floated around and the hesitant attitude to try something new was persistent - even though I had proven that it was more effective, time and time again. The *problem* was and is that I'm all about the new. Backing down is often not even an option, because it's not a problem but more like a glitch.

Although my anxiety seemed more manageable, in this period, I experienced several attacks. A big one occurred at the hotel, right in the middle of the day. Again, the paramedics came; the whole show, everyone worried, it was so embarrassing and awful. The entire situation made me so upset, as some individuals such as the HR leaders, were thinking, oh honey, you can't take it. There was a lot of judgment, rivalry, and competition in the air.

One day, while sitting in my office, the ultimate dream job call came in. I was presented with a job opportunity in global operations at the headquarters office. The excitement was over the top. This had been my dream ever since I began my career in this company. I always used to say, I need to get to that round table and tell those people how it's done. They really don't know or have completely forgotten what it's like to be on property; how is that possible?

The interview process went well. In addition, I received recommendations from my previous director and a few global operations leaders I collaborated with throughout the years. Humbled and grateful, I accepted the offer and soon began preparing for the long drive from San Diego to Washington, DC.

9

FULFILLMENT & RECOGNITION

Career Growth, Yet No Longer Fitting

Another big move was on the horizon, East this time. I was excited and nervous. A new beginning, and this was what I needed. Headquarters was intimidating. I felt a bit out of place and didn't know how to manage things. Luckily, I had a few friends whom I worked with on other on-property projects. Being an active POC (proof of concept) contributor, testing services and products with my teams and guests, the corporate operations teams recognized my dedication and recommended me for this job, which made me feel so grateful. My ex-boss from Tucson was there. I really loved her; she was a genuinely real, driven leader, and an impactful role model. I used my gift of adapting easily to the environment, although inside I was very anxious, restless, and overly stressed.

Being receptive to all the new information, trying to figure out the new terminology of my assigned project, what my role was, attending meetings, rushing from one meeting room to another, working with an enormous IT team and multiple departments - I was in the middle of it all. I represented hotel Operations in a multi-discipline project that touched many areas of on-property inventory operations although it mainly revolved around revenue management functions. Sometimes I felt like I was just there so these other individuals and teams could say, yes, operations approved, but I didn't really get it, and sometimes they weren't trying to make things clear for me, on purpose. After a while, I understood more about some developmental components, the implications and impact on everyday hotel Room Operations, so I tried my best to stand up and make changes. It was brutal.

I would drive about 9 miles, which in Maryland means about 45 minutes on the highway to get to Bethesda, where the corporate office was located. My routine consisted of waking up early to spin, getting ready, and heading to the office. I would park and walk toward the entrance, and with each step toward that door, I could feel the knots in my stomach becoming tighter. The thoughts and feelings were assertively convincing me, I made it, I'm here; behave as if you belong, because you do, but inside, this other voice was getting louder and louder. You actually got here as you said you would, but this is not you; this is not what you are to do.

Serious internal conflicts began to surface, hearing my heart say, you proved you could do it, but you can clearly see this doesn't fit. It was an ideal, but it's not your path. Do you see it now?

I had established a relationship with a medical specialist since I was taking all these meds for anxiety, and whatever else doctors decided to label me as. In San Diego, a wonderful psychiatrist started taking me off some high-dosage medications. I was so happy when she said, these meds are not right for you, and the dosage is way too high. No wonder you're shaking. It took about 8 months to slowly reduce and integrate something else, coming to a point where I was taking less of everything. I knew there would soon come a point where I didn't need to take any more medicine. Throughout this period, I kept seeing a therapist to help through everyday life.

The following Spring, I went to visit my family in Italy. My brother-in-law, who is a very perceptive person, said to my dad, Enrica is not doing so well. I was literally gray, with a palish pasty hue on my face. It didn't matter if I put a really pleasant guest-face on and make up, it was obvious. My dad wouldn't discuss it, he didn't want to touch it, and I was trying to hold it together in front of him, thinking he had to have this idea that I was the successful one with the big job and that I could take care of myself. As always, since I left home,

I guess I was always trying to prove myself to my dad, constantly anxious about his approval and acceptance. Let me share this event; here is what happened, and this person said this; and here are my accomplishments, and this is what I experienced here and there; oh, this story, and the other story. Trying to make him part of my life, which only revolved around work. We didn't talk much about anything else, just my work and how fulfilling it was.

I was the daughter who left at 19 years old who was lost, *according to everyone back home*, who couldn't manage her money, who married a returned missionary and failed, who married another guy who took advantage of her for 9 years, financially, and then that fell apart too; she keeps moving, she says for work, but why can't she stay in one place and just stay there and establish a foundation. She's living like a gypsy.

These are the thoughts my dad had about me and my life. Never mind explaining the nature of hotel life, growing in the company meant moving and experiencing different types of properties, cities, and even countries. I was a person with an immense drive, determination, and an open mind. Aren't these good qualities to have? I would say to him. No, he would reply, just try to settle instead, buy a house, save for retirement. My insides would revolt every time we had to have this conversation. Settling? What? I've been *settling* on so many levels. We're just not on the same page on what settling means, that's for sure, but that is absolutely ok!

Once I achieved a role at the corporate headquarters, I felt like the golden child nevertheless, I was a mess. During my family visit, the following thoughts filled the air: she'll be gone soon, back to her life; I don't have to see or hear it. I don't know how to deal with her. Years later, I realized it's actually ok to be so completely different.

Yes, I was gray and felt a deep sadness inside that I didn't know where it came from. I had it: the corporate job, the nice salary, a 4-story townhouse, and a nice car. I could go shopping and spend a thousand dollars on suits whenever, eat out a few times a week, travel for work, and make an impact on a bigger scale. However, I was becoming averse to the attitudes of those I worked with. Nice people, sure, but something was awakening inside of me, recognizing that what I thought was being overly distracted back then was a heightened sensitivity. I knew I could relate and connect to people deeply, but didn't realize I was also picking up other types of information. Years ago, it was common for me to joke around during meetings or training programs, saying, I can hear people's thoughts and have to interject, let me explain it another way - I am going off on a tangent once again, sorry. Having bullet points to stick to my program was a must. Department meetings would last way longer than they should have. Training classes made me so anxious. Again, I thought I had a communication problem, but what was happening was that I was simply receiving too much input and didn't know how to manage it.

For the longest time, I had trained myself to ignore this aspect of myself, despising this form of awareness, and try to stick to my talking points. Then, I started practicing observation, feeling things rise to the surface, such as emotions and thoughts, not just my own but discerning those of others.

The process of observation was my anchor, which started when I began mindfulness practice back in Scottsdale years earlier. I kept practicing daily and started learning other meditation techniques, including alternative healing methods.

This opened the door to a new level of heightened sensitivity that was already present, but more awareness on my part made it more real, more tangible. I simply wanted to understand, oh so I'm not "crazy" and there are things I can do about my discomfort.

Five months after moving, I decided to finally walk into this holistic studio I kept seeing almost every day. I had researched different forms of yoga and meditation, and attended a Buddhist meditation group that would meet late on Wednesday evenings. It was fulfilling, but what was missing was something where I could include my body. Why are things so separate? I thought, feeling totally annoyed with the fact that I had to wear trendy clothes and make-up to go to these fancy studios. Of course, nobody has to do that, but we are consumed with what others think, appearances, and outer layers, and so was I. The practice and principles of Hindu Yoga truly resonated with me and still do, but I couldn't feel affinity with any of the teachers or studios' vibes I visited, which is too bad, really.

This led me to another studio where I began learning about the ancient SunDo philosophy of energy circulation, the principles of KiGong, energy medicine, and the teachings that made these ancient practices accessible to the modern world.

I almost immediately went through this strange phase of being furious at the world - a strong fiery rage that made me want to tear everything down and rebuild. Why aren't we taught the ancient mysteries of healing? Why don't we talk about energy and spiritual senses? Why are people still needing to take medicine for mental health? Why couldn't I help myself sooner? Why couldn't I bring these teachings to mom for healing? Why are we still dying of cancer?

The Body is a Portal - Our Work is to Open up to It

Through my training, I learned about the wisdom of our physical body. Until then, I was only focused on taking care of my body on the surface, enjoying going to the gym, lifting weights, becoming obsessed with outdoor cycling, and then indoor spinning. Of course, I wanted to maintain a fit look, so I could feel comfortable and fit into nice clothes. There was also such stress relief when I worked out, and knew it was really good for me, a lifesaver in many circumstances.

When I started learning and practicing how to *feel energy* moving inside and outside the body, a whole world opened up to me. Something buried deep inside, my inner intelligence, was like, oh yes, this is the way; there is nothing else that is more important than feeling energy. I instantly knew I was experiencing more of myself since I walked into the training studio that first day, following the inner knowing and desire to learn as much as possible and then *do that*, whatever *that* was. Things weren't clear as to how or what and it didn't matter because I just knew this discipline and practice was right for me. It was a strong calling. Something inside of me came back online and pushed me forward along this path.

My teacher and spiritual mother, as she would call herself, Master Ahn, was and is a powerful guide for me. She's always been able to make me think about simplifying life, which meant I had to simplify my thinking. Since my whole world revolved around thought alone, I had to come back to zero, to the space where nothing and everything exists. The physical training was incredibly opening; however, I realized my energy bodies were weak, spent, and congested. It didn't matter that I had focused so many years on being physically strong and fit. Quality of energy, such as strength, endurance, and resilience, are certainly linked to our physical form, but not completely. My spirit was bright as it has always been, but it couldn't get through to my soul, resulting in an uprising in my body.

I started attending regular training classes, healing sessions, meeting the other students and teachers, and really enjoying this practice. Nobody had to wear pretty clothes, and I was extremely interested in learning from the people who were also guided to practice this discipline. While I felt very comfortable in my body, that we were working on the inside, not the outside, attracted me to go deeper. The discipline, structure, and sense of order resonated with me like nothing had before.

As I went deeper and deeper, taking more advanced training programs, I couldn't stop that inner voice screaming to be heard. It would be a good path if you dedicated your life to this type of thing, don't you think? You know this - find a way.

In late 2015, I took two of the initial instructor training courses plus more advanced training from my teacher on a bi-weekly basis. The training programs were quite intense on a physical level and allowed this incredible initiation phenomenon to occur.

When I first felt what I could only identify in words as my true self, I was devastated about all of the *ignoring* and *avoiding* I carried out up to that moment. The thought of how much she, my true self, was and *is* trying to communicate, how sweet and loving she is toward me all the time. How much encouragement, no matter what, and how much confidence and wisdom she has. I have never felt so deeply. I have finally touched the energy of my heart, my essence, and felt so desperate to stay in that space. This connection phenomenon with the power of my heart, whatever we want to call it, was a true sense of home. Nothing else mattered.

I had similar feelings when I woke up to the fact that mom was dying and there was no more hope for her healing. Mom and I shared a special spiritual connection. We knew our soul and spirit were bigger, brighter, and wiser than this body and our thoughts. So, I connected with her heart in those moments of training initiation, reminding myself of the awakening when mom left. I had decided back then to go after important, meaningful experiences. Connecting to another aspect of myself, such as my energy, a glimpse of my true soul vibration, was another nudge to focus on what's really important.

I know she helped me throughout all these years, finding my way back to my essence, which is the same essence she is made of, that we all share as one humanity.

When I could reconnect with these truths through the sincere and simple guidance of experienced spiritual teachers, it was like a strong bell going off. It doesn't matter what or how you choose to *do* and *be* in life, but you must pursue a life of high-doing and purpose; this is why you're here. The impact you made has trained you for the next phase. These are words I kept hearing over and over.

Consequently, I kept taking all the training programs and classes I could afford, fully immersing myself in this discipline, practicing, while conducting my own extensive research and self-study activities. Everything felt and sounded like I was already aware of these principles and practices, not knowing how. I purely felt passionate, confident but humble that I could share these experiences with people by guiding them through simple sequences that provided benefits on so many levels.

Words from Master Ahn:
"As soon as you declare that you will heal yourself and train yourself to be a self-healer, a new life will come to you. Also, you will save a tremendous amount of time, energy and resources. More so... you will

enjoy a higher quality of life. Life is too short to wander around. I truly hope you don't waste time suffering from your illness and sickness. Your time is so precious. I believe your soul came to this planet to grow spiritually and reach a higher level."

A few years went by. During the Thanksgiving time frame, I moved back West to Arizona. I loved Arizona so much, and my partner's family lived there. We liked the idea of being close to people who cared for us, except we didn't know then that it wasn't the case. Our expectations and apparently strong relationship ended quite poorly.

Being able to work remotely, I would fly back to Bethesda every three weeks for about 5 days. I had hired an outstanding senior manager to take over some of the implementation tasks of our project. Once he was fully onboarded, I decided to take some time off. Months before, I had planned to attend a transformative training program, which was on my mind for a while and knew this was the right time frame.

I started regularly teaching group classes in late 2015. Every chance I got to go back to the studio in Maryland, I would try to teach a class, but then it became a bit challenging with flights and my work schedule, so I tried to at least go for regular classes in the evenings after work. It was a way for me to recharge, to see my teacher, Master Ahn, and to reconnect with myself.

I had soon begun to experience what some have called silent quitting, starting to withdraw, and caring a bit less about the broken processes the project was settling for, from an operations standpoint, at least. I was hanging on to a very thin string, experiencing feeling heartbroken as parts of me began to die a long time ago, but I kept trying to keep it all together; just a bit longer, I would say to myself.

My body had been giving me signals for years. I was leading my life through the lenses of *very good ideas*, but not entirely my own, going along because I identified with them as my true identity. I always had a strong gut feeling and high intuition, although calling it something else, also replacing these sources of information with what my rational, logical, and calculated mind would tell me to do otherwise. These *ideas* - or set of projected frameworks of righteousness - are just like another box to categorize and put people into. Is this still ok for me? Of course, everything inside of me screamed, no, with huge stadium size banners, sirens, fireworks and any other light and sound show to catch my attention. Wow, so loud in there - ok, I think I got it.

This time was different. I felt like my soul had started a huge strike, created a demonstration that included millions of people, some crazy manifestation of an uprising that had to make me reflect. Ok so, I think I got it. There I go with my rational mind trying to make sense of it all. If it doesn't make sense, that doesn't mean it's not right. I'm so tired of things having to *make sense*, making sense for who? And what does it mean when something makes sense? That's very superficial, don't you think? Questioning the rationale became a super interesting practice for me. First of all, it's always so loud, but that doesn't mean it is right. Question, and be suspicious of what we think and hear in our head, it may be totally wrong.

My only way to handle this was to stop everything. Too much happening? Then stop, cancel this and that appointment or task, eliminate, and simplify. Sit quietly and just feel.

Remembering when I chose to take this leap, to lose it all and undergo this huge severing, I didn't know what, why, or how. It took me two years to actually resign from my 20-year career, but I just knew it was the right thing for me. A logical, cautious person with good ideas planned out for their lives will consider this choice reckless, impulsive, even stupid, but I chose to believe in myself and jump.

10

THE BIG WAVE

Soul Calling

A strong wave can cause immense destruction and dismantling, but can also reveal a whole other world beneath it with unique treasures and potentials.

I had been extremely stretched mentally and emotionally, feeling agitated and heartbroken. I went on a few more flights to D.C. for work and kept up with my meetings and tasks, but I was growing more exhausted, and the tormenting restlessness was getting worse.

There was one path I could pursue, which involved working at the retreat center where most of my holistic training programs would be conducted, thinking of approaching that avenue. With my hospitality experience, I would be of service by supporting the management of the resort operations, and would also be involved in the healing work conducted there. Being surrounded by such beauty of Nature, the incredible energy of Sedona, and the high-vibration work - yes, I loved this idea. It felt right.

In Spring, I went to the first phase of a training program that was mandatory in order to be working for the company that managed this retreat center. It was a beautiful experience as I met many peers with similar stories. I worked hard and could see more of myself through the expert guidance of the master-teachers.

Toward the end of the program, I had to really decide if I would move forward to the second phase - which involved another advanced initiatory training program. It was an easy decision. Everything inside of me told me I had to proceed. This was my most important action toward my silent resignation. By taking this step, I knew I was moving forward with my decision to leave the corporate world.

Starting the second phase of the program, after just a day and a half break from the previous course, I spent time contemplating, expanding in a safe and nurturing atmosphere, allowing myself to just BE. I dedicated 100% focus to this training, gaining clarity and taking care of my heart. The group in the second phase was quite small; we all bonded well. We had a few very seriously intense initiatory healing practices. It was a process of remembrance, ritual, and ceremony that activated parts of my soul that were very ancient. The fiery coals under my feet, floating on air as I passed through this etheric gateway, accessing deep levels of awakening within my body, all aspects that represented another catalyst. I felt strong and confident. A new life source cascaded down into my being. What worried me before lifted. I experienced this knowing that no matter what I did, there was no mistake and that I could choose whatever I wanted, even staying at my corporate job. What needed to happen was this lightning rod within me to hold me steady, to hold that powerful inner light, to maintain my energy line strongly connected to all of my minds and vibrations in order to function more effectively without being strongly swayed one way or another. This was *the work*. It didn't matter what I did for a living. Only this inner world was of prime importance. I felt like I had just put on a new pair of lenses - this was a new way of seeing life, lifted, peaceful in the chaos, an unstoppable smooth wave.

While driving away from this intensive program, I experienced what can only be described as going through a gluey substance about 10 miles away from the retreat entrance in the desert. I was exiting this sacred brighter space held for us by the land, our higher selves, guides, and our master-teachers. Stopping the car briefly as I felt I needed to take deep breaths to continue, it felt like when you go to a higher altitude, up in the mountains, and need to slow down your steps. Keeping that light inside, I kept driving toward home, feeling the difference, though, the lower vibration - not negative, by all means, just slower and heavier. It was palpable.

It wasn't easy to speak of my desire to move forward with what I had harbored for some time. I had already been in contact with the retreat center leaders a few months prior. I now had to really make a plan to resign and start my new assignment.

There was still another unknown, and I was ignoring it for the moment. I had a *Jason*. Our relationship was very important. I had always felt very strongly, without a doubt, that Jason and I are closely linked in our mission at this time on Earth, so I wasn't about to leave this aspect of my life. No matter what life circumstances we experienced, we were committed at a soul level. Running away to a monk-like life was appealing in more ways than one, but not my path in this life. The retreat leaders and I tried to arrive at a workable solution by providing Jason with opportunities onsite, while he would still continue working on his creative expression as a video editor.

This was a time of confusion and strong waves of commotion inside and out. I couldn't figure out what was best. Again, an uprising deep inside. I requested a leave of absence from work. I was on a three-month break to care for my health on all levels. My legs experienced some unusual swelling. It hadn't happened before, and I knew it was stress related. In addition, I couldn't really keep it together, crying at anything and was especially torn. What should I do? Why do I have to worry about everyone else? I took some time to look at my life, heart, and creative solutions.

Here was the deal. I felt very strongly about making a huge change. I knew I had completed that phase where I lived in a box. It served me well for a long time. I felt so good about everything that happened in the past, without harboring any form of regret, yet I was literally making myself sick just thinking about going back to that life. That was clear. It needed to end.

The desire to dedicate my life to service in another way was the only thought and drive. I had found a different way; still continue to teach, but my teaching would be through the lens of personal experiences, sharing the beautiful training and insights I gained. Knowing I was just a baby in this field, a newbie with a lot to learn, I would grow and gain greater wisdom by teaching. I am still learning, practicing, and teaching. I mean, that never ends, right?

Should I be a *hotel person* at this retreat center? I wouldn't be doing holistic training; this was made clear to me. That is what I really wanted, but of course, one needs practice to be able to hold the space. All I wanted to do was to be part of holistic retreats and learn. I could run the resort operations with my eyes closed, but I wanted to do something more. *There it was.* I heard it. If I go there, I will *only* be a hotel person. I need to focus on something else now.

At first, the conflict I was having revolved around Jason's agreement on both of us moving toward working at the retreat center, but now the deeper dilemma was revealed. You're going from one box to another. They are too similar. If you were going into another box that's at least toward your heart's desires, then sure. It was clear, thank you, I said to myself, I understand. It felt so good when I said, ok, then I will not go work there. The teachers will be disappointed with this choice because they've been waiting for me, but they are so advanced they must understand.

When I spoke to my teacher, Master Ahn, she scolded me like a child. She was under pressure too as she recommended me and provided a path for me. It was a privilege to be considered for this role. Initially, I thought it was a great opportunity, and I committed myself. Although confused, wanting to please others, I had to sort out my mind. The thing is that in moments of deep awakening, we make choices that are right for us. Then our left-brain ego directs our attention to things, people, and places that hold us on a particular path. These are not necessarily *bad* but present us with a choice. I could have followed my initial intention when I felt I wanted to be in that light, but after the waves of confusion and working hard on grounding, I found the balance within to see what was best for *me*. This was my choice. It's difficult to explain in words. This was the time in my life that felt like severing parts of myself and stepping into a new way of being. I knew I was brave, but I also knew it was only the beginning of a lot more. I simply couldn't grasp or understand but I trusted in myself.

After this decision, I spent an entire month resting - it was the only thing I could do, sitting in the sun, reading, studying, and continuing to train, finding myself in an empty-void-period.

Rest and stopping everything were medicine. Another phase presented itself. Thinking, what if I manage my own studio? I could go work for somebody. My teacher is in DC, and going back is not an option, it's too congested. I should stay in Arizona, mom even suggested that.

The message came in like a lightning bolt - I should open and manage my own studio. You're close enough to other studios to receive regional support. It will be great, I hear - my never-ending optimism instantly created a spark. That was it. I could combine my experiences. I can do it! Telling myself joyfully, I will do it!

In September 2017, I completed the certification program to open a franchise studio, and three days later, flew to Korea where I received my attunement and uniform.

Korea

My journey to this magical land was exceptionally impactful. I was going through this strange revolution within. Master Ahn had arranged for me to participate in the Maryland KiGong team for the Seoul International KiGong festival. I could practice with the team remotely, it was a beautiful, slow, and simple routine, but I was at the front of the group, and the group was in a triangle formation, so when we were going to be performing, I wasn't going to see them at all. I was the apex of the pyramid. Not only was I intimidated about doing this KiGong flow in front of what seemed like ten thousand people, but also because I couldn't practice with them in person.

We got to Korea. My dear friend and training-sister Romina was my roommate. I loved her. She is from Argentina so we could speak Spanish sometimes. She was lovely and I felt I could be myself with her. I was going through some strong emotions about leaving the previous life of being a corporate leader to this journey of soon opening my own business and having to be solo in a new venture.

One day in a sobbing blow-up, asking her to really listen to me, I had a breakdown. I think I scared her a little bit. She was talking to me as if she was talking to her 4-year-old child. So sweet, trying to calm me down. These are some words and sentiments I was trying to express to her. *I am so sick of leading. Why do I have to be in front of the group? Nobody in the group even wants to practice; now that we're all here together, we need to practice, and people just don't give a damn. We can't be so unprepared; I mean, how unprofessional is that? I don't like mediocrity, and can't do half-ass.*

A few of our teammates just didn't care that much, and this really triggered me, making me wonder, *why should I care then? Canceling this performance is an option, and since I'm in charge of this group, pulling the plug is no problem for me. Since nobody cares, I will back out of the competition. Why do I always have to pull it all together for everyone? Being in charge is making me so sick. I just want to be quiet, not talk to anyone. I wanted to be alone at the back of the bus, just sit back and have others do everything. For once in my life, I want to be led, and have someone just tell me what to do. Hearing myself, I know this all sounds irrational. Well, the fact is that I can't even properly communicate whatever is being thrown up out of my mouth right now. I see it in your face. You're totally misunderstanding me. This one, over here, is completely freaking out, you think. Well, yeah, I am. I am really exhausted.*

I've been on overdrive for 40+ years. Nobody knows what's happening to me. My family doesn't care. Jason is worried. What about my sanity? There is nothing I want to do but sit at the beach somewhere and read, without carrying such heavy weight on my shoulders. Basta! (Italian for stop) I can't do it. I want to be left alone. Then the inevitable guilt shows up as I always tend to cater to people, which is a boundary, or lack thereof, I continuously face. I don't want people to misunderstand, which they often do because honestly, how can you truly see what is underneath all this nonsense coming out of my mouth?

I get it, I hear myself, but you're my friend and you need to listen and just be there without judging. I see it in your eyes, you're judging me. Ok, yes, I know.

There it was, I let it out. To be honest, here in print, I greatly modify my tone, minimizing the hideous blowout of anger, sadness, and grief.

I then started trying to patch it all up – saying to myself, how do I fix this? *Your willingness to be here, and listen is greatly appreciated. I'm very sorry I was acting a bit crazy, and you're very kind to still be here listening. Please forgive me. It's not ok for me to be like this. Thank you again, and I'm sorry... again.*

I had a meltdown. Romina behaved very differently in the following days. She distanced herself and left me alone. I was hurt. Once again, I was being misunderstood, but she was also respecting and honoring what I asked for, which was to be left alone. Why can't I just blow up, and someone be present and impartial, just listen? Ok, then. This is clear now. I am the only one who can be there for myself to do that. No need to talk to anyone anymore. Nobody really cares or can fully understand, even if they have good intentions. I let this heaviness digest a while and worked on allowing it to move on.

Sitting in the back of the bus, I observed myself and made peace with my sorrow. My nature is to be a leader, though I recognized there has never really been a time to rest, resulting in extreme exhaustion. My aura reflected this. It was fiery red and orange, some dark reds holding such heaviness and hurt, right in the center of my chest and outer layer of my field. I was carrying so much pain. We had taken aura pictures during our training programs and would regularly do so to see the changes before and after specific types of practices.

Mom wasn't there for me to ask her what to do. She would support me no matter what, I knew it. You see and know the truth Ri, don't worry, honey, you can do anything - her voice and words resounded in my heart.

We went to magical places in Korea. I saw traditional villages, got lost through the streets, found ginseng and tea stores, and stopped at a traditional Korean restaurant. Left my shoes outside and walked in. I was alone and only knew how to say *no meat, please.* Soon, a few group members showed up in the same place, and we ate together in this beautiful restaurant. We sat on soft cushions at a low rectangular table. I was so comfortable in this environment. The people, the writing on store signs, the atmosphere, and the layers of decorated wood of the traditional home structures were strangely familiar to me.

We arrived at the bottom of Mt. Moak. We took our time *entering* the mountain, walking through small paths, rocks, and passageways, and crossing streams. There were places to rest and enjoy nature. Other hikers were walking quickly up and down the mountain trails; we stopped to meditate, enjoying the beautiful day, and fully taking in the messages of this mountain.

We arrived at the top. There was a peaceful monastery with a beautiful temple. I had a sense of being lifted high into the clouds. Not only physically, admiring the magnificent views, but energetically and spiritually.

The monks that serve this sacred mountain had prepared a warm barley drink for us. It was so good. We could rest and take our time exploring. I ventured off to one side and found a dirt path. It led me to a small opening with an incredible view. There was a burial mound. I had seen many of them during the road trips across the countryside. These burial mounds have a dome-like shape emerging from the land, covered in grass, and marked by a tombstone with beautiful writing. There is a distinct style of burial mounds in Korea, similar to the ancient Etruscan tombs in the central coast of Italy where I live, but unique in their own way.

Approaching the burial ground, and very mindfully asking permission to enter this space, I realized this was the peaceful dwelling of an old woman who cared for the temple for years, dedicating her life to this mountain. Turning around and looking out, I began internally speaking to my mom. How amazing would it have been if she had been there with me to enjoy this amazing journey together? She would love this experience. Starting to perceive that electric-buzzing sensation, I began feeling so strange both mentally and physically. The sense of peace and calm was strong, recognizing that tranquility as a sign that mom was right beside me, enjoying the panorama holding my hand, and interlocking arms, as we normally would.

The vibration, buzzing sensation suddenly felt like a daze. I was in a cloud. The feeling in my chest was of returning to a place I had been before. I started seeing flashes and then clear visions of a life on the mountains, in this land, as a man in ancient times. I was strongly called to pull that energy back into me now. The sudden feeling of knowing filled me as if I was a giant vacuum or magnet and could pull this memory and all the energy that came with it back into my heart. I began making energy movements and half-bowing motions with my spine and my arms with a strong sensation of reverence for these memories, honoring the wisdom, and expressing gratitude for the light beads returning.

As I felt more alert and less in this daze or cloud, I faced a strong sense of melancholy, of homesickness. I knew I had to return to the group as it would soon be time to descend back into town, but I didn't want to. Why couldn't I stay here? Remembering this feeling distinctively, and thinking to myself, I belong here. I can stay, right?

Although cell service wasn't available since we began the journey toward the top of the mountain, I thought of calling my dad in Italy, perhaps catching a signal from the surrounding mountains. The call went through, and he answered. Just checking in, I said, but inside feeling like it was time to say goodbye. I was crying and felt mom's presence grabbing my hand to give me strength. The feeling and tears showed me parts of me were dying, and preparing to step into this new me. I was saying goodbye to my dad because I was to stay here for a while and find myself again. Mom was saying in my mind, you're ok, it's ok. After hanging up from that 2-minute check-in with my dad, I took a deep breath and stood there empty, taking in the mountain, breathing.

As I began walking toward other parts of the complex, there was a sense of being lifted from all heaviness. Walking toward my friend Romina, we shared a warm, loving hug without exchanging any words. We entered the sacred temple. The teachers and staff had prepared mats for us. We began sincerity training, bowing meditation, and as perfectly laid out, I was in the back, the last one to get in.

Communing with our higher minds in this sacred space was magical, something that cannot be put into words and can only be experienced. The air was filled with a sense of *being*, the complete being that we are, an immense sense of peace, and that nothing is missing or needing to be fixed. So beautiful and true.

Time to go back down the sacred Moak mountain. I remember this moment clearly. Someone said, ok, everyone, let's begin our descent, and I froze. I started crying uncontrollably; just like that time at the airport in Rome when I was going back to Rhode Island after my second visit home since I had left. My mom's watery eyes, my dad's worry, my heart was contracting so much. I literally lost pieces of myself back then.

I couldn't stop. I did not want to leave this mountain. Others started the long walk down. The master-teachers guiding us reassured me it was ok to take my time. I sat down on a step and sobbed. One of the monastery staff members, a sweet man with a bright, loving face, came to sit next to me. He was saying some words which I could not understand, it was Korean. He was rubbing my back with such tender care, very softly, respectfully, being unintrusive, delicate, and transmitting a beautiful light. Telepathically we were talking about the deep connection to this mountain and the land. I knew I was having a full-on conversation with this beautiful person as our eyes met during this exchange. He knew what I was feeling and what I was experiencing, demonstrating such a kind demeanor, encouraging me that it was ok. I asked him, can I stay? I need to stay, don't you think? He made a motion with his body, sitting up with a straight back and open, bright face, and said to me, you have a bigger job. This, you already did. Now you have to do another job. And just like that, my heart was calm. I kept crying, feeling homesick, but what he said went straight into my heart, and yes, it was true. But I need to find out what it is. He says, it's ok. You don't need to know everything.

I finally got up. It felt like 10 minutes passed, but it had been over an hour. I walked toward the path to go down the mountain trail. A few hundred feet down, I saw one of the two master-teachers who accompanied us; she was waiting for me this whole time, giving me space, and just patiently waiting under a tree. I mindfully walked down the giant rock steps, sobbed more, and kept looking back; the man waved goodbye for now. You can come back another time, everything is ok.

As I walked down, I gained a sense of calm that was so deep. This wiser self was holding my hand, keeping my chin up. You're alright, you're going to be ok, this is what I was hearing from my higher self.

It was time to head down toward the base of the mountain. As I approached the bottom, this sense of courage filled my chest. Taking deep breaths, I raised my head feeling brave, holding this new energy that was so powerful it was bursting from every pour. The recognition of this fire inside was extraordinary, making me feel this sense of awe. It was a full immersion and exchange with the energies of the mountain - ancient, wise, profound beauty and power. I decided to keep quiet, not share the experience, feeling it was so precious and needing to integrate its messages, which took quite some time.

We arrived at a resting area where we could do some gentle training and recharge our batteries after a few hours' journey back. Afterward, we received a meaningful lecture from one of the on-site senior master-teachers, another powerful woman with stellar light emanating from her eyes.

A few days later, I started diligently practicing for the KiGong festival. I would find a spot at the empty gym, then find an open conference room or the small hallway by the laundry room and practice as much as possible. I eventually called the group together, and we began practicing outside on the hotel deck. It was nice. I would play the beautiful Mykol track on my phone, and we would follow the movements while trying our best to match the waves of the sound. I was hopeful. It wasn't going to be that bad. Oh my gosh, I was still so nervous - who thought this was a good idea? Oh yeah, Master Ahn. The days leading to the KiGong festival in Seoul were great. We saw the beautiful countryside, the vast mountains, and valleys. The towns and people were amazing.

The final performance went so well, with our low budget, low-quality uniforms, and we were happy and relieved. It was a success, at least for me. I wasn't so angry anymore, I was delighted to lead the group, and I was going to prove to myself I could do it, even if I didn't like the whole idea in the first place. We heard some wows and cheering. Our group was so supportive and loving. That was what it was all about. Sharing and being joyful together. This moment reminded me how much more important this was than having high standards and trying to be perfect. We were loved and supported; everyone was so encouraging and genuine.

After our performance, a huge weight was lifted. We had a massive dance party. I let loose and danced like a crazy woman to all my favorite EDMs artists (electronic dance music). It was ecstatic, allowing my body to move wildly, and finding myself smiling while tears poured down my cheeks. This was a bright, loving atmosphere. Still so torn, wanting to stay here, I promised myself I would absolutely come back.

Small Business Owner

When I decided to resign from the corporate world, I had already withdrawn my retirement funds and waited until I accrued my yearly bonus. There were no savings, but I was determined to go down this path, planning to be a leader in my community by opening a franchise studio in beautiful Prescott, Arizona. I pushed through by qualifying to be a franchise owner, pursuing the final certification programs, deciding on a location, and moved forward without looking back. From corporate leader to holistic studio small business owner. What a jump.

Some of the external changes I went through included cutting my hair short and taking off my giant Citizen wrist watch and never putting it back on again. Refusing to wear a suit jacket no matter what the circumstance, I finally started wearing tie-dyed t-shirts and fun, colorful pants. I wanted to express myself in ways that made me feel more myself, following my own preferences and no one else's.

I knew pursuing this opportunity was the right thing to do at the time, but another part of me also knew it wouldn't last very long. I knew I had to go through this huge learning curve, which would make me grow exponentially. Master Ahn had told me, it will be hard, but you will grow so much; it's going to be so hard because you're isolated. There is no other sister studio near you, and you will not have any support. You have to rely on your inner strength, there is nothing like having to do everything and take care of yourself at the same time.

I didn't want or ever wanted any type of bypass or shortcut, but I simply couldn't ignore my self-reliance mission, my strong will to be a leader and not follow. I actually did not like the idea of being a franchise, initially at least. Since my hospitality days, I have understood the challenges of being a franchise owner, but also the freedom that comes with it. I worked for two franchise properties and opened one. The incredible support one receives under the corporate umbrella more often than not guarantees success. This was, and is, a holistic practice. The idea of a franchise isn't good for me, I thought, but it is in the holistic field, so it *must* be different. I will move forward with this. I can do it.

Truly doing my best, I learned so many valuable lessons that I never would have experienced if I had gone to work for someone else. So many tears were shed, both of disappointment for being taken advantage of so many times and for such beautiful people opening up and learning how to take care of themselves differently, expanding to their own natural healing power. This experience gave me so much and I would absolutely do it again.

Developing and maintaining discipline as a spiritual practice was vital, which led me to carve out dedicated time for my own training daily. It was essential to continuously return to a state of centeredness, making time to clear and prepare the space and myself not only for my group and individual sessions but for my own well-being. Although my teacher was still in touch with me and she could help me remotely, it was still very much a solo job. Headquarters sent a more senior teacher to introduce my practitioners to advanced training programs, which was great. I felt so honored that I could hold this space and experienced this huge growth inside of me as I started noticing that the quality of people coming through the doors was changing. I was receiving people that I resonated with more, and also people who allowed me to see what I needed to work on at a deeper level.

All our life experiences, including people and apparently random things, such as messages on the radio, books, or something falling off the shelf, are all teaching moments. I really started to pay attention more and more. I had always known this throughout the years, even if just intellectually, but when I started to really notice, I began recovering multi-layered expressions of this phenomenon in my everyday life. The language of the universe speaks *Enrica* - and any other name frequency out there, now and in All-time. This is a technology of communication we can describe as a *language* and it is unique to each individual intelligence. What a Whale or Blue Sparrow means to me may represent something slightly different to another person. The universe is always presenting and crafting this beautiful sea of language we're swimming in - a vibration - precisely arranged and beautifully designed in collaboration with our purest, highest Mind.

The training I received is rooted in the ancient principles of SunDo, which refers to Mountain Taoism in Korea, Japan, and China. SunDo revolved around practicing and developing states of *internal alchemy*. These practices included internal and external forms of QiGong or KiGong. I will refer to this vast amount of teachings, principles, and practices as *KiGong* since I trained in the Korean tradition.

This teaching was delivered through the three eras of enlightened masters: Han-In, Han-Woong and Dahn-Gun. There were 7 Han-Ins in the first era and 18 Han-Woongs in the second. The third era had 47 Dahn-Guns and they are the most direct ancestors of the Tao tradition of Korea.

This enlightened society existed in the far distant past. A society that shared similar healing practices as those of other ancient people around the world transmitting the wisdom of star families.

Although shamanic QiGong practices were kept secret for ages, several aspects were introduced to Western cultures in the late 20th century. A few teachers in the last 40 to 60 years transmitted these teachings, and they even helped resurrect ancient wisdom presenting it to modern society.

My formal training journey followed the standard path to becoming an instructor, teacher, and healer through a lot of practice. I dedicated my efforts and focus to deepening my spiritual senses, moving on to learning and studying, and practicing various healing modalities.

I don't like presenting things as a resume. This is definitely something linked to my corporate career. I witnessed many of my colleagues *parading* at various work events, whether a going away party, some formal training, or awards ceremonies. I found myself doing the same sometimes. You're talking to some peers at a training program, and you share what you've done, where you've worked, this and that. International experience was always a big deal. When I told people I opened a hotel in Rome and worked in Mexico for 7 years, people would turn their heads even if they were conversing with someone else. Ok, sure, I was proud of my achievements, but I have always been a very humble person. I couldn't bring myself to brag and act so inflated. So, when I saw some of my peers act as if they were on the *Price is Right* - wanting *themselves* to be the prize, I often wondered about this need for attention, vicious comparison, and competition.

As I opened my studio, I felt a bit uncomfortable when someone asked, can I see your credentials? One day shortly after the grand opening, a nice lady came in and inquired what I did. Noticing the various signage and posters for Taoist yoga, mindfulness, and healing, the woman mentioned her long experience with acupuncture and familiarity with energy concepts. She then asked to see in writing all of my qualifications, and would call me if she thought my background was appropriate and acceptable enough - these were literally her words.

This was interesting, I thought. The interaction didn't bother or trigger me that much. It came more as a realization that a lot of people do need a *resume*, as they need to make sure you are who you are based on where you studied and who you studied with. Accepting that it is very important for some people, I also knew deep down that you couldn't demonstrate on a piece of paper if a person could help you or not, and this is true in any field.

Well, so here I am. I did a whole bunch of amazing, advanced training and still continue to study and learn, which will never end. If I ever have some type of sponsor - someone who can pay rent and all my bills - research, study and discovery would be my life, turning into a new version of Indiana Jones with amazing gifts.

Since I was a child, ancient wisdom has always intrigued me, developing a deep connection early on to ancient Egypt and ancient Greece. Periodically, it was normal for me to become completely consumed with revisiting my old studies and notes about ancient people worldwide, making connections and intuitively listening for the meaning of symbols. When I learned about the Central and South American cultures, I dedicated my studies to Maya and Inca civilizations. The original plan, years ago, was to study archeology at the University of Viterbo, but then I changed my mind when I received a scholarship to go to BYU (Brigham Young University). Deep down, my dream of becoming like Indiana Jones persisted, motivated to teach, travel, research, discover, and learn as much as possible along the way.

Living in Arizona turned out to be a beautiful experience. I had always really enjoyed the mystical Native American culture ever since I was little when mom brought my sister and I to Oregon. Something awakened inside of me. The sound of a Native American flute, the drum, the chanting and dancing, the ceremonies, talismans, crafts, and jewels. It all felt part of me, so familiar. I was here, I know this.

Similarly, I had been attracted to Taoism and Buddhist philosophies for years and continue to study today. I knew I had past life connections to all these cultures. It was common knowledge to me. Even when I was young, mom and I would speak about this topic often. Although she was Mormon, she would talk to me about the concept of *having done this before* or *it's a memory from another life*, and it all made perfect sense to me. How ridiculous is the idea that we only live this *one* life, and that's it. I mean, why this one single life, with all of the events unfolding in *this* particular way. That is a bit of a simplistic little box we are putting our life in, don't you think?

When I felt very close to a culture, a sound, a tradition, I knew it was awakening a vibration inside of me, a recognition - a resonance - *oh yes, I know you, I know this*.

As I began practicing various healing arts, not only was I growing as a business owner and leading in a different way than I had done for 20 years in the corporate world, but I was also growing as a healer and spiritual teacher.

I would be teaching a group class, and although I had a nice program selected and rehearsed, it became normal feeling guided to speak specific words, practice a particular KiGong flow, and lead a certain type of visualization journey, other meditation practices and so on. I was a bit startled at first to hear my inner voice, not anyone else, but my soul, along with my guides. I was allowing this effortless transfer to occur more and more. Whatever I thought would be the class flow is now becoming this instead. It fits, now. People respond well; some say, oh I needed exactly what you said or what we did. There was a feeling that whatever I was bringing through was simple, sincere, and pure - a bigger opening, allowing a different energy to flow more and more. Surrendering and allowing the *coming back online* of more energy-spiritual senses, these experiences made me feel I was on the right path.

I am convinced they have always been there, but now I was consciously allowing my perception to expand to include physical, energy, and spiritual senses. I often remind myself and share with others - we need to walk around with all of our minds, not just in meditation or when there is some heaviness and we need rest, all the time. Take your minds to the store, in the car, in the kitchen, in all interactions. This is the work.

Later that year, my little 15-year-old Tito passed away. He was getting so tired, suffering from incontinence, overall difficulties with movement, and slowly becoming blind in his left eye. Back in Maryland, he had developed glaucoma, which resulted in enucleation of the right eye. It was a terrible ordeal, but after the procedure, he regained his vitality and did so well with just one eye. It was the Tuesday before Thanksgiving when I realized it was time. My dear friend Joy, a vet herself, recommended we call Dr. Dalia, a wonderful, loving friend who was able to come to the house at 8:30 pm that evening. I sensed Tito's soul separate just moments before the full effect of the injection. He was finally back to his joyful, energetic self, in the spirit realms. Although we were grieving, allowing him to be free was the most heartfelt decision to make.

The next day, while leading my morning class, I could sense his presence. It was so precious, although tears rolled down my face, especially during vibration training, when the lights were low, and the group couldn't really tell. He hung out for quite some time during the following days, then began to appear in dreams and journeys as a loving companion.

Spiritual Name Vibration Ceremony

A year after opening my studio, I attended a deep awakening program conducted by a very senior master-teacher. She is a beautiful spiritual teacher who led our very small group through an intensive 7-day process of physical training, expanding energy bodies, and opening and merging fully to our spiritual bodies. In this program, we could connect so deeply with our Soul to perceive and experience our *Soul's name*. Once we could receive the name and its vibration through our energy line, our teacher could help interpret it to put it into words. We would be assigned a soul name in beautiful ancient characters and sounds. These characters, symbols, representing the essence of the name vibration - included Chinese radicals, ancient Korean Hanja and modern Hangul alphabet or a mixture of all three.

The importance of the soul's name and feeling its vibration is a very ancient principle. The *name* was one of the *nine* bodies in ancient

Egypt, representing the power of speech, holding the individual's personal power and mission. It was called the Ren, and the hieroglyph depicted a mouth and a wave, such as the symbol for primordial waters, Nu. The name was sacred, and at times, held secret. The ripple effect we create with sound and words reaches the visible and the invisible.

Only after learning about and practicing Light Language would I gain a deeper understanding of the power of energy words. Receiving my Soul's name during what you can call a profound shamanic journey experience was like being struck by lightning and turning on a different expression through my energy line, the spine and internal energy system. Our spiritual teacher who guided this intensive program did not call this experience a shamanic journey, but from what I had experienced in other healing disciplines, it had strong similarities. The preparation for this awakening and opening was extensive physical training, fully stimulating and purifying our energy system, activating the deep circular breathing and energy orbit experience. This occurred over several days. Although we were all experienced students and teachers, we each had a deeper activation of our unique healing power. The journey to become fully empty, or should I say *spacious* enough to merge with the entire universe, required an extensive vibration training session.

Many are familiar with the practice of shaking the body, which is very ancient KiGong healing work. Well, most practitioners shake their bodies for a few minutes as part of a whole sequence of meridian opening exercises. When the vibration training is close to three hours long though, something extraordinary happens in our nervous system, brain, energy centers within and outside the body, and along our energy lines. The training is about merging the physical body with our higher vibratory bodies to expand fully and simultaneously hold a deep state of presence. Space and time, and the elements converge. It's like seeing yourself return home after a very long trek in the desert. This is definitely not for everyone, that's for sure.

This particular practice, simply referred to as vibration training, includes many forms of creating *vibration*, such as body tapping, shaking the body, dancing, or moving the body with the flow of energy. It creates a sense of freedom.

Our rational mind prevents us from fully letting go and trusting our innate healing powers, so I've come to appreciate how it may take us several minutes to fully surrender, trust and let go. It's a beautiful way to honestly watch our head-brain try to make sense of it all, categorizing, telling stories, reminding us of why something is this or that way, preventing us from fully connecting. It's quite interesting.

Once more, I want to mention the power and elevated frequency of sacred words. The ancient Korean-Chinese character for emptiness or *nothingness*, *Mu* - Chinese Wu or Ma - which really refers to a state of pure spaciousness, depicts a shaman with arms open to the sides, with a shall or mantel over his shoulders, dangling from his arms; he is dancing, communing with the spirit realms through shamanic dreaming and journeying, moving his body to achieve a higher state of consciousness where he can have clear vision into other dimensional worlds. He can access his own innate wisdom and that of the land, ancestors, and guides. This is the state of nothingness, Mu.

Since I like to draw correlations between symbols, when I came across the Egyptian hieroglyph for the *primordial waters* known as *Nu*, I heard the words - the same concept of all potentialities held in the realm of the vast ocean we are part of. Water holds both Yin and Yang energy. Thinking of the Yang aspect of water, it creates potentials through the strong currents. It also reveals possibilities that were previously hidden. A place of nothingness, as well as beginnings and regeneration.

All symbols hold deep, multi-dimensional meanings. I like to see the world through this form of mystical science and technology.

Back to the practice of becoming nothing or space itself, a deeper transcendent state of presence is the key to transformation. Can we hold that space continuously? Well, we also need to function in our left-brain ego reality; balance is what keeps our minds together. This is the main work. Continuously returning to balance and flowing harmoniously through life. Literally surfing - with strong legs and the ability to adjust to the incoming waves, feeling the smallest changes under our feet, maintaining deep focus to see ahead clearly, anticipating the appropriate level of flexibility and adaptability needed, with a light, fluid upper body and a strong, stable lower body.

Vibration principles and how to use our bodies to achieve elevated states of consciousness drew me to these practices. Across many ancient cultures and still practiced today are the shamanic traditions of transcendence, navigating the invisible realms and connecting to our expanded selves, our ancestors, alleys, and guides. In my experience, delving into this beautiful East Asian series of rituals and ceremonies, I felt a profound connection to this work, as well as a realization that these ancient people - East Asia and ancient Khem - had the same teachers. I was also in awe of the elevated exchange between facilitators and practitioners. There is a different level of light activation. It all felt like home.

My soul name was revealed to mean *the current that moves the oceans.* This is what I wrote as they asked me to describe my vision in one short sentence. I spoke of my visionary journey to the spiritual teacher, who could see it as it was happening, and she shared her insights on the meaning. The name she assigned to me was *Dae Hae,* which literally means 'grand - dae' and 'ocean - hae', and then she refined it as *heavenly ocean.* Using Chinese radicals to write the Soul's name has a meaning all on its own. Why not write it in roman letters? Each line of the radical represents a specific quality of vibration. The sound, given in the ancient Korean language, also has its own vibrational quality and frequency. We can translate the words and how the characters are depicted. However, it will never transmit the same frequency.

Dae is a profound multi-dimensional word. A literal correspondent is not really available. It can mean big, large, grand, cosmic, celestial, massive, the big bang, high vibration.

When my peers asked me for the meaning, I would often joke, *big wave, like a tsunami,* or simply *big ocean.* We would use our soul name within our internal groups; teachers started calling us by our soul name, and it resonated so deeply.

In the same period, I was led to review what my birth name meant. I had read this years ago in Italian, but have forgotten. The name *Enrica* comes from Germanic languages, and it means *Signora della casa o della Patria*, translated to be l*ady of the house or land - ruler of the house, land*. I was intrigued by the meaning of words and where they came from, and when reading the ancient names of goddesses and gods, I often researched their origin, creating connections to similar sounds, symbols, and letters across the ancient world. In what way do these symbols and archetypes relate to me? I would ask and soon began to meditate on the symbols.

As mentioned, I always resonated strongly with ancient Egypt and promised myself I would one day experience a journey with the two sisters' group led by Normandi Ellis and Amy Auset Rohn. What an experience. It will be literally entering into the portal of my heart, gathering more and more beads of light.

Entering these sacred sites, opening to transmissions of light, and rediscovering the ancient voices is life changing. This is a dream I look forward to experiencing soon.

Yes, I am Enrica, but I'm also Dae Hae.

Delivering Beads of Light - Inspired Message

Flow of creation beneath the surface. What lies in the unseen worlds - Potentiality. Creation. Flow. Giving and receiving.

Soul vibration through heart and voice. Creation from nothingness - manifested sound in the realm between worlds, between the above and the below - expression.

Speak inspired words, imprint your vibration into the flow of expression. Express the highest vibration.

Life of higher doing. Life force of source moves through. Deliver the merging of yin yang, Earth cosmos, humanity divinity - the harmonious infinite alignment evolution.

11

MERGING EAST & WEST

Deepening Connection Through Symbols

My morning routine includes communicating with my Soul. It became the most important part of my day. I usually train throughout the day to help me center, process information, recharge, and reset. In recent years, I started incorporating a practice that I've always resonated with, bibliomancy. Asking about the meaning of a dream, a thought or emotion, a physical sensation, asking my Soul to speak to me through words, symbols and through drops of inspiration, and it always, without fail, comes back to me with something to consider and explore - often a hint, most of the time a clear-as-water answer. I developed a devotion to light oracle cards years ago. I say *light* oracle cards because I don't know how to describe them any other way. A certain light vibration emanates from everything. If it resonates with my own, then I know it would be beneficial to interact with it, while in other circumstances, I may feel things may be detrimental or draining, and I simply don't associate with them - including people and situations, of course.

Some oracle cards made me feel light and expanded, while holding or looking at others made me notice a contraction. As I was studying the Awakening of Osiris, I came across Hieroglyphs Words of Power and accompanying Seshet oracle cards - works by Normandi Ellis. Since I first communed with these symbols through meditating and practicing active dreaming with these divine messengers, I developed a deeper connection with my guidance team and higher minds.

I learned the meaning of the names Ast (Isis) and her sister Nebhet (Nephthys). Ast literally means *the seat*, representing the place or home where the heart is. Nebhet literally means *lady of the house* - the home is the temple - the temple is the body.

This may be a superficial concept to some, but for me, it resounded as a profound buzzing sensation through my entire energy line, and the chambers of my heart. I heard the words: you hold the yin and yang within the heart, the dark and the light, both parts of the light spectrum - it is the same energy, vibrating at different rates. Holding such force within and seeking balance throughout life is the mission - the drive to align and hold within to expand outward.

The affinity I felt with both of these great leaders-goddesses, Isis and Nephthys, was so powerful. They are my teachers and guides. I feel this vibration and presence. I, too, hold these beads of light-wisdom. These messengers watched over me throughout ages, and as I began going deeper, opening up more to the vibration of noticing symbols and meanings, I could practice working with these energies in a more profound way than I had before.

Each day, I take time for my spiritual connection with my soul and guides. Sometimes they explain to me the unfolding of physical transformation; other times, they provide me a priority list of what I should do next; sometimes, they remind me to check in with my heart. They always, always encourage me to be seen, to be myself, to share life stories, and to *BE*.

Dreams ~ Visions ~ Journeys

The Tall Wave

Seeing myself as a stunning tall being, walking barefoot in a wide-open space in the snow, I have a beautiful flowy dress and mantle, a headdress, and long whitish hair. A large winged being flies closer to me from behind; it's a hawk of incredible size, and as I walk forward it lands right behind me. I am walking tall, with a smile, confident and strong, coming to an outlook area; it's a cliff. In front of me is a massive, tall ocean wave. Piercing through the waters, there she is, Whale. Mermaid-type beings waving hello, some other sea beings I can't begin to describe, and the massive Whale, right there, waiting for me. Bowing to her, we greet each other and connect. While hearing the melody in my heart, I start making sounds to resonate with her. Wow, so beautiful.

Suddenly, Hawk takes me up high into the skies, we rise and fly. The wind on my face is so intense. Hawk is wearing a harness of some sort, I crawl under him, and he's flying me over the water right on top of Whale. He lowers me, and I gently land on her, resting with my belly, chest, and side of my face on her back. Ah...it feels so wonderful just lying there, so happy to be back. My dress and mantle reach the water, and my feet are submerged. I feel her breathing and see myself hugging her. Getting up and looking into her eyes, we welcome each other once more. I turn and lay down face-up, enjoying the sun. She's simply gliding with me right on top of her; it's magical. A little seal appears, she comes to say hi, nibbling on my feet and leg, then dolphins show up too. There is so much excitement that I'm here. Receiving a bright beam of light from the sky, I suddenly find myself holding a clear crystal in my hand. It is brilliant, bigger on one side, then thinner on the other. I bring it to my heart, putting the crystal in a pocket on my chest. There is a belt wrapped around my waist, coming up to my chest like a harness with straps and pockets. Diving straight into the ocean, deep down to the blue city, I come to an area where I slow down, float in front of massive doorways, then proceed forward. My stay doesn't seem to be long. The Whale is above, hovering, watching, waiting for me; the other ocean beings are there too.

In a flash, I am then back on Whale. She brings me back to the surface. It is time to say goodbye for now. I look up and notice Hawk is coming down to pick me up and fly me back to land. Looking back, saying farewell to my friends in the ocean, I pass over a beautiful valley with a long windy river and tall trees. Hawk then drops me off on a cliff over the ocean where I am receiving cleansing winds from all four directions. I am operating the crystal with my arms extended, bringing this energy all around me, moving in beautiful energy motions guided by the crystal and the winds. Looking down toward the shore, I immediately find myself in this place, on the beach. There is a large fire. I see myself communing with the fire, alone, dancing, shaking, singing, and seeing through the flames. I am participating in creating a certain quality of Fire, infusing this energy in the sand into the Earth. This fire has a specific purpose for the land and the people. The wind pressure is so strong, noticing this force all around. My body begins to feel more and more, and I am fully back in the physical, resting and breathing.

The Winged Angelic Being

I sat with indigo gabbro, my companion stone, and played whale sounds. One guide came forth, the tall blue being. As he came in, he put my ego-self to rest, holding her while floating in the air, allowing her to rest. She tried to come in and out with thinking and was gently brought back to a resting state. A large white female-being emerged; I saw her come forth, standing tall with a beautiful white silvery glow and long white hair in the wind, or maybe this was underwater, everything was in slow motion and so smooth. This remarkable being had something on her shoulders that looked like some cover or shawl. As she came closer, I could see she had large white feathers on the upper back, they were wings. Her body was strong and built, and she wore a robe-like wrapping, with one shoulder and abdomen exposed. She looked like a female gladiator with objects on her shoulder cover near the collarbone and neck, a feather tool holding it in place. Around her waist she wore what seemed like a belt where she carried some items.

I noticed she had fishlike scales or bumps, more like what you can see on the top of a crocodile or a turtle's shell. There was a ridge above her ears, turquoise in color, it ran behind her head, and from the back of the head, it came down the back of her neck under her white flowy hair. As she raised her head, her eyes were closed, her arms open to the side, and she spread her wings. We were floating in the ocean of energy, so beautiful. She made me feel calm, strong, and centered, creating beautiful sounds. I asked if these sounds included her name as I, too, started chanting the same sounds. She said this is what I can call her. OH RI AH SSA. I chanted this three times, then at the end, I heard in my mind's ear that there was an accent at the end OhRiAhSSa'. I was in awe and so grateful. The other guide allowed

156

my ego-self to get back up. I opened my eyes and was fully back. Thank you!

The Elderly Priest-Scientist

I see myself as an older man. Looking carefully, he is wearing sandals, although his feet are covered by a long dark gown. It seems like a Franciscan gown, although it is clear to me, he doesn't belong to this particular order. The gown has a large hood and a belt with something hanging from it. I recognize myself to be a priest but also a scientist, a well-known person traveling to where I can be safer. Someone is accompanying me, and there are a few other people close by holding some of my belongings, and an ox carrying many items. There is a dog. It's Tito's soul. He is walking right next to me, protecting me. I give him a little fruit treat that gives him energy and extraordinary powers.

Appearing as a long-haired, bearded elderly man, I have a critical role with certain capabilities. Humility, quietness, and a preference for solitude define me. Many people fear me. Where am I going? I ask in my mind. A map becomes visible bringing my gaze to the northern region of Greece, revealing a path that runs through the land toward Turkey. Although temporarily staying in an area to rest and find shelter, I am headed to central and Far-East Asia to meet the masters of the East.

The trees and animals speak to me while walking in the forest, headed to meet with a leader who does not receive my message well. After delivering information, I continue on with a purpose. My whole being exhibits confidence, courage, wisdom, and peace. I carry ancient knowledge that can only be shared with very few. Some people follow me; we guide and support each other simultaneously while being students and learning together. Noticing the way I walk, it is with absolute purpose and peace, there is no such thing as fear or worry, completely free in the moment. There is a strong connection with the dog, my companion and partner for ages. A circle of stones comes into view. The dog sits like my dog Tito would, facing toward the outside of the circle. Although alone, there are others in the distance ensuring safety and holding space.

I begin offering ceremonies, rituals, and prayers, seeing myself warming a stone in the middle of the circle with my thought alone, as if it was a little kettle, then throwing some herbs on it in gratitude. There is wind. Nature is communicating through many sounds. Turning and looking around, receiving all the information coming toward me, my field expands to include all my senses within the entire area. Something is guiding me that is beyond what I can recognize now. It is mesmerizing to see how much humbleness, sense of calm, care, and foresight this person carries. So much knowledge of the natural world and so much spiritual wisdom. He needs nothing and no one but embraces with great compassion all who want to grow and learn.

Tanarassius. I kept hearing a name in my mind. Over and over. This is the name - sounds and letters resembling: Tanarassiuss, or Tenarassius.

Healing Journey to the Upper Realms

Waking up with a tension headache on my right side, I sit on my chair, quieting my mind and asking for healing. As I begin focusing deeply on my intention, my requests become chants. I expand, focusing on my center-zero-point, and visualize my field, suddenly finding myself in a different space, surrounded by endless waves and motion - the ocean of energy within my being and beyond. I can see my body and ocean-like waves moving all around. Symbols light up, showing different patterns of infinity signs inter-weaving with each other inside and outside of my body. Then a bright golden rod manifests as my energy line. Moving above my body, and seeing the pattern from above, it looks like a flower, in constant movement all around the vertical axis of the gold energy line. Next, a tunnel-like horizontal axis crossing the golden energy line at my 6th chakra comes into view. There is another one now appearing at the heart level and one at the lower abdomen, with diagonal lines shooting out in all directions - points of attraction, contraction, then expansion and flow. If looking at this image drawn on paper, the phenomenon of light strings would resemble a star - the axes (vertical and horizontal axis), with the addition of diagonal lines. The message in my mind is, these are portals - the points where the lines converge. Starting to detect a sudden upward movement, within the dream, I hear myself say, oh, we're moving up – completely aware of this change. Asking for guidance and help in reaching a level where my guides could come down enough for us to meet and interact, I immediately have a huge welling in my heart, and tears roll down my face, sensing we are getting closer.

Finding myself in a holding space for a few moments, I focus again on expanding even more, and the upward movement starts again, going even higher. The air feels like a vacuum. There is pure silence. I hear myself say, help! - and immediately feel my hand being held. A being who looks like a small child appears. Only the upper part of the body is visible, the lower part is a bright flowy woosh as if this little angel-looking being doesn't have legs or they mesh with the long clothing. Then I notice all these birds. They are flying around me as an escort team, made of bright white glowing light, leaving a cloud-like trail as they fly. Their song while accompanying me to another holding space is magical. We go through some thick layers of the sky and arrive at quite a large space. Beautiful light emanates from all around. The floor is light blue, as if I am just walking in the sky. It's not really a floor, although there is a path, there aren't any walls as the entire place is open. The being next to me escorts me forward, and I immediately see many, many paths appearing in all directions from the single point where I am standing. My consciousness is split into all these paths – a trail of Mind moving outward through these lines.

Becoming aware of different guides approaching, I know I am about to receive information and guidance from all of them. While this is happening, part of my consciousness zooms out into space, floating around, making circles and dance-like motions with the stars. This is a space filled with pure joy. While enjoying this consciousness dance in space, I sense continuous upward movement. Knowing she, part of my mind, is still here with me, but also knowing she is headed somewhere else, I hear myself say, I'll go meet with the others while you're here having this meeting - be right back, the view from up there is way better anyway. This part of my mind and consciousness is observing the upcoming process of recalibration and delivery of guidance, where I meet with my guides, but she also gives me a different perspective, while enjoying herself connecting with other soul family members.

Appearing in front of me, I see a series of images projected like in a movie theater, they are so beautiful. Here are some images presented to me. I witness myself kneeling in reverence, greeting a master-teacher, looking so happy to see my mentor. Wearing a long white gown, I have long hair, and appear bright and beautiful. There is another image where I am sitting on a carved wooden bench with mom in what looks like a Victorian garden, with lovely flowers and nature all around. Then, I am shown seated on the floor between the Sphinx's paws, receiving messages from her, speaking energy words to the land. In another, I stand with my arms open, then reach up and touch the forehead of a giant elephant. The next one shows me lying on the floor, playing with kitties, so sweet. Followed by many flying birds that constantly bring me messages, I am speaking with them. These are wonderful images.

There is so much being shown in rapid flashes that my conscious mind may not grasp everything fully. While receiving a great deal of information, I keep hearing the words, let this integrate, and it will come to your awareness at the right time. The last image and place I see shows me admiring the sunset at the ocean, walking on the sand toward the water. Whales and dolphins are close to the shore. Walking right in and swimming toward the whale guides, I find myself crying tears of joy. There is such loving energy coming from the whale's eyes. She's holding her flipper wing out, and I am holding on to it as I swim.

Suddenly shapeshifting into a giant being, I see myself being able to sit on the bottom of the ocean while half my body rises out of the water's surface. Turning, lying face up, dolphins jump from one side to the other over my face. It fills my heart. We are playing. There are many messages being delivered as I float there in the gentle waves. The whale is beneath me, supporting me. After turning over and looking into the water, I lay on her as she swims. We flow in wave motions as many, many whales appear all around. They are chanting a greeting, and we are together. It's so beautiful, and I am filled with joy and love in my heart. This chant – the song and frequency of the whales – is familiar to me; it is a song resounding in my heart-mind. The infinity signs continue to appear as wave motions while I perceive a lot of movement around my body, which initially startles me a bit as the physical sensations almost feel like a strong pressure massage.

It's time to return to the open hall space. Sending a goodbye greeting to the whales and dolphins, I descend to the area where the little angel and birds guided me. We gently fly into the lower layers of the sky, feeling the magnetic pull toward the Earth, and slowly fall back into my body - with some considerable pressure, but in slow motion.

As I come back through my golden energy line and anchor, I am in awe of the feelings in and around my body, experiencing waves of energy massaging my field, with enough pressure to feel contraction then release - in and out, side to side, up and down, infinity signs everywhere. Extremely calming. Descending through my energy line, I pull everything back into my body, past my feet into the Earth.

Opening my eyes, and feeling a bit dizzy, I stay with the sensations for some time, sitting quietly while the raindrops-like beads of light are coming down, expressing such gratitude for this journey. All of a sudden, these words resound in my spiritual ears: be with the waves, stay in the heart, and expand to see the bigger picture; we are here to help and guide you; you have what you seek, you will see more, be and express everything you hold.

New Paradigm Healing

The year after opening my studio, I experienced a profound healing modality that helped me shift in a major way. Although changes were subtle at first, I immediately recognized something was happening, and needed to adjust to it gradually. I started receiving Angelic Earth Resonance™ healing sessions regularly. During the sessions, I was exposed to Light Language. I had never heard of or experienced this type of energy language and healing technology. The first time my body absorbed these vibrations, my nervous system allowed me to fully enter a deep state of stillness, my head-brain went quiet, and I could fully trust whatever was happening. My ears and left brain-ego certainly thought these sounds were quite strange, thinking and saying to myself, what does it mean? But it didn't matter, my heart recognized it. I was so comfortable, my armor started to crack, and energy could seep through. Subsequent sessions were so supportive and magical. Soon able to perceive my guides with more clarity, I trusted the integration process and noticed significant shifts in how I conducted my own training and healing sessions. It was difficult to intellectually explain or fully understand what was happening, but I felt that this type of vibration was activating other packets of information that I was ready to incorporate into my journey.

Some months later, I attended a Light Language course facilitated by Jennifer Wrobel, my friend and teacher. She is a powerful guide with a sincere heart and desire to raise people's consciousness in her own unique way.

I loved this class. Although I can't deny that it was mysteriously strange at first, it allowed me to open up to this powerful healing modality, so much so that soon after, this was all I wanted to do. I began listening to the powerful activating words of Judy Satori and Jamye Price, strongly resonating with these frequency transmissions. It was an interesting process starting to feel a difference in vibration as I allowed myself to speak energy words. I would do some training to center, clear my mind, and create a sacred space to commune with my higher self. Then, I would ask for a transmission for something specific; for example, feeling peace and calm or helping me with my headache. Sometimes I just asked to bring through whatever was most appropriate for me at that moment, even if it was something that my system would need to integrate sometime later. Without getting in my way with thinking too much, I would create space, enter a state of presence, receive, and express through movements, sounds, and light whatever was most beneficial for me.

Clearly able to recognize significant changes in my voice, my body, and my heart, I went through a few months of different types of sounds coming through, as well as movements. The energy transmissions brought very different feelings. I can't really describe the sound of these energy words, but the feelings were crystal clear, recognizing different types of vibration. I felt so comfortable bringing these through as if I had done it before, and simply hadn't practiced in a very, very long time. In this period, there were some deep shifts happening as I experienced profound active dreaming journeys, visions, and teaching transmissions.

Coming to me as an inspired realization, the practice of natural flow KiGong, which I would experience on my own as part of my spiritual training, was a form of Light Language all along. In my training we called it *energy dance* - becoming one with universal currents and expressing the minds guided by the highest intelligence running in and around our bodies. In a complete state of presence, surrendered to the purest form of guidance, the inner healer and teacher leads us through healing and transformation. I was always deeply connected with movement; perhaps this is why I became so interested in learning about the principles and sequences when I was first exposed to healing martial arts disciplines. I recognized the impact on the mind and could feel the profound healing effects.

While continuing with my daily classes and sessions, my business began to struggle during the pandemic, experiencing difficulties getting people to the studio in person jeopardized me financially. Still, I was able to get more and more people to join lessons online, and that was a blessing.

All of my free time was dedicated to working on myself, although I was growing tired of struggling and feeling restless. The uncomfortable feelings revolved around resentment toward the franchisor because there was no support, I mean zero. It was all on me. I would ask myself, why wasn't I part of the region? Why wouldn't they include me in their weekly training, updates, and support meetings? I was linked to HQ, which was pretty lame because they are simply way too busy to help manage a small-town franchisee.

Earlier in the year, I had the wonderful opportunity of supporting my teacher, Master Ahn, in a beautiful retreat program in Sedona. She brought a large group from Colorado, and I was able to gather several practitioners and dear friends to join. It was amazing participating and co-leading the group, creating such a spark as this was all I wanted to do. My goal was to create meaningful opening experiences for people in a safe, elevated setting, such as a retreat program.

I did experience a sense of lack, though, something was missing. Whatever I was already teaching was and is fantastic, but I also wanted to include Light Language and whatever else was ready to emerge from me. Buried by this sense of restlessness, I couldn't figure out exactly what it was. Emptying my mind would reveal more space to see things clearly. Here it was; I was bitter that the corporation ignored me because I was a franchise. Feelings of blame came to light, and thoughts such as, I'm failing because I have no support. All of my other peers who graduated with me as franchise owners had several other studios nearby and a regional manager who could lead advanced training programs and was available to provide extensive support for them and their practitioners. That is one reason they are so successful - successful meaning they are financially stable and can keep their doors open. I know for some of them it wasn't easy, and they each had some serious difficulties, but having a giant entity behind to offer support made all the difference.

There came a time when I was already privately doing my own training programs. When I asked HQ if I could officially lead specific courses on my own, I was denied. This was very frustrating for me, although I completely understood why. Again, a corporate boxy mindset, all justified by too many unpleasant experiences in the past with individuals of poor integrity and ethics. But that wasn't my case, why couldn't I get support? Why wasn't I included in the region, again I asked.

I've always held a high sense of integrity and ethics in my work and professional life, therefore respecting my franchise contract agreement was the right thing to do. Although opportunities would present themselves for me to merge modalities in the studio or even rent out the space for other types of work, I was always hesitant and shied away from these circumstances, losing the potential of creating additional funds.

In Spring, I decided to sign up for a year-long apprenticeship in Angelic Earth Resonance™ healing modality. Jennifer guided the group through a powerful inner and outer transformation process. Learning and practicing this beautiful body of work, we each developed our own unique signature, and with time and practice, we would continue to expand and open more and more to the codes received and exchanged.

I began providing a few of my clients with this form of healing modality. I started offering services outside of what I was offering as part of my franchise. Opening to this form of work was so much more complete for me. Healing offerings were so empowering, impactful, and more aligned. The shifts I personally experienced and profound growth were only possible through integrating this powerful body of work with the ancient East Asian energy practices of KiGong.

Asking what I would really do with all of this, aware that there was more wanting to emerge, I knew I had to continue to practice and be of service in this way. However, feeling clouded and uncertain on how I could merge these practices and expand from there, I intuitively heard the words: *there is something more, just stay the course. Continue practicing, learning, and being. You are exactly where you're supposed to be, energetically and spiritually.*

Dreams ~ Visions ~ Journeys

The Little Girl Down the Hallway

I am in a large country house - a castle, with brown brick walls and wooden doors, cold and damp; seems very familiar to me. I find myself in a very long and wide hallway with massive wooden doors on each side; it is wide enough for a carriage to go through it. Holding what looks like a toy tennis ball, and throwing it down the hall, I'm playing with cats who like to chase the ball bouncing down this hallway. I keep walking playfully, seeing all these doors on each side, and have a definite sensation of descending, as if moving downhill with a noticeable inclination.

At one point, I feel I'm going too far or too deep, stopping and looking back for a moment. The hallway seems never-ending, but I keep going until the end. There is a solid entryway, resembling a fire door with a window. Looking through the window, it seems like the end of a railway carriage, but I can't really see anything. Once I decide to walk back, it becomes quite hard, given the incline. I get the sense I should hurry, having been gone a while, and starting to feel a little too isolated. It's rather scary down here. While I keep walking forward looking on both sides, the doors remain closed. Arriving at the landing where I started, I have a brief exchange with someone, or something, overcome by a strong, overwhelming, sinister feeling. There is a sudden movement and sounds coming from behind me. In a flash, I feel something or somebody quickly rushing up this hallway, it followed me. Completely frightened, not expecting anyone to move toward me so rapidly, I look back to my right, and behind me is this little girl with red hair and a long dress. My sight is blurry, unable to focus well, but I can sort of make out her features. Scared, thinking this is a ghost, I ask myself, what does this mean? This is a part of me, I hear; she woke up, hearing me walk down the hallway. This time you got all the way to the end, and she could finally get out; as you walked back, she came following – my mind completely aware of what I was hearing within the dream. Looking at her, I feel worried and scared, then asking for my vision to gain clarity and focus, I can suddenly truly see her. She looks down and acts a bit nervous, as if she's in trouble or did something wrong. I immediately soften, no longer confused and startled, bringing my upper body forward closer to her. She acts shy and scared.

I wake up yelling, *no, I have to speak with her!*

I keep trying to reenter this dream for several days. Only after I stopped thinking about it, I found myself there again early one morning.

The little girl appears again. We are outside the large house with the long hallway and all those doors. It looks very old, not taken care of, probably abandoned. I kneel to see what this little girl can share with me. As I come closer to her, focusing my gaze, I can see her eyes clearly. A rush of energy suddenly fills my body as if being run over by a train. The little girl is me as I suspected in the dream days ago. She extends her arms to show me her hands. The palms and fingers are severely burnt, evidently due to a fire. She was hurt. I hold the back of her hands and look into her eyes. We both cry. I asked her to tell me what happened. She makes some sounds and cannot speak. Asking again, please, I am here, you can speak with me, she opens her mouth and shows me her tongue is completely cut off. She cannot speak because someone cut her tongue. I understand her strong feelings now and hug her tightly for a while.

I woke up crying. I was scared of this frightening, dark, little girl, but she is so hurt, burnt hands and no tongue. How can I see these characteristics show up in my life?

Traveling with Mom

I am at the airport, traveling with a carry-on bag, wearing a nice suit, and heels. It seemed like a business trip. Mom is in the distance accompanied by other individuals, who are helping her with luggage, while I'm getting some salads for our trip. At last, we come together and prepare to board. It's an exciting and happy time, feeling completely thrilled about this trip. Just the fact that she is there with me gives me the best feeling, knowing I'm not alone on this journey. The other people, two or three ladies who seem very familiar, are assisting us, getting things in the right place, the luggage ready, and helping us go downstairs to the correct terminal. They are simply there as helpers before the launch, so to speak. Suddenly, we find ourselves in an empty, white space. I couldn't see anything anymore and this caused me to wake up feeling restless and upset, wanting to see and understand more. Everything was white. Where is everyone?

Healing in the Big Cat World

Meeting Lynx, my companion, I ask her for help upon entering the inner world. As I look around, there are many beautiful cat beings coming to welcome me. A large black panther approaches me in greeting, while Lynx is further down the path, waiting for me. This is a big cat world. Lynx then walks me to the three tigers. The one on the left is enormous; there is one in the middle; she seems older, slightly bigger, of a different shade - a little whiter and grayer. The one on the right seems like a younger male tiger. All three are healers. Lynx makes me stand with my back toward them as they slowly surround me, while she sits right in front of me.
Telepathically, they show me that there are two rods in my lower back that look like porcupine spikes. The one on the right is much bigger. They burn and are very painful when one of the tigers tries to remove them. Worried and in pain, my eyes look up to Lynx, but she reassures

me that the tigers are here to help me and to trust this process. While I try to endure the pain, I suddenly feel my body being pushed forward forcefully. Within the dream, I realize it's my left-brain ego. The strong motion is my ego snapping me out of this process out of primal fear; the burning feeling pulls me out quickly. Aware I'm no longer in a state of pure presence – spaciousness - I still feel the daze of dream space, hearing myself say, why are these spikes there? They need to finish, despite the apprehension of the pain. Can they finish? I must be brave and go back. Please finish! Thank you.

Preparing for the Long Journey

I'm in an airport-like setting again. This time the terminal is extremely large. Just waiting around for the trip to begin, I notice there are many people and some look very familiar, I know them. There are a bunch of other people just waiting for the plane or ship to leave, and I get a sense this is going to be an important trip – there is a lot of excitement in the air. We are all waiting and preparing. The terminal is very bright and so large I can barely see where it ends. Suddenly we hear announcements, and some people say, ok, they're getting ready for us; this will be a long trip, but we're all ready, aren't we?

Everyone knows we are about to get on an enormous vehicle, although we can't see it yet. It's all so exciting. We expect to be shuttled to the area we can board, because we know the craft is just too large to dock at the terminal, and we simply can't walk over there. We are aware this is a trip we've all been waiting for and that it will take a long time to reach our destination. Although I am standing there alone, looking around, I don't feel alone. There will also be other individuals close to me who are about to show up at any moment, and I am confident we will find each other eventually. As usual, I am early, ready to go, observing everyone preparing their belongings and gathering with others. This is going to be amazing, I say to myself.

Gathering in Grief

Startled from waking up crying and feeling intense chest pain, I take deep breaths, then re-enter the dream through the last image in my mind.

There are several people standing around close to me. We are waiting in line, gathered to speak to someone. I can see who everyone is waiting for as there is only one person in front of me. He is known as a spiritual guide. Everyone is wearing what looks like a black scarf over one shoulder. Something must have happened because there is a lot of crying and grieving. We are there to receive counsel on what to do next. The guide has a short beard, brown hair, and wears a long robe. We all have similar type of clothing with this black shawl or scarf over the shoulder. I realize we belong to a specific order. We were called together to review what happened, take care of each other, and prepare for the next phase.

Council of Light

I am in line. There are two long lines with people gathered single file. It's almost my turn. A very large, bright light is shining toward the people the entire time. As I get closer to the front, being exposed to such bright light becomes unbearable. I can describe it as an enormous old-fashioned lighthouse beacon, or large, old Hollywood set Fresnel light. My eyes start to hurt so badly that they start to swell up, while I cringe and fold in two from the pain.

As I come closer to the front of the line, the shades over the beacon begin to shield the intense light. Whoever is operating this light knows the effects on us in line. Suddenly, I am taken to what appears to me to be my doctor's office, thinking they have to take care of the damage to my eyes. I can see myself talking to my doctor, asking her if I should get acupuncture to help me heal. She just smiles, no words. Then I see my spiritual teacher, Master Ahn. She's in the same doctor's office. They both tell me to start breathing through my lower dahnjon – belly breathing. They want to see how much I can pull into this energy portal. I am nervous, thinking this is a test, but begin to breathe through my dahnjon as instructed, while they observe.

I wake up, and notice my lower back pain is about 80% less than when I first got into bed. Some stiffness, but nothing like the day before, when I couldn't even put my socks on. Applying oregano and clove oil to baby it, and proceeding with my morning bowing training, I feel strong and grounded. Deep inside, there is a strong sense that I was shown a doctor's office with my real-life doctor and spiritual teacher as cosmic beings were administering some form of healing.

In deep meditation, later that day, I tried to re-enter the dream asking in my mind what this type of intense light was. I immediately saw huge, beautiful letters spelling something out. They floated in the dark starry sky and the sparkling letters slowly appeared spelling, *Council of Light*. I was so amazed being able to see distinctly these big fancy letters spelling out for me: COUNCIL OF LIGHT.

I fully came back, feeling my body, smiling, and saying out loud, I like how you guys have to spell things out for me so bluntly. Thank you!

12

A TURNING POINT

Grief – How Long Do I Hang On?

After completing the year-long apprenticeship, we had the celebration retreat through group healing sessions at my studio. We prepared my training room with four healing tables, and created a wonderful space surrounded by instruments, essential oil sprays, herbs and incense, music in the background, healthy snacks, and beverages. We, practitioners newly appointed as successfully graduated apprentices, worked on individuals, sometimes two at a time, partnering with one or two other practitioners as a team. I resonated strongly with most of them, and it was truly a magical experience, especially working with Jess, Jane and Lauren. I felt my training room literally come alive even more with the high frequency we were transmitting. There were guides from many dimensions, angelic beings guiding and supporting us as well as the receivers. We were expanding brightness in all directions, and it was palpable. I could have gone for days. We were definitely exhausted after eight hours of doing this type of healing work but charged and uplifted at the same time.

Group sessions are extremely beneficial and powerful. During our year-long training, Jennifer would have us experience going deeper and deeper as we worked on one person at a time as a group. We would take turns being on the table, receiving.

I had personally experienced many openings and expansions, not only when I was on the table but also when I was transmitting, holding space, or just radiating, supporting the group. Strong energy moved through my body in one particular session like it hadn't before. It can be described as a powerful fire, a very ancient energy. I suddenly let the loudest scream out through my mouth, as hard as one could ever scream, three times. It gives me the chills recalling those moments. Being conscious and aware of what was happening while expanding into a deep state of presence at the same time, so much so that I could experience with other sense perceptions a huge current running through me, powerful enough that my physical form could not contain it. I heard myself scream but wasn't fazed at all by the fact that this whole scenario could have looked so over-the-top and would have most definitely alarmed the surrounding businesses. Once the session was over and fully returned to a more *awake* state, I felt quite embarrassed and somewhat silly, but deep down, I knew it was ok. Something deep was released; it was unsettling but beautiful at the same time.

Fire Of Release - Recorded Experience

About an hour ago, we had the last class of our apprenticeship. It was beautiful. As usual, I went last before our teacher Jennifer. The experience during this group session was deeply meaningful. There was lots of movement, building, and building until suddenly, I shouted so, so loudly, not once, but three times. Right before that moment, I found myself in a void vacuum-type space, then out of nowhere, I screamed from a place deep down with an irresistible urge to let go. There was no time, just a profound, quiet void. I don't know exactly what I was screaming about, but it was so powerful, that I perceived it as a total rebellion against all the shallowness, wanting to break free and push through yet another layer. I felt a significant and memorable expansion afterward, a sensation that made me feel very comfortable, calm, with colorful brightness emanating from all around, like a feather, floating in this radiant light. Finding myself in a deep state of nothingness while fully conscious of my physical awareness, my throat started to feel uncomfortable, which made me realize I actually screamed out loud. My body wasn't particularly sore, but my throat was depleted.

I was so tired when I got home that I needed to rest, and before going to sleep, I asked to be shown what was important for me to know. In the early morning hours, a series of images appeared in my mind screen. Many memories, various scenarios, from long ago to recent times, all flowing in chronological order. I heard myself say, *these are all the strengths and qualities you have gained. Look at your strengths and move forward.*

A lot of anger and fear was released. In this vision, I could see myself expecting to be shown the root of anger and fear, but I instantly heard these words, you don't need to actually pinpoint it or see it.

Things were clearer. Whatever had been accumulated consciously and unconsciously, I needed to empty myself further to make space for more brightness to enter. Feeling much better and ready to face forward again, I woke up and opened my eyes. Looking at the clock, it said 733. For days, 633 would catch my attention. I smiled, thinking, this just means to me, get up, and let's keep going - up the spiral we go.

It was Lion's Gate. I had a wake-up call. Why keep going? I felt so exhausted. Although I was receiving a federal small business loan to stay afloat, the message received was clear to me - this journey was complete. After experiencing more of myself – sensing with expanded awareness, I was no longer fully committed to my franchisor. I struggled with feeling guilty and resentful at the same time. It was my choice from the beginning, anyway. As I relaxed more into my decision, I felt more settled and knew it was right for me. Although painful, this was the best choice, and proceeded with the plan to close my studio.

Grief took over. I cherished my teachings and loved my mentors; to be honest, not all of them, although some were extremely powerful teachers - the brightest people I know, on a physical and spiritual level. Everything started to feel a bit too tight, it didn't fit anymore. It was the same feeling I experienced when considering leaving my corporate career.

My entire life had been all about work, having spent 20 years in the corporate world. I identified with my job completely, thinking it was me, but actually, it wasn't. Adapting well was and is a strong quality

I hold, even when I don't entirely like everything, however there is a time when we come to a full realization that we must go in another direction in order to grow. Every step of this process is very positive; there is nothing negative about it at all, except many times fears take over and paralyze us.

Once the decision to close the studio sunk in, all the logistical things that I disliked had to be handled. Consulting a lawyer for a full review of my commercial lease was the first step. I was going to break a five-year lease, so what would happen? It was so incredibly stressful as I absolutely detest any form of bureaucracy - all ridiculous and really heavy for me.

I finally set up a meeting to speak to the landlord's representative. The studio was located on Native American tribe land in a large shopping center. The lease process was a bit different than regular commercial lease dealings. After explaining the circumstances, she appeared to be extremely understanding, and we were able to come to an agreement. The plan was in motion, and I could proceed with the next steps. We agreed to close within the month, which led me to the bitter process of informing all of my clients, most of whom, the more active ones, were notified all in one day via phone. I spent hours crying, making myself strong between each call. It was difficult. They were so sweet, understanding, and some began to grieve too.

The closing process involved clearing the space and moving everything out. I was able to sell a few items to my teacher, who had moved from the D.C. to Colorado by this time, and could sell some things to a few of my clients. I kept all of the decorative scrolls. I knew I could use them in the future, plus they hold a special vibration, which is very meaningful to me. This whole thing was a brutal process. On the last day, when we had to leave the studio and the plaza, Jason and I stood in the empty training room, looking around. I gave it one last sweep, then we both laid down on the soft floor, held hands, and played one of our favorite chill tracks as loud as possible. Our sound system was fantastic, and I used to absolutely love being transported by the music, especially when I was doing my own training. We cried a lot, then finally got up, said goodbye, and locked the doors.

I haven't driven to the plaza since that day. A huge part of me literally died. I know that I will always hold the codes of my teachings; they're not *mine* by all means, but I will always carry what I received inside, cherishing the high vibration connection to this ancient wisdom. That is part of who I am now. Nothing changes this fact whether an organization says I'm affiliated to it or not. I'm not part of anything, belonging to nothing and everything at the same time. I can say I just belong to *myself*, and that is plenty, choosing to continuously strive for higher vibration rather than being part of a box. All of my learnings, all of my experiences, and even all the heaviness are remarkable treasures to be honored. I consider all of these my teachers, and would do it all over again. This wonderful experience was needed, chosen, and carefully crafted for what I am becoming now and in the future.

My teacher, Master Ahn, came to Sedona one day. After picking her up, we spent half a day together. I love her deeply. She took care of me by giving me a restorative healing session, which always included a journey to connect with my soul and guides. We revealed a memory this time. My guides showed me the experiences I had gone through these years were part of my path, but they also wanted me to remember something in particular.

I was reminded of a recurring dream, where I could hear myself singing a popular song. Although I cannot remember the exact title, it goes something like: *out of this town, out of this town...* it was a very famous song by a female artist, being played on the radio constantly in those days. I must leave this town - asking myself, what does it mean? No, that can't be right. This message kept repeatedly resounding in my dreams - non-stop, over, and over for days. I totally ignored it.

A new phase started. Grateful for what I learned, knowing I found more of myself and now moving on to the next cycle, whatever those next steps would be, my focus was trying, as best I could, not to micromanage - always very interesting and powerful as I see *letting go* to be a process involving many dimensions and facets of release.

The soul always has a way of getting us to what destiny we chose, although there may be so many different ways to *be* in this life. There is no definite path to follow, just the path we chose at any given moment. A strong suggestion can be ignored, and then another opportunity comes about. It's not the longer or shorter road, the faster or slower way. I never experienced regret. Even when I was miserable and suffered so much, my whole being does not regret any experience; instead, there is a sense of awe and wonder at how amazing my inner guidance system has been, presenting the next steps, never losing hope in me. I never knew back in Rhode Island that I was about to end my life, but something inside me said to *turn this way instead.* It wasn't possible for me to see, maybe it wasn't my place to fully understand back then.

I'm not saying everything is completely clear now, but there is so much more awareness, that's for sure. Often, I like to describe seeing light through a crack of a slightly open door; it begins to open more and more, allowing more light to shine through, giving the opportunity to realize that there is a lot more on the other side of that door - incredibly more real, natural, and true.

Feeling extremely grateful, my heart is full, still protecting itself, sure, tending to the hurt and showing up for myself first no matter what, then practicing *being* me as I keep opening just like flowers do, following the laws of the universe. This is my process, and honoring this process is the gift of trust.

Training – Depths of Feeling

How deeply do we need to push our body? Why in the world does one need to do a certain type of practice and repeat it over and over for an extended period of time? These are common questions that come up during training. Depending on what an individual's needs are, still (or static) postures as well as flowing movements may need to be practiced for a certain amount of time or repeated one hundred times, three hundred times, one thousand and so on. Sometimes, we just need to push our bodies that much to fully open up. Here is my experience with pain and taking the journey of going deeper, facing levels of the mind through the body.

I always knew, conceptually, that our bodies hold so much information; however, early in my training, I was able to experience and fully recognize this notion with my whole body, not just with my *thinking*. There is a huge difference. We hear this all the time and know it intellectually, but many of us don't really recognize it as a universal law; in addition, we have difficulty understanding the *feelings* in the body due to some form of block, resistance, and disconnection. There is nothing to believe in here. We are literally magical beings, and our body holds precious information. It always wants to return to its natural state of harmony and balance. A certain sound and light vibration live, adapt, and thrive in our body, and we may not fully perceive the vast amount of information we hold, whether we are intentionally aware of this or not.

Deliberate avoidance or pushing any sort of heaviness away in a deep dark corner is an understandable process we all go through sometimes in life, consciously or not. I think of this phenomenon as an actual technology. There are times in life when it's absolutely necessary to avoid and disconnect, but other times this survival, protection, or habitual mechanism becomes a distortion, no longer useful or valid. It doesn't matter at what level of depth distorted information lies, it's there and we need to *clean house.*

For the *body* to align with the energy-spiritual fields, our multidimensional minds, it (*she*) continuously needs our assistance. When we pay attention very deeply to the language of our body, we open up to a new level of communication with our heart-mind, with a higher quality of vibration - our true voice. The body is a very important portal, the gateway to a refined conversation with our soul.

Sometimes we just want a shortcut, wanting to lead with the heart directly, but if the energy of the heart is not mature enough, we experience instability on multiple levels, with potential detrimental effects in various aspects of our lives.

We may arrive at a level of discernment where we can identify if a specific type of healing, practice, even food, supplements, or individuals, will enhance and brighten our energy bodies or be harmful and dimming, often struggling with an unchecked internal whirlwind returning to the habitual thoughts and emotional patterns which inevitably cover an aspect that truly wants to be free.

As an example, in KiGong, practitioners may be guided through various movements and postures, some of which may even seem extremely simple on the outside. One may ask, how can this be beneficial? They may be asked to repeat a particular movement again and again.

The rational mind will inevitably ask, why does it have to be so many times or for this long? It may begin to rebel, create stories, lose control of thought processes, and feel resentment. Who made me come here? Do they know what they're doing? This is kind of ridiculous, and it will definitely not help; I decided, this can't be good.

Aside from all of this internal chatter, what happens is that upon completing the exercise or sequence of forms and postures, one almost always experiences a deep sense of opening. Something changes physically, through our nervous system, the brain, and fluids in our body, and in the energy-spiritual fields as well. Energy flows deep through our meridians and energy centers and purifies the space inside and around our physical body.

A deep sense of relaxation arises, and our nervous systems are infused with *new* information. It's literally like switching the channel. From being in front of a news channel, fed low-quality information and distortions, you are now in an open space with greater vision, clarity, and ability to see farther and in more detail, like being out in Nature. In this space, true healing occurs.

So, when we practice a certain form of training, we challenge the innate resilience of our minds through the physical body's intelligence.

The pure intelligence we hold within our bodies matches the energy vibrations of the following statements: we are strong and have perfect health; we are open, stable, and continuously receive empowering vitality from all sources; our filters know how to purify and reset effortlessly; we carry the brightest light deep inside ceaselessly shining outward and receiving a vast amount of brightness from the cosmos moving inward.

We've become too used to managing and operating through our thinking left-brain ego. This phenomenon and aspect of our mind is merely incomplete as it gives us the ability to pay attention to *only* a sliver of what is actually there.

Just analyze the electromagnetic spectrum to learn how much visible light we can actually perceive with our eyesight – it is less than 1%. On a larger scale and dimension, we think we know, but we really don't, since we equate *knowing* with *seeing*. This concept alone should make us very humble that there is so much that our physical bodies *do* and *know*, while we simply get in the way by focusing our attention on that 1% alone.

The same concept goes for what we intend when referring to *mind* in the West. When I talk about the mind or *minds*, I do not refer to the thought processes that occur in the head-brain. This is why I call it head-brain. It is a processing system, a beautiful instrument of tuning, sending, and receiving, it's a device and tool for one dimension of alignment and direction.

These are all critically important qualities, however, thoughts are not us. Thoughts are just like the five physical senses. We should pay attention, but really....is it taking over the management and operation of Life or is it being utilized as a helpful tool?

Observing and considering the quality of thoughts is absolutely vital, however, continuously purifying our filters, maintaining centeredness and neutrality, then analyzing what the thoughts are actually telling us is way more interesting work.

What about the *mind*? Ancient people thought of the heart as the seat of consciousness. The heart-mind creates an electromagnetic field much vaster than the brain's. In ancient Egypt, the heart was left in the body, while the brain was discarded.

Aligning our heart fire with the fire of our spirit, of truth, of our highest vibration was divine work and what led the individual toward their true destiny - no matter what fate has handed down through generational patterns or current environments.

I experience the principles of mind as multidimensional, including many layers of awareness and evolution processes, and began recording guidance and instructions as I receive insights through my spiritual classroom daily.

Since I began my training journey, I was fascinated by the internal happenings of the head-brain while practicing still-KiGong postures, energy accumulation practices, and other physically challenging work. This was a different level of mindfulness practice. The left-brain ego would, and eventually does, begin to literally flip out. It rebels and doesn't like any form of stimulation to open and allow more light in. The body reacts as if it was stuck in a rusted, old broken car which is 100% the manifestation of the head-brain defense armoring system and misinformation. From the outside, one may even look peaceful, but inside, there is a war, a deep conflict between who's in charge and who's more stubborn. The soul's voice is soft, gentle, and kind - always. But what is loudest and most obnoxious? What catches our attention more? What is it that makes us distracted from *seeing*, truly seeing? Yes, of course, we can't really see clearly if the thoughts are so loud, if our body is shaking and cramping up, if we're convinced this is not helpful, and if we're cursing the instructor. This makes me smile because I totally experienced all of these feelings physically and emotionally multiple times.

Cycling has always been a great passion of mine, although it soon turned into a bit of an obsession. Back in San Diego, I bought a professional indoor spinning bike, after completing an amazing instructor certification program in LA - the bike became my best friend. I would spin almost every day. My body was so fit, my minds not so much, but I looked in shape and was so strong. After moving to the DC area, I was able to have my very own gym room on the top floor of our townhome. It was an everyday occurrence, even on weekends, to get up extremely early, spin for about an hour, while blasting the best EDM music as loud as possible in my ears through headphones. My legs were so strong, my heart resilient, it felt so good. This was my medicine back then. When I started KiGong practice, I immediately felt a different type of strength and resilience, but I couldn't put my finger on it. I simply didn't have any reference point.

They don't teach us this stuff in school; what energy, what does that mean? I began the training involving still-KiGong postures. This is energy accumulation training where practitioners hold a particular pose for a certain amount of time. Many of you may be familiar, but for those who are not, it's not something like a headstand, although it could be, I suppose.

Imagine a person hugging a tree. There is a posture often called the *holding tree posture*. Standing with feet hip-width apart, sinking into the knees, tailbone tucked in just slightly, lifting arms as if you were to hug someone. Imagine holding a wheel in front of your chest. Shoulders relaxed, elbows down a bit, relaxed face muscles, gaze toward the space between your fingers, unfocused, or eyes closed.

I don't think anyone has ever died from holding a tree posture, however, after about 10 minutes, one may begin to experience an explosion of feelings, physically and on other levels. After 30 minutes, it may be unbearable.

Well, I thought, I am so strong, I can totally do it. Bring it!

The reality is that I couldn't hold that posture for very long. I was so disturbed. What is happening? I must be tired today. There is no way, what is going on? So many thoughts clouded my mind. Using my abdominal muscles and thighs to resist in that posture as much as possible, I was focusing on the physical alone. My teacher kept saying *relaxed – focuse*d repeatedly and would guide us toward achieving a relaxed body with a focused mind. What? What is that? I was having the worst time, unable to understand, but was even more intrigued because I do like challenging myself. It was also very disappointing for me that I couldn't do this type of training at first, it's not like I was weak by all means. A light bulb went off - physical strength has something to do with energy, but *not* this type of energy. I kept asking myself. Why can these little, fragile, petite, elderly ladies hold this posture as if they were Olympic athletes?

Why do we have to suffer? Why are you telling us this? You may be asking now. The truth is that our bodies hold a lot of information, processed and unprocessed - we have an important job and responsibility, which is paying attention, not with *thinking* alone, but with *feeling*.

In order to properly digest information, we may use other types of energy-technology for us to make improvements, to upgrade. We may not need to fully recall every detail of the past to overcome traumatic events, returning to outdated frameworks. Maybe it's no longer useful to continue to avoid or neglect parts of ourselves, and we can certainly begin to stop identifying with ideas such as, my grandmother had it, so it's my destiny; it runs in the family genes; I'm old; I have a disease; I had an accident; my wife left me; my father doesn't love me; I can't find my purpose in life; my children despise me; I don't want to be here.

Words carry vibrations, just like all thoughts and emotions. We can help our body open up, release, and nourish its natural healing qualities by recalibrating the sources of information. This requires us to be fully centered and grounded, by cultivating a neutral level of consciousness.

Neutrality is a sense perception just like touch, smell, or eyesight. We can develop and stimulate our neutral senses through this type of training or body stimulation. Can we be willing to go deeper until the loudness of our left-brain ego subsides a little, or even better, can we be willing to expand to include the subtle, gentle voice of our higher minds? In neutrality, we can become deeply present, but *deep* should not be mistaken as contraction, like going into a cave. Instead, I see it as going into the alignment space within our energy line and then expanding outward where we can experience more, becoming fully aware of what our physical body is processing, paying attention to all of our senses - including thinking, and then begin to include our higher senses, welcoming our minds – the higher vibrations, the faster pulsating frequencies of our source.

I do see this whole process as very natural, and everyone

experiences it in their own unique way. It's the evolution of becoming. We're unfolding into more of who we are. As we continue to remember the vibration of our essence - entering this aligned space, focusing within then expanding outward - we can recognize presence as a sense perception as well. Through pure, sincere devotion to our higher consciousness communication channels, we can continuously evolve, learn, and grow. It's a natural level of mind we must remember and connect to as if our life depended on it, because it actually does.

All of this describes the beauty of work that encourages our bodies to heal – the physical form and the energy and spiritual bodies. I'm only sharing my personal experience, and I feel very strongly about this. Sometimes in our lives when we need a special type of guidance, specific outside resources to show us something, maybe even the help of medicine to allow us to get to a space where we can sleep, rest, and reset our nervous system and think a bit more clearly. I have gone through many of these processes myself, and feel so glad I did because it helped me when I had no other tools available. However, there is a time when talking about our wounds is no longer useful. The body wants to help us become the best we can be. Holding a pattern of worry, anger, and sadness will inevitably ask us to pay close attention as it comes to the surface. Inflammation, a twisted ankle, a strained muscle, a degenerative disease, and so on. There is no such thing as an accident or mishap.

One thing that I will do my best to convey. We never, ever, did and are doing anything wrong. There is nothing to fix. We are not failing if our body is hurt, if we have inherited a disease, if we feel lost within our heart, or are processing deep heartbreak, which may manifest in anger and resentment. Our job is simply finding a way to love ourselves more, how much? As much as we can and then, from there, expand even more so that we can embrace more of ourselves.

Wearing our trauma as a backpack is a heavy burden that may prevent our growth. We can't see it all the time; it's back there, and we may unconsciously work so hard to keep it there, but it's heavy, no longer relevant, and it's time to leave it behind. We tend to identify with *what happened to us* and stay in the past. I strongly believe it's essential to uncover the root cause of sorrow, but I also strongly believe (and experienced) that if we can recognize with our entire being, not just with our head, that we are not limited to *our story* in this life, that we are much more that the story, deep healing can occur. Our story may not be entirely ours, how true is this story, really? Are we wearing someone else's ideas? No need to overthink now. Opening and softening is what needs to happen. More light cannot enter if we're contracted and identify with the small mind. Open and soften, it's time.

We are not our information; it is simply ours to manage. We can gain huge strength from focusing inward to fuel our own inner fire and let lower vibrations move outward as we increase our inner light. Cultivating higher frequencies states of consciousness doesn't mean avoiding or wishful thinking; it's a practice driven by our soul's desire to use the lower vibrations reflected in the outer realities as tools to raise the bar even higher. The *story* becomes the instrument and catalyst to assist us, to lift us, into greater potentials.

We must love ourselves enough to be willing to change *jobs*, to fully step into new roles. What I mean by that is that our primary job needs to be to get to know the minds, to interpret the messages of our bodies, to listen carefully to our heart, to observe with interest and devotion all of the information we are consuming, to live as if we had no other focus but the love for ourselves.

This is when we find that inner knowing: nobody else can really resolve this or that situation for us, it is all in our hands. This feeling should not feel like a burden, another task to take on, another person to take care of; it's not that type of feeling. It's a sense of responsibility that elevates us to an empowered state, with a bow and arrow, with an angel sword, with a tall staff like Gandalf, holding the sphere of bright, colorful light that is our higher mind and lifting it up high so that everyone can absorb the brightness while we help them share their own, as we inspire others to become their own inspiration.

As we brighten and lift, we are becoming a new version of humanity. This is the most important and valuable work out there. The rest functions as a support system. Even the heaviness of people or circumstances, including collective turmoil, and what Earth is experiencing are all signposts, directional markers pointing the way - over here, look at this closely. There is no good or bad, there is no right or wrong.

The practice of opening our energy bodies is beyond our psychic abilities; it includes the mind of the body, which is intelligent and holds incredible wisdom. The shortcut or bypass would be wanting to experience and navigate energy-spiritual fields with psychic phenomenon alone. My view, as you've probably gathered by now, is that this perspective and practice is incomplete and unstable.

When reconnecting to our energy and spiritual senses, many find themselves not fully anchored to the wisdom of the body, or at least only to the first few layers. Learning how to effectively clear, ground and center is probably the most basic foundation one needs to *master* and continue to sustain diligently as the process of mastering never ends, it simply evolves. We must become humble experts at being fully grounded and centered.

Connecting to the spiritual realms is like coming home, it's a meaningful and needed practice, however, through my experiences, I quickly realized I was more interested in learning how to feel complete and whole, wanting to experience my spiritual bodies along with my energy bodies and my physical body too, all at once, and then expand from there. I would often ask myself; how can I get them all together and have one nice big department meeting?

So, when I began practicing different ways of accessing emptiness - spaciousness - presence, including my body, energy, and spiritual senses, I was able to hold more energy. This is the endless process of opening to consciousness, to the movement and flow of our minds. I think everyone needs to develop and cultivate this capacity and continuously focus on improving because not only is it the natural state of being - expanded forms of awareness - but it supports us in becoming brighter, literally, which leads to living in-joy.

Practicing this state of awareness supported me in showing up for myself differently, allowing me to reach a deeper level of connection to myself, which resulted in being present for my own clients in this way too, with the highest devotion to my integrity, ensuring I could provide and hold a sacred space where we could feel the freedom to open up.

As I continue to grow, I am so grateful for being guided through the process of awakening the mind of my body and heart. I know for a fact that I could have easily gotten lost in other mindsets, unknowingly feeling incomplete and most likely unable to perceive pure high-vibration messages from my true self, higher consciousness beings and guides. The connection to our whole self is not a few steps process, it's continuous, but it's absolutely essential.

An indication of missed connection, or simply not deep enough, would be experiencing significant swings of imbalances in daily life, such as dysfunction, low vibration projections, misguided information due to unpurified filters, and mismanaging our spiritual senses with a careless, superficial focus. Once again, building a strong basic foundation is key, because it allows us to improve the quality of our minds and cultivate presence through the body's spiritual alignment.

13

DREAMING AS HEALING PRACTICE

Minds Speak Through Journeys

Being a dreamer and visionary has always been part of my nature, even though this quality and aspect of my personality was shut off when I was so small. My early years are a bit hazy, but there is the distinct memory of the time when mom heard me speaking to my team as she was getting ready for bed and asked me about it. I cast it off as something mindless and silly, not wanting to scare her or for her to think I was extremely strange; besides, I was already feeling odd and inadequate since my sister absolutely despised and hated me, so I couldn't jeopardize things with my mom.

Throughout the years, though, I always paid attention to my dreams, those that would occur in my sleep and those that would take shape as visions in my mind screen during active-dream time. I would often write them down in notebooks until keeping a digital log allowed me to record my journeys very quickly. Handwriting is still a beautiful way to connect and always delivers inspiring messages; over time I've been guided back to the simplicity and pureness of this practice as it provides a powerful link to merge with the minds.

I would continue to daydream and travel in imaginal worlds throughout my teenage and adult years, without ever telling anyone. Years ago, I came across the work of Robert Moss, and about fell off my office chair when I watched a short intro for one of his Dream online workshops. His storytelling voice and style was captivating, and the content certainly medicine for me at the time. I couldn't get enough of the recordings from the workshop, feeling so relieved. Tons of people dream like this, and we're not only talking about sleep-time dreaming. This is fantastic, and we also get to learn how to go back into the dreams, ask questions, and learn.

During the same period of time, I also discovered the work of the Monroe Institute, and while still living in the DC area, I considered going to the Gateway workshop in person, but it didn't work out.

Through studying the work of Robert Monroe and practicing myself, I realized that I shared some of the same experiences before, having vivid recollections of lucid dreams and astral travel since I was a little girl, but simply didn't know what it was called or even how to describe it. I was one of those people who had always been told, it's *just* a dream, not only as a child but even today. A sense of encouragement fills my heart when my inner voice lovingly reminds me, it's ok that others don't see it or understand and accept you for you, the dreamer - walking in two or more worlds simultaneously. As I began focusing on uncovering this part of myself on a more profound level, I started experiencing huge awakening experiences in my dreams.

Dreams ~ Visions ~ Journeys

Somebody's Watching Me

I am in Cancun and see several images representing memories; the house where I used to live, the hotel, my team, the delicious juice made from the rind of pineapple I used to buy from the street vendor on my block, the warmth, the humidity, the water, and sun. Some bad times, some great times. The mosquitos while walking the little Tito, the way to the hotel, waiting for the taxi and bus when I didn't own a car. A series of memories from that timeframe. It's like I am watching this other person - me - my adventures and experiences, asking, who is that? Feeling like she's this whole other person, separated from me, pursuing her dreams of freedom.

In a flash, I find myself in another world, escaping from something or someone. At first, it's a place that seems like a gym. I am trying to find an elevated quiet space, up some stairs on the roof, busy moving some things around, closing lockers, and trying to find peace and quiet. Someone is watching me. They follow me, but keep their distance. I'm not too frightened, noticing they're simply observing my every move.

Presented now with the image of another location, this time I see myself on top of what looks like a tower or lighthouse. My sight is focused enough to gain a good look at the man following and watching me; he has Asian features, and is also quite tall and slender, wearing a tailored suit. Moving some books around to make myself room to hide, I try to find a space to sit comfortably. The books are unusually large in size and while rearranging them on a shelf, I keep looking around - there he is. Now it's a bit daunting, why is he watching me? There are no words exchanged, he's just standing there. I start to wonder if he's looking out for me or just needs to report my next move to someone else. Meanwhile, I am desperately trying to get away from it all. There is no more room for me to move around here, everything is so tight. Crouching down by a small window, I can make enough space for me to wait. The man is still there, just watching. What am I supposed to do next?

I wake up, and I'm startled. Why is he following me? Who is that? *In the sleep-awake state, these words arrive in response, he represents a part of you - observing what you are going to do next, why are you running and trying to get away from him, from you?* I immediately recall the series of images from Mexico shown to me right before, wondering if it's related; *of course, it is* – hearing in my inner ears. It's so wonderful that I could clearly hear all the sounds, vividly see colorful details, and be fully aware of my feelings. Asking, what is the name of that drink with pineapple? Tepache, I hear right away. So good!

Once fully awake, the left side of my head was pounding with a tension headache. *Why is this happening to my head so often? The message coming through tells me, adjustment and integration.*

189

Merging with the Universe

Awake within the dream, I am given specific instructions. Create a connection between the crystals within the Earth and the crystalline structures held within our bodies. Hovering over the waters, I am supported as if sitting on those ergonomic no-gravity chairs, enjoying being held between worlds, in an expanded state of trust. An image appears; the energy connection between Earth's many particles and my own, shown as the physical body and the entire cosmos, linked then merged through the empty space, the Amun – the invisible intelligence. The space I am hovering in is an ocean. Weightless, it feels so good, a spacious emptiness restoring connections.

In this state, I hear something - an interesting sound with strong vibrations and frequencies, it's quite distinct. This is communication, an intelligence that simply exists with no beginning and no end. It's moving, sending and receiving - clearly detectable. The Movement now expands - it becomes an echo all around. I am so comfortable, more myself, so peaceful and relaxed. Laying back, I close my eyes and enjoy myself, as if I'm recharging, knowing I am part of it all. Loving words resound in my ears, yes just like this, open up, even if just a tiny little bit to the enormousness of energy structures all around. Everything, down to the smallest unit, has a beautiful form that constantly interacts - sending, receiving, and collaborating - with harmonious Movement, the ocean of consciousness. I am in an ocean of frequency and buoyancy, the calm space of All-time.

Contact - Missing Time

I find myself in a large laboratory-like structure. It seems like I am working the overnight shift because I'm changing into pajamas. There is a big room with computers and equipment everywhere.

In the middle of the night, I go outside and look up; something is in the air, it feels like strong electricity. I see flashing lights all around, and bright lightning-like beams. Although it's hard to figure out what is happening, I know something is very close. There is a humming vibration and electric static in the air. My body is shaking, although I don't seem afraid; this whole scenario actually feels quite familiar to me.

It's so cold and I suddenly fall into an altered state. My body is lifted, floating in mid-air. Something is happening to me. I am bathed in this humming, static electric energy. It's so strong, but I am completely comfortable, it almost feels like I'm getting a massage.

Many hours go by. I know this because I see myself in the area in front of the building once again, but it's the middle of the day, and I'm still in my pajamas. Noticing my location, I am further away from what I remember last, behind some large panels that are part of the control mechanism belonging to the equipment inside the building.

As I run back in, I find my robe and put it on right when Security comes in. They ask if everything went well overnight; before I could answer, another person walks in, followed by a whole team of people. They get to work quickly, jumping on all the equipment, computers, and phones. They are gathering and analyzing data. Something happened last night, we comment, and we have to go through what was recorded by these machines. Feeling so tired, I get a coffee and try to find a place where I can change and feel more normal.

As I record this dream-vision, I immediately recall a similar experience the night before. In addition, once I opened my eyes, I remembered a past life regression where I was a scientist in Los Alamos working on undisclosed programs - could these be memories from that time?

I am alone in the building, there are huge windows from which I can see the night sky. I am guarding the area and monitoring various phenomena. During the day, my team members have the responsibility of deciphering data collected overnight; I am the one in charge of the work at night. Suddenly, sounds fill the air. Going toward the windows, there is no sense of fear. I then proceed with going outside. It's so cold, and I'm definitely not properly dressed. I'm in pajamas.

There is something in the sky, it's close, but I don't see it with my eyes. I hear very unique sounds. Suddenly, a huge craft in the sky appears to my right. It is massive, oval in shape, hovering, tilted to one side. Then it quickly moves toward the right and suddenly disappears. There is a mountain cliff in the distance where the craft disappears entirely; I think it flew behind the huge land mass, and maybe it did, but from what I saw, it simply disappeared.

Analyzing this phenomenon, the sound is very unique. There is such strong wind too and it's so cold. I feel excited, with a sense of familiarity, and so happy to see it again. Heading back into the building, I prepare some more coffee, look for layers, like pants and a robe, and continue working frantically. I see myself sitting at a table with all these computers and different kinds of equipment I can't even begin to describe. Such large buttons, some types of radars and data analytics instruments. It's very messy and looks like I've been so busy working that I couldn't straighten out or even dust. Who can work this way, I say in the dream, seeing myself as the person in charge, and telling the morning crew to please clean right away, we have lots of work to do.

This made me smile, so typical with the compulsive cleaning and all.

Conflict at the Threshold

I see myself in the corporate world environment. There is an atmosphere of needing to build relationships so that one day you can get something out of someone, not genuine or completely authentic. People have a habit of behaving dishonestly. Going from one person to another having conversations, I feel completely restless and frustrated. Curious to find out why I was shown this scenario, I am unexpectedly pulled out of this scene and now find myself in an empty house by myself.

There is an Asian-looking man. He looks familiar, I say, within the dream. We act like roommates; while I'm walking around being frustrated, talking to myself, and venting, he is just there for me, paying attention and listening while brushing his teeth.

These words are shared with him: I want to really express who I am, enough of this bullshit persona - half-ass being oneself. I don't even know what that means. Who am I? He agrees. We're having what seems like a true friend's conversation, feeling very open and honest with him, and on the same page. In the dream, I pause for a moment and say to myself, how do I know him and when did I see him before?

The next moment focusing on the feeling, realizing it's so nice to have him there with me. Such a sense of relief.

He says something striking. Who you are is not really coming out. It must emerge fully, truthfully, without apologies, without feeling like someone will be hurt. Your voice is repressed, and you're frustrated. What do I want to say, express, do, create? As soon as I speak these words, I remember who he is. The realization that he is a part of me is strong and vivid. There is no judgment or misunderstanding, I know I can tell him anything. What a nice change.

I'm at a critical threshold. I want to go forward, then get stopped by something. My body hurts sometimes, it's resistant. Why am I fighting myself from crossing this threshold?

Evolution is Effortless with Trust

Why am I seeing so many scenes with *transportation*? What is the metaphorical meaning? Airports, terminals, actual planes, trains, mom being there many times. I don't remember dreaming of her so frequently. Now she appears in transportation-related dreams almost every day. This is a transformation period, taking off, preparing for a new journey, and leaving things behind. I always see luggage in each dream, some very heavy and large. Then the luggage becomes smaller, like a carry-on, much more manageable. Mom is in the background, there to support me. I am responsible for making the journey - leaving, transferring, going to the next stop, and the next station.

Instant clarity - more of my pieces and aspects of my soul will come in to help me with what's to come forth. Fear should not overwhelm me. Looking back, I recognize parts of myself returned right when I needed them, without me even trying or knowing how to look for them. I just lived as best as possible, sometimes knowing I was following my soul, other times without a clue. Parts of who I truly am need to be reinstated, as if they're hovering in the air close by, ready to jump back in, to fill me up a little more. The entire picture is not yet fully transparent and clear. This is a time when I really don't know what the next step is. I feel like a volcano about to erupt. In the past, knowing what was next, looking ahead, crafting well thought out plans was a superpower, a useful skill I was very proud of. Now it's so open, totally up in the air, and I just don't really know.

Focusing inward, and becoming really quiet, I hear my soul's voice. Support is here, you will know when to let go, trust completely, not knowing is OK. Emptiness will open a vast amount of wisdom that you already discovered, collected, and carried through all-time. It's foggy and blurry now, but it's getting clearer. Step out.

Your brain has been processing. Stop. Just Be. You are fighting what is. Evolution is effortless with trust. Now is the time, no need to continue running in circles. Stop everything. Who leads the heart? What does she want to say? What does she want to create and do with her gifts? Remember all the gifts.

The next phase is surrender, opening up to everything without knowing, controlling, or planning. All those skills are valuable, and you've managed them well. When needed, they are there for you. Now is a time to expand, to create openness with no boundaries, to initiate growth, light connection, and be empowered to bring more light inward. There is too much effort into persona structure-form, what picture is being revealed? Instead, there is no effort in just being connected, allowing all that is - infinite information - to come through the heart, and whatever that is, it already reflects aligned order. No control. Allow the ingathering and outward expression to be. Then parts of you, the real you who holds wisdom, can shine, share, expand, and brighten. Your heart grows to an amount that will change all life. It is a time to elevate from these contractions. What a relief to have an expanded view – aware of so much more amazingness and an infinite number of connections to be made.

There are 5 levels of conscious mind awakening before connections to these levels are fully restored. From 6 to 12 the super-conscious is engaged, then 13 to 72 will allow all memories and wisdom from ancient experiences to be reinstated. Bringing healing to the lower unconscious worlds from the beginning of all-space-times. It is the natural process of upgrading. A new processor is installed. Only the outer connections are active to calibrate, to test the circuitry; the wiring is fragmentary and undergoing repair. It needs to be able to handle the enormous load. Resistance and rust-like mechanisms causing contractions are phenomena due to persona disorientation. Time to dissolve, to let in silver light for re-haul - recall. So many old chips and data bits. You don't need these anymore.

Do you see the difference in your eyes, the eyes of nature herself? The snow falls off the tree, it does not resist. Fall, do not resist. Then look at the tree from below, recognize you have always been part of that tree, although you couldn't see. From below, know you are still one with that tree but are now here lying in the white sea of snow, a different stage of water, another contributor to the ecosystem. As we navigate level 6 of conscious mind, there is a quick jump to level 8 by just surrendering to everything.

I suddenly hear myself say the words, although feeling unprepared, not knowing, I stand empty, with no particular wants or needs. Yes, in this state, other aspects of mind can fall back in. Welcoming and streaming in more of myself, the feeling is whole - so very natural and enjoyable.

Need For Rest After a Long Journey

I am traveling across oceans on a large cargo ship carrying various trailers, including my belongings within a container. Feeling anxious, I notice there are people all around me, related to me in some way, but unable to determine what their role is. The journey was so long. I have been feeling pretty unsettled about this big move, and extremely relieved now that the ship arrived. I find myself in what seems like a large suite bathroom. There are two parts. One is more like a guest bathroom, the other more private. That's supposed to be my bathroom. There is a large bathtub with some high-end faucets on one end. In the dream, I suddenly am aware that I've been here before, there is a memory of this space, although unsure where it comes from - where did I see this scene last? It's an amazing place and hear myself say, it's time to stay here for a while, finally - enjoying a bath and resting. I get undressed, then put on two robes, thinking, why two, extra coverage? Headed to the other bathroom. I see myself in the mirror and look so round, all bloated and swollen, resembling the effects on a dead body after being left in the water for a while. There is some skinny tan lady who's getting all dressed up as if going out. We're supposed to be preparing to go out, she says. But I don't know if that's the right thing to do. I'm actually so tired, headed back to the private bathroom and resting there. I have a strong feeling of needing to be by myself. This was a big trip and I don't care about anything right now, except a nice bath, alone time, and rest. This bathroom is so familiar to me, every single detail. Others are waiting for me, but I am not interested in being with them, sensing they don't care much, and wanting to separate myself from that whole thing altogether.

Meeting the Dolphin Race

Awake within the dream, capital letters spell out: NEXT INITIATION PHASE... with a space between the words. These large capital letters are emerging from the background of another text, resembling ancient writing. I have a clear perception my guides really want me to know this and feel so grateful they are literally spelling it out for me. There is another word in there - letters A C T LL V T. Maybe ACTIVATION, ACCELLERATION, OR ACCELLERATED. Something like that. As I'm recording, this last word is fading, but I can clearly remember the others, as well as saying something like, wow I guess I really need huge capital letters, thank you so much for your patience with me.

After seeing these letters, I find myself being greeted and surrounded by dolphins. Approaching a dock and getting closer to land, they come toward me. I'm traveling in a small vessel that looks like a capsule, very high-tech, something I've never seen before. It's not a normal boat, it's completely enclosed and I'm inside.

Upon arriving at the docking area, the little dolphins come up to me just like puppies jumping on your feet and legs when you come home. Wait, how can they be out of the water? I realize I'm actually submerged. At first, I thought I was in a vessel over the water, but this whole environment is underwater. I see them clearly now. They're different kinds of dolphins. Their bodies are of a deep blue color, and they have huge eyes. I'm trying to get into a building, coming out of the capsule, and keeping the dolphins calm since they're so overly excited. How adorable. I feel like I know them, then see and hear myself, let me get through c'mon, hold on there you guys - aw, so sweet. They are making their sounds, and their eyes are so huge and sweet, a deep, intense blue. The shape of the eyes reminds me of those of a cow except they are much bigger. Wow. I get a sense that *these dolphins are a rare race or species - maybe prehistoric, but then I suddenly realize I'm actually in the future. This is a different Earth. I see myself as a third person turning around to see my expression, looking back at me, over here, standing with my mouth open, a surprised look and a quirky smile on my face.*

The Harbor

I am on a vessel and arrive in a harbor whose surroundings resemble a fiord in Scandinavia. Looking out the windows, there are what look like massive cargo and passenger ships. One in particular is extremely large. There is snow and ice everywhere, I am wearing a seriously heavy coat and many layers. It is so cold. Once we dock, it's evident the wharf is crowded with people. This area is a waiting station. There are hotels and businesses, each one bustling with ship passengers and crew, a scene similar to a jammed airport. I am walking toward a large hotel building, needing to check-in, and notice there are other people I know well all around. In order to check in, I have to type my last name into this glass screen, but mistakenly misspelled my last name because my fingers were so cold, and I was typing really quickly. The attendant smiles at my fast typing, and after verifying some information, through what looks like advanced technology, the system knows who I am regardless of my mistake. I say, wow, so advanced, nice – I'm impressed! Then get a key of some sort, a very unique type of entry pass.

Within the dream, I return to the imagery of approaching the harbor. I visualize the letter 'O' as the location was announcing itself to the incoming ship. Perhaps this is Oslo, I think to myself, but immediately I also have the strong feeling this place isn't on Earth, or at least the current dimension of Earth. Maybe it's some future or parallel life. I have to research, what other harbors in a cold environment start with O?

Surfing on Ice

On a ship again, ice all around. There is a captain with me. We jump off the bridge onto a piece of ice, which starts floating away from the boat. I fall and feel myself sinking into the ice. It doesn't break, the sheet of ice is just sinking. Moving slowly and rolling on one side so I

197

can get back up, the sheet of ice moves in the water away from the ship. I get a little scared, but the captain seems to be calm. We bring our weight to one side, trying to head back, but then we decide to go the other way, pushing our weight toward the other side. Suddenly we find ourselves close to land, noticing the water levels are extremely high. The ice sheet moves so close to land that we can jump off. I stepped off the sheet of ice onto a sidewalk. There are buildings all around and a green pick-up truck catches my attention. After looking around, I can see two other trucks exactly the same. I am able to look inside one of the trucks and it seems familiar like I know who it belongs to, but then I move away. An older man close by who looks like a fisherman with a beard and a wool hat is standing there, watching.

Relieved I am no longer on icy water but feeling totally out of place, the captain is still with me, which makes me feel a little better. He says, alright, let's check out this little village, c'mon.

I see myself thinking, within the dream. There is a shift happening into a different time-space. The green trucks may have to do with my bodies, the high seas maybe with my unconscious rising, the sheet of ice I am floating on, then sinking, then navigating with my weight, maybe that's my thick armor that's acting as a bridge to another space-time. The captain is my higher mind, leading me with a stable and calm demeanor. I wake up, always feeling grateful for the messages.

The Machine in the Inner Earth

I find myself in a space deep within the Earth, under many layers of water. It's a structure. I am in a vehicle in front of a gate. It's a massive platform that allows one car with a driver onto it, then it elevates to a large surface. I am next in line. The person controlling this platform elevator is friendly. I recognize him as the cashier at the property in Mexico. His name is Ariel, an extremely caring man - he's smiling and reassuring, waving me in as it is my turn. There is a sense of anticipation, but I also seem a bit worried. What is this? Is it safe? I see how it works with the person in front of me. It opens up, the car moves onto this platform, then Ariel pushes some buttons, the gate closes again, and moves up like an elevator onto the upper level. I *don't know, but I feel like I need to get out of here. When it's my turn, I go onto the platform, hear the heavy metal and machinery sounds as I come right out of the dream state. Anxiety wakes me up.*

Later that evening, before going to bed, I asked if I could be shown more about the previous night's dream and if there was another way to help me better understand.

I am shown the upward movement with the car, in the large machine within inner Earth. My emotional state in the dream is frozen, in awe, consciously observing from a distance. I move from one level to another. I see cars, and someone there to watch and guide me, with a friendly demeanor that should make me feel like everything will be ok – hearing, no need to know what or how. Seeing this whole scene from the observer view provided greater insight and reassurance.

14

ANOTHER SEVERING

Separation ~ Resentment ~ Fear

I was so nervous when I had to speak to my landlord about the lease on my studio. She was a very nice woman, but her goal was to protect the Tribe's interests. I was just concerned and worried about the repercussions of breaking a five-year lease so far in advance. How much would I have to pay? This idea kept me up at night, however I couldn't take it anymore, so on a Monday morning, right after class, I called her and asked if she had a few minutes to stop by so we could talk. Feeling so anxious, she finally arrived and sat down. I had been rehearsing my speech for the past week. Her reaction was very open, respectful, and understanding. She knew it had been a difficult past few years due to the pandemic. Both businesses next to my studio closed, one right away after the first lockdown and the other some months later. We arrived at an agreement I could digest, and soon after came the time I would tell my clients and friends. That following week I began calling everyone.

Before speaking to the landlord about closing and coming to an agreement, I contacted the franchisee headquarters to see if there was a remote chance they were interested in taking over my studio. I explained to them that I would leave everything and facilitate the handover with the landlord. They considered and asked how much I wanted to sell the remainder of my franchise contract. I was completely shocked because I just hoped they would take over and relieve me of this immense financial burden, but more importantly, I wanted them to keep the studio alive so my clients would continue this beautiful training practice. My response indicated there were no expectations to sell. I just wanted them to take ownership and to send someone to manage the studio. Continuing alone, with no support, was impossible, thinking the company - a big corporation - could manage and handle it. The president was very interested and gave it some thought.

The answer that came back differed from what I was hoping for. The only reason they declined was simple, they didn't have anyone to assign to my studio. The entire company had been extremely short-staffed in instructors, main trainers, and studio managers for a long time. I knew about this situation from my teacher, Master Ahn, as she would explain how they simply didn't have enough people to support all the studios in the country. They were trying to get more people from other countries to come to the States, but it would take a lot of work due to the language barrier, at least at the beginning. The organization needed to pull someone from another location, someone qualified to manage a studio on their own. Most studios have more than one person handling the operation, between instructors and master-teachers, there are many more resources. One person managing this type of holistic studio is rare and difficult. They realized it was a great opportunity but simply couldn't send anyone. Nobody could handle this alone, they said.

The words of my teacher, Master Ahn, resounded in my mind. It takes work to manage by yourself. We need community. You will experience huge challenges and growth by yourself. Although feeling upset, angry, resentful, and very sad, I had chosen this path and actually knew I couldn't have done it any other way. It was a difficult time also because I could clearly see that the lack of regional support since I opened my doors was primarily because, as a franchise, sharing revenues with corporate studios wasn't possible. They weren't able to support me because they wouldn't get anything from my studio besides commissions and franchise fees funneling upstream. I knew this, but it became heavy for me because our work was to guide individuals through beautiful holistic practices to learn more about themselves and how to navigate life. There were so many opportunities to share income, send people to regional workshops for more advanced training, host shared community events, and allow clients to experience other instructors and teachers. Why such a black and white approach? I had a deep internal conflict about this, unable to understand black and white. Why not a whole bunch of grays – unique circumstances call for adjustments.

I know this strict delineation of responsibility and structure was set in place as a protection mechanism for the company, and I fully understand it. However, I saw it and still see it another way. We are people, and each situation is different. Flexibility *also* makes good business.

Ultimately, I recognized it was ok to feel this way. Either side was right. Nobody was wrong, and there was nothing to fix, really. Even if I had a million dollars to keep my business going, I realized this period was coming to an end. On one hand, something felt incomplete, as in the work I was doing, thinking there was definitely more needing to be done; on the other hand, a sense of completion became apparent, as this phase was ending, it was ok to step out and away.

I must clarify that any resentment or frustration I experienced and held at the time soon dissolved, feeling extremely grateful for what I've learned, my growth and all facets of this experience. It's part of my life as I still practice and share these beautiful training methods. Nothing can ever erase that.

This phase literally felt like another severing from a corporate mindset. I now choose to no longer fit in. I turn away from *fitting in* with everything I am inside. There is no such thing as one way. I always felt this way, but continued to make myself fit in, unconsciously in some respects. There is actually nothing wrong with conforming in some way or another, especially if the individuals, environment, underlying *mission statement* - what they represent to you, resonate with who you are. The key is to know who you are first, then not to get lost or buried in what you chose to associate yourself with.

What about *my* mission statement? During this time, the need to embrace freedom was especially strong.

Another strong wave is rising, only able to see a small portion, unknowing what comes next, I'm paralyzed by the burden I sense on my shoulders. If I was alone, I would spend my time recharging in complete silence, getting lost somewhere on a beach in Malaysia. All the *what if* scenarios floated through my mind, a normal mechanism of feeling scattered and trying to find what direction to move into - always so many possible scenarios to consider, plan A, B, C... it keeps going. Penang looks good, how about Arequipa or Porto.

My nervous system was overwhelmed, and I began experiencing severe body pain. I know this process, I'm in the midst of ending and beginning. It's ok, remember the training.

Self-care was essential, making sure I checked in with myself and did whatever I could to make myself feel better and more comfortable, even if it was only 5 minutes of quiet breathing.

Dreams ~ Visions ~ Journeys

An Apocalyptic Scene
I'm driving on a bridge, and there is so much traffic. Suddenly the bridge is shown on its side. I am able to pull over, noticing some people are following the road and as it turns to its right-side cars roll right off of it, falling over. Somehow, I can go straight, driving on the side of the bridge. Suddenly, I slip down into a ditch, tipping the car on its side. Outside of the car, unhurt, I look up into the distance to see how in the world this happened. Everything is moving slowly. Grabbing my phone, I try to call Jason. The bridge is fully twisted on its side - so much destruction with all these car crashes. Then in the far background, I can see the structure that caused this massive destruction. I know I'm ok, but am in complete shock more than anything; looking around, it seems to be a future time. Suddenly, I am presented with another scene.

Finding myself in a very large store, it's a bit futuristic, and again, destruction everywhere - an apocalyptic-type environment with strange people walking around, talking to themselves as if they have lost their mind. There is a bit of a line at checkout, and then I realize where to go for faster checkout. A lot of items are missing, including equipment, and carrying bags, a very poorly organized situation with a staff person trying their best to help the people but clearly seems overwhelmed. I have to go back in after retrieving some bags, unable to carry everything in my hands. Looking down at what I purchased is an extension cord, some soap, other electrical cables, a hair dryer, which I almost leave behind, but I quickly think it's best to keep everything I can find. After paying and getting out of this store, I walk into what seems like a hangar-type place, with an emergency response set up; this makes me feel distraught, anxious, and really glad I could get out of the store. So many nervous people, but I had to get a bit of supplies.

In the dream, I say to myself, wow there is a mess inside my mind, is this why they're showing me these disaster scenes?

On My Way Out

Two people are talking about me. The conversation is about what to do with me and what to do with each other, how to merge themselves with me, from three becoming one.

Not knowing who the two people are, I have a feeling this is an ending, like someone is about to die. Within the dream, I see myself suddenly understand. The image shows me these two people, both women, but one had more masculine features, and then me as this third person without any apparent female or male attributes - very neutral. Right, Left, Middle - me in three different aspects.

The next scene shows me in a training program at a retreat center. There are many people I know well, other instructors and teachers. We are gathering for the main session. I sit down in the back, as usual. One of our most experienced facilitators, teacher, and guide is there, Master J, he hugs me. As I'm walking away, he stops me wanting to talk. He asks, what do you need to do to improve your condition? I respond, if I could have one person help me run classes, I think I could expand and grow more. Then, my tone and comments make me aware I'm complaining, realizing I sound like I want other people to fix the problem for me. If I can just have one other person run classes besides me, somehow that would make it all better. I hear myself inside, yea, but is that the real problem? Master J asks because he wants to offer spiritual assistance. He knows I am struggling, and is so wonderful for having such a pure open heart, it brings tears to my eyes. We share a sincere look that everything will be alright. I return to the meeting room to find my seat. Suddenly, sensing I should just leave, feeling like I'm just an outsider, I don't continue to participate and prepare to exit. The people around me are some of the brightest, most genuine individuals I've ever met, wanting to make a positive impact within their communities; some of them have trained with me in many courses, there is a deep connection, appreciation, and respect. However, something is off, I feel disconnected. I am free to leave of course, nobody is making me stay. As I get up to walk out, nobody seems to care or is bothered by me leaving.

I take a nice walk around the beautiful, peaceful grounds, feeling truly content. Upon waking up, the words and feelings during that brief conversation with Master J fill the room.

Some parts of me want someone to help; other parts of me say I do not want to be part of any organization, but I love the work and know the healing potential people can experience. I feel so disconnected and have been lazy in my training. My body hurts, and I know better.

Ancient or Parallel Worlds - Aren't They the Same?

This is a place I have visited before; I am certain of it. I have a few options on how to get there. The option I choose involves shooting off some aggressive beings who look like humans, whose purpose is to scare or attack and take us down. On this wide dirt street, there are lots of people on the sides of the road, watching who will attempt to cross the road and move forward - I say forward because it's understood that by crossing the street, it means moving onto another time and space.

There is one person I know I can trust. She's younger, takes my arm, and forcefully asks me if I'm ready. She has this intense sense of urgency. It will be rough, she says, but we have to go now and push through. I said yes, let's go! She takes my hand, and we start crossing the road. It's dark. Someone is coming from the lower right side toward us, I can barely make out who or what it is. It's clear now, a small child - oh no, it's a dark shadow being and it's moving really quickly. At this point, I realize it looks like some sort of zombie coming at us viciously. The young girl helps me swing my arm to hit this being with my purse, but little damage is done. It bounces back and comes at us with even more fury. Scary! It's now trying to pull my arm off, attempting to bite us too, while we're trying to get it off of us. It appears as though we're moving quickly, but this being is slowing us down with incredible strength. The next moment, he's gone - we finally get rid of it. Good thing she was there to help me, my body seemed so heavy and frozen, I wouldn't have been able to lift my arm to defend myself.

The young person who helps me, obviously familiar with this location and knowing what to do, drops me off in front of what seems like a massive ancient city complex. Some parts look a bit more modern but still very historic, others are clearly very ancient. I know everything is going to be alright here. As I look up at the ancient stone wall, I am mesmerized and immediately feel like I recognize this place.

Like in the movie Inception, where huge city blocks fold onto each other, I am walking toward the tall wall, then just like pulling down a shade, I move it so that I'm able to climb up and walk through an entrance. Afterward, it folds back in place, allowing me to walk onto this large terrace. It has several doorways, halls, and windows. Walking forward slowly, looking around, and recognizing all the details of this structure, just as I remembered, I look into a large amphitheater. A few elderly gentlemen in the background are talking about the coming of Kukulkan - Quetzalcoatl. They speak Spanish, and I recognize the story very well. They are sitting around having their afternoon coffee, and I'm just enjoying them telling the story.

Then I am presented with a vision of two parallel worlds, gaining insight as to why the complex is familiar to me. As I am walking down the wide halls into the opening, there is something strange happening. From my standpoint, the images go back and forth between the very ancient past, to more modern times with people touring and taking photos. Am I tracing steps? I hear myself say. This is a place I know, where is this? Am I there and here simultaneously?

207

Strange Otherworldly Being

Staring at a being with reddish, sunburned looking skin, I think it's me - yes, it is me. I try to focus my sight more, and notice she has a strange shape. The head is much greater in size than in an average person with large slit-like openings where the normal eyes would go. Strikingly, this being has three eye-looking features on the front of the body. One is located on the palm, another on the torso, under the rib cage area, and one below the navel. They look like wounds, but as I focus more, it's evident they are not. The being is just standing there with arms extended to the side, showing me these physical characteristics. I approach her and hear myself say, it's going to be ok, reaching for one hand to better understand if the opening is a wound, like an open cut, or if she is bleeding, but there is no blood, and it isn't an open lesion. What appears as an opening is a small fold, unlike loose open flesh. This is how it's supposed to be, I hear in my mind, they are made this way. The being seems to be crying, or maybe it's me inside - I am the one crying, feeling scared and shocked.

There is someone else on the left who seems like a much bigger person in comparison, like a giant. He has been there the whole time. I am kind of freaked out at this point, but get a sense he is supervising. Looking back at him in the distance, he looks like an older man with a big gray beard resembling a shepherd. I turn toward the being with the eye-openings again, and with both hands she points to the eye located on the lower abdomen area. As she holds her hands there, I immediately know to focus on my lower dahnjon (dantien) - that is all I need to do. I can see myself, within the dream, contemplating why there is this strong feeling that she is me or part of me; speaking to myself, what do all the eyes represent? Is this a real being in another world? Why is she indicating the entrance to the lower dahnjon? I think I already know why - it's the key to the other soul portals. Catching myself over-analyzing this whole scene in the dream, I stop and simply observe.

I wake up upset, feeling like I'm not paying enough attention to the information shared. It's there and available for me to access, but what happened?

The Way to the Unknown

On a vast outdoor field, driving a little Fiat 500, I am approaching a road where there are some baby cows; they kind of look like puppies. I carefully try to get through, navigating between them, noticing cars coming from my right that suddenly slow down to stop. Instead of a car, I now see myself on a bicycle. It takes a lot of work to gain momentum. A few of the little calves start to follow me onto the road, they think we're going to play, and I am worried they will get run over. I have to get going, and with a sense of urgency, I try so hard to pedal faster, but there is such resistance even though this is a flat road. It's extremely dark out. Cars are parked all along the side of the road, and they shine their headlights my way. It feels as though I'm pedaling uphill, hard to keep my balance, while trying to shoo away these little cow-puppies who are following me. Looking ahead in the distance, I begin to accelerate.

My cell phone rings. In answering, I say something like, yes, heading out now, I'm coming. Suddenly, it's pitch black. I try to get the flashlight of the phone to turn on, all while keeping balance on this flimsy bike, pedaling so hard into this dark road. I am scared because there could be an animal, or an obstacle and I wouldn't be able to see them in this darkness. Hesitant to move forward, I get the light to turn on, and can see ahead a bit more. The headlights behind me are still shining. These cars are all stopped because of something, but I don't know what it is. So weird, I'm thinking.

I'm just focusing on riding this bike in the darkness on this flat road that I perceive has an incline, struggling so much. Thoughts resounding in my mind, this is your road to the unknown. Use the tools you have to help you see the way. Resistance, difficulty in pedaling, and keeping balance are the attachments and pull from the past. The many cars from one side shining the bright headlights are guides, showing the way toward the other side of the unknown. The little calves-puppies are the baby parts of self that need to be left behind. It's time to move onto the grander, unknown path.

All of a sudden, I'm able to see further down the road, although it is still so dark. Then the road disappears completely. It's like going into an abyss. The phone call was from a person in one of those cars back there along the side of the road, shining the headlights. They encourage me to keep going, helping me think about the flashlight on the phone. Yes, I can use this to make light. I do have what I need to move forward. The pedaling now still feels hard but manageable, as I'm slowly gaining momentum, knowing I can do this.

I wake up with these words and feelings - so beautiful, thank you.

Being Chased

It's been a strange period with a streak of scary dreams.

I see myself in the middle of a city, up high in a building at a gathering or party. Suddenly I am being chased by a whole gang of people. Looking to the periphery of my eyes, I'm able to see escape routes. They are catching up to me, although feeling my body move, I definitely need to go faster. They almost look like zombies – a scary scene since they were moving at incredible speed. My mind returns to the top of that building on an outdoor fire escape landing, watching the other me run for my life.

In the dream, I am so confused, hearing myself say, wait, there are two of me in this dream! I'm here observing, but I'm also down there running. This is awesome. Completely surprised, watching this whole scene like a movie, I briefly wake up, startled, but am then able to go back in - the entire experience feels so real.

It's so dark in these streets. I realize the need to move faster with my right leg, it's a bit slow. The left is fine, but my right is getting stuck, almost like it doesn't want to go anymore, but we have to get out of here! Suddenly the whole scene is shown as a film strip negative, like the old-fashioned reels, in black and white.

My left side needs to move more quickly, but in the dream, I say the right side. It becomes clear for me. Everything is backward, actually everything was opposite, I should say.

Looking around while running, the buildings resemble some familiar place. There is nobody on the road but me running for my life. Someone is close to me, and I am forcing myself to go even faster. I wake up with extreme anxiety.

15

CHOOSING TO START OVER

Am I running?

The entire year leading to the decision to close this chapter of life can be described as the initial *reordering* of priorities, opportunities, resolutions, and reconciliation of much internal conflict. I had seen some beautiful openings into potentials I couldn't fully grasp rationally but knew with my entire being a new beginning was approaching and I had to get ready.

Guided to prepare and use my organizational skills - a superpower - to plan the next phase, I had been thinking about another online opportunity that would allow me to work from home and live anywhere, even if it was temporary. Wanting more freedom, thinking, there is no point in living here with all this heaviness, maybe this is the time to move on. Am I running away? Are *we* running away? This phase feels complete and so why not walk toward a new start?

Jason's experience over the past several years had been deeply devastating. I do believe when we experience a heavy disappointment in life, it is an opportunity to learn how to love ourselves more and expand our ability to connect with our true selves. It certainly isn't an easy experience to navigate, but nobody can do it for us.

There was this lingering, painful blockage of feeling abandoned, surrounded by a lot of fear and sorrow. It had been very hard for me to see him in this condition, and although I was able to help sometimes, I really couldn't take all that away. It was a very challenging time for him, for both of us, but I knew it was necessary. He experienced a huge wake-up call regarding his own family dynamics, and buried wounds that had been avoided for years. Nothing is actually completely fixed, when is it ever, but a level of evolution happened during this time, which helped in moving forward.

We can become certified tutors of English as a foreign language and choose to live anywhere in the world. We don't need to be here. The studio is closed, we have no reason to stay. The family doesn't want us to be included in their lives. We have each other and can take care of what is important to us.

I want to clarify that this may sound a lot like, oh poor me, poor us, nobody likes us, we're the *victims*. No. Sure, we were hurt – sometimes feeling sorry for ourselves, each in our own unique way. We chose this area to settle down and open a business because we hoped for a deeper family connection. Some things were broken and worsened due to bizarre misunderstandings and stubbornness from all sides.

Running away is not the answer at all, but forcing your story onto others who live in a completely different story is never appropriate. When circumstances feel like we're trying to convince someone to accept us, that is when we must realize it may be a lost cause for now. The heartbreak only comes from the fact that we have an idea of how a parent or sibling should behave. That is our story, one story, and it's not *the* complete story. Nobody is ever right or wrong.

We must simply choose what is important for us and use the experience of pain, for example, as fuel to create the life we want, with freedom and openness, with the sense of empowerment that only what our true heart-mind sees is the only thing that matters, with enough clarity to choose what is best for us, when we feel completely neutral and centered. In those moments, the choice of direction is clear, and the path will be paved without micromanaging.

We realize, once again, that continuing to work on ourselves, allowing healing to occur in a ripple-effect way, moving outward from within, is the most important endeavor of the heart. This is key for our own journey. We can include others' perspectives and exchanges, but only if aligned with what we are all about, while maintaining dignity and honor for what we want to learn and experience.

As this chapter closed, I would see similar patterns resurface when I returned home. Another opportunity to go deeper.

Dreams ~ Visions ~ Journeys

Contact - The Tic Tac Craft Again

There is a UFO, actually, there are a few of them out there. First, I can see myself looking up at the sky, out in an open space along with some people I know. It's a large opening with hills in the background and lots of green all around. I notice this bright white sphere, clearly moving in an arc-like motion, like a rainbow, from left to right. The UFO slows down, stops, then quickly moves back toward where it came from, but seems lower to the ground. It's now moving in a straight line going back toward the left of the horizon, while the next moment, it returns toward where I am standing, flying right above my head. Quickly running back, trying to follow it, I'm able to see this white sphere quite well. It's made of bright, shiny metal. Now the size looks to be considerably smaller, like it suddenly shrunk, how did it get so small so quickly? When I saw it in the first place, it was far, far away in the sky, and much bigger, but as it came closer to me before whipping back toward the space behind me so rapidly, it looked much smaller. So cool, I hear myself say within the dream.

I run over a little hill and head behind a building, in someone's backyard. This place seems familiar, a beautiful modern house. I'm in the backyard, with my eyes fixed on the metal ball. Suddenly it stops about twenty or thirty feet above me. Two other spheres appear. One is closer to the one I am following, and the other is a bit farther back and higher, just there hovering, while I'm clearly able to see the sunlight shining off the surface. I then remember grabbing my close friend Carrie and hugging her, even though my face and eyes are fixed on these objects. I snuggle her next to my neck and head and say to her, look Carrie, do you see, can you see them? She responds, yes! I guess I just wanted validation, to see them for myself.

Walking toward them with a sense of curiosity but also a bit of anxiety, one of the spheres comes closer down. My heart is beating so fast, unsure what to expect. It looks like it's becoming much bigger and changing to a different color. The shape now resembles a soccer ball, whitish gray with some shapes on its surface. I say to myself, it's an icosahedron or dodecahedron! I also notice it's sort of soft, based on some movements I'm able to detect, making me think this soccer ball-like sphere is actually breathing. Before it looked like metal, with the sunlight reflections, assuming it was a hard surface. After coming close to me, it just shoots away, down toward my right, then behind me, and it's gone, just like that.

I turn to look at the other two. One starts coming closer; the one that is higher and farther away. I get even more excited, thinking, this one wants to connect with me. It is close enough that I can see it at about forehead level, it's changing shape again looking like a soccer ball, but this one now becomes a little more oval, like a Tic Tac. The surface of this one moves too - it's breathing - making wave motions with a certain rhythm. It then comes close enough for me to reach out and be able to hold it.

While holding the sides, I notice it's not that soft even though my fingers can sink into it as I squeeze a little. I'm being very gentle holding it, suddenly seeing handprints. Wait, they're not mine! There are invisible hands right where mine are. I get startled as I can see my hands are right where this being's hands would be, I can see the indents of fingers and palms, extremely close to my hands. There is no one there, but clearly someone else beside me is holding this object. I let it go, moving back a few steps, still curious, amazed, but startled a bit.

I wake up gasping, saying to myself, wow! Did you see that??? Did you see that???

Two Beaten Versions of Me

I am sitting on a chair with my face torn up as I'm being beaten. Someone else is sitting beside me but slightly behind, also being hit in the face. Within the dream, shocked, I recognize this person as another me. The light in this environment is extremely low - maybe it's my sight, unable to fully focus or we're just surrounded by darkness. Sitting there with our hands bound behind our backs, we look exactly the same. Almost unconscious, crying, there is a lot of blood and bruising on my eyes. I feel so much pain from watching this entire scene. Whoever is beating us holds so much anger.

After waking up, although I was unsettled, I thought, we must see what's happening here and be done with all of this - so disturbing. We all have some dark sides. I want to see, no more hiding. What do you really want?

Violent Conflict

Running down a hallway with a sense of urgency, I find myself in an enormous building. The hallway where I'm coming from opens to a landing where I see a person on her knees looking after someone lying down; she looks back at me and yells, no, you can't come this way now.

There is someone else, maybe one or two other people, and the area is blocked. It's almost like a paramedic's situation, but I sense it's definitely a temporary diversion, what I'm seeing is not really what it seems.

Feeling anxious, I realize as I look back to where I came from that I'm actually running away from something or someone. As I take a few steps, what looks like an insane, unstable girl rushes toward me. She has long dark hair, and looks furious. I'm about to have a huge fight.

I get in self-defense mode and run toward her, starting the attack. We're both super powerful, extremely strong, punching, swinging, hitting, and screaming. We look at each other, and I begin to shout, yelling so loudly she starts to do the same too. I hear myself say, wow, so incredibly loud and vicious!

We release so much anger, fear, and maybe just fury from this confrontation, but it's almost like an invitation to keep fighting. As I fight, we swing each other from one side of the wall to the other, back several feet, then shove each other to the other end of the hallway. This is crazy, violent, loud, and over the top. I am hurt but still standing. She is on the floor and looks super angry, but she's beginning to struggle.

I'm able to run toward that open area; there is a door that I didn't notice before, I try to close it, but I see this tiny black kitty who seems hurt as he's moving very, very slowly, so I can't just slam the door. The girl is crawling, walking hunched over, trying to reach me, but I must wait for the kitty to cross the threshold. I'm just watching him as I hold the door knob, not helping him. That's weird, I think, why I don't pick him up and close the door is beyond me at this point. A part of me starts to shout within the dream, hurry, get the kitty! He finally comes through and I'm able to close the door.

There is a lock, and as soon as I secure it, she gets to the door. The fury and strength of this person is palpable, but at least the door is locked, and I'm safe. There might be a chance that she can make it through, but this is over for now.

During this stressful event, I watched this scene and clearly recognized that the crazy, violent, angry person was another version of me. I was savagely fighting with this other self who didn't want to die. It felt like this was one last attempt to keep me stuck. It realized that I was leaving and completely freaked out, wanting to kill me.

I finally reach that open space down the hallway and meet this other lady who seems to be assisting who arrives from the long hallway – a greeter of some sort. The people I had seen at the beginning - the paramedics over the person, the blocked path as a diversion - are all still there, but I can now make it through. I'm hesitant, but there is no reaction like before, so I'm able to pass.

I wake up overly shocked by this huge fight and violence in my battle, but also realizing this is a powerful message. I could not pass until I let that go, release the old who is angry and resistant to me leaving, acting as if it should kill me to keep me there. More work is

216

definitely needed, but a huge opening is happening now.

Standing Like a Mountain - Freedom

I am interacting with two other versions of myself, and they are being quite confrontational. However, within the dream, it's clear that I am not even slightly affected by anything they are saying to me. It feels like I am being instigated, maybe they're trying to aggravate or push me, but I do not react, displaying a completely calm and confident demeanor, while watching their sinister intent and struggle in provoking me. I stand like a mountain, with a peaceful smile on my face, nothing can negatively affect me, and there is no resistance on my part, no need to react in any particular way. I feel proud of myself and certain I will be ok no matter what. As I stand tall, with my head raised, chest open, the other selves start to withdraw, backing away in the distance. I am free.

Darkness - Projections

Such restless sleep lately.

I see images of familiar people surrounded by a dark energy. The darkness is emanating from their body, moving in and out of them. Thinking to myself, here is their true nature. I felt that in the past, but kept ignoring it. Feeling completely disturbed within the dream, I can see some parts of this dark energy being directed toward me, but I'm also aware the person isn't fully mindful of what they are doing. Disliking what is happening, I think these might be projections of people that mirror areas of my life I need to look into.

I recognize there is dark energy behind the surface and that I don't want anything to do with that. Whatever that energy is, it does not belong to me and has no effect on me. It's simply a waste of effort on their part. While observing this scene, I also see and recognize some heaviness leaving my heart, on its way out of my field.

Many energies and beings surround me in these dream scenes, catching my awareness. Some are very close to my body, others are far away but watching as in a boardroom, observing what's happening. I have a sense of reverence and gratitude, but haven't expressed it within the dream. I want to reach a point when I am conscious enough to thank whoever is there. Their support is deeply felt.

My lower back has been killing me. As I ask for help to move through this pain, something, or someone approaches. Even though I am so distracted by my mental chatter and physical discomfort, some work is being done, perhaps it is not yet completed. I will continue to train and focus.

A Friend to Help Me Relax

There is a fox in front of me with something in her mouth. She looked happy and harmless, but I'm startled upon seeing her. Standing there, she has messages for me.

In the following image, there are some people. Some I know, others I don't recognize, it's a bit of a chaotic scene. People are just standing around, preparing to head somewhere. We know each other, although I don't recognize the place. There is a person lounging around while I'm standing. She is sitting on this long couch holding a soft granola bar, and hands one to me, too. She says something about chilling and relaxing more, let's just sit and enjoy this snack together. She bites into hers, and while I unwrap mine, I have a distinct sense that there is something in this bar, some plant medicine that would help me relax, let go, and chill.

I realize the need to release, just be and flow, as I feel extremely wound up tightly. In her company there is a definite sense of calm. She has long, black hair with beautiful curves and clothes wrapped around her. I'm finally feeling very relaxed and comfortable.

Ending - Beginning

I am standing in front of a tall, granite sarcophagus, trying to get up on my toes to see inside. Barely able to reach that height to fully see, I know it's me inside this enormous box, despite the fact that I have another appearance.

In the dream, I am telling myself, this is a message that this part of my life can lay to rest now, and a new beginning is evolving into manifestation.

Even if the process has already begun a while ago, I am now consciously catching up to it, feeling like I am 9 months late stepping into this new timeline, knowing nothing is really ever late. My awareness is expanding in different ways to now recognize I have fully stepped onto a new path, able to only see fractions of it for now.

I continue to move forward, walking at an intentional slow pace, uncertain and unable to clearly discern my next steps; only about two feet ahead is visible, my mind becoming more comfortable with unpredictability.

In the past, I have always made so many strategic plans and thought things through. Now I fully welcome the space of the unknown. I'm asking the source and universe to show me as I step forward without a preconceived plan to cloud my path.

Planning the Next Move

Why not Peru. How about Penang, Malaysia, or Vietnam? I would return to Korea in a heartbeat, but Jason wasn't persuadable. He was still processing some aversion toward anything that had to do with my teachers, as he felt they didn't do enough to support me with my business. His own perception, not entirely the truth, but it was his way of digesting the past several years, which was fine. I couldn't convince him to go to Korea. Not the right place to move to for now.

The goal was to live a simpler life so that we could focus more on our creative work. We wanted to create a comfortable space to express our creativity while continuing to listen to the nudges of our true selves, take care of our minds, continue to overcome self-limiting beliefs, learn, grow, and just keep going.

Although I absolutely love Arizona and considered just moving town, there was a deep call to make a bigger jump. The United States has gradually felt more dysfunctional and unsafe, plus the cost of living increased exponentially.

All over the world, things are so similar. There is no better or worse, but there are significant differences, and we had to consider what was currently more important for us.

When people would ask me, where was your favorite place to live? Giving a clear answer was very difficult because I loved everywhere I had been, and I can say with 100% certainty that people are the *same* all over the world. I mean, people are people, right? Governments, systems of control, education, and health care are strongly influenced by the 1% of the population, the rest are in survival mode for the most part. This occurs all around the world.

I definitely don't hold a cynical view, but I didn't want to paint things in pink just because I needed some relief and rest. I also see that no matter where I choose to live, I get to create my sense of home; it's only and always up to me. You can live in the middle of any massive city with a huge divide in social structures and still feel you're home, safe, content, and can lead a joyful life. So where to?

I had received messages in dreams that I would continue to connect to the ancient mysteries through specific geographical locations. However, there was also a feeling of disorientation with way too many options, having always been drawn to the lands of Peru and Chile, but also just as strongly attracted to Asia in addition to the Atlantic European coast, Portugal. Then a sense of clarity and direction occurred.

This is the time to return to Europe and reconnect with the wisdom of the land where I chose to be born. A warm feeling surfaced along with a sense of assuredness. It was the right path to step onto – given the gift of processing the loss of soul fragments from long ago when I was too little to remember, and bringing light to what I've been carrying from my mom. In addition, I hadn't been there during mom's illness, struggling to have more time with her before her passing. Moving back would give me the opportunity to experience and share more time with my father.

The idea that I could take a short flight or drive to visit and listen to him telling stories, felt like the direction I should move toward. Returning to Europe felt like the perfect next move.

I began to seriously research Portugal and Spain, mainly Portugal. My heart was and is asking me to physically enter the space where I could reconnect to ancient mysteries and Earth wisdom from Atlantean times, knowing deep inside that I lived in the Iberia peninsula, specifically on the Atlantic coast, in the distant past. Furthermore, there are strong connections with the entire Mediterranean region.

I easily concluded that it made more sense to move back to Italy, to land at my dad's house, then find a place to settle and experience this new chapter.

The transition was not easy. Moving is always a huge life-changing event, whether one moves across a state or to another country. In addition, we had a Charlie. Our brave Australian cattle dog was rescued from the United Animal Rescue organization, and since we loved him so much, he simply couldn't be left behind.

Years prior, I had traveled from Seattle to Rome with Tito, my little cock-a-poo, and two cats. It was brutal. In addition, as I mentioned, I had moved back to Mexico some months later, bringing the little Tito with me. It's so hard to travel with dogs that are not small enough to travel in the cabin with you. Our lovely vet had traveled with her dogs to Africa and was like, oh yeah, they're fine, but it was so hard. We certainly considered another option, but it wasn't feasible, so the little one came with us. We both cried nonstop when we had to hand Charlie to the onboarding crew in Los Angeles. We were about to begin our Iberia Airlines journey to Madrid and then continuing to Fiumicino Rome airport. Poor little guy. Every little vibration from turbulence made me cringe.

Dreams ~ Visions ~ Journeys

The Waiting Space
I find myself back in a place I've been before, in dreamtime; it's down

the street at a convenience store. The feeling and attitude are quite different than when visiting in the past. Preparing to run away, I grab a few things in my backpack and leave. While at the store, just wondering what's happening, I feel like I am homeless, waiting around for I don't know what. The atmosphere is filled with a strange aura of loss, heartbreak, and despair. I am not really stuck there, but there is nowhere to go. In the dream, I notice the need to check what time it is, as if time has any meaning here, and it shows only about an hour went by, although there is a sense many hours passed. Time warps, I am consciously aware it's not relevant within the dream, so the fact that I was keeping track of time is interesting to me. The environment looks cloud-like and foggy, I can't see things clearly, which makes me think perhaps it's my vision that's blurry and unfocused. Then a realization emerges - this is a specific waiting space.

The scene changes as I now find myself on the outside, there is a different outlook from here. The location is the same, the convenience store, but somehow it turns into a different type of business, it now looks like a pawn shop. I am wearing my favorite black t-shirt and am carrying my training sword, which I decided to sell at this shop. My vision is much clearer and focused now. After parking a flimsy scooter, which is about to die, I walk into the store. Two heavy-set ladies, wearing a black t-shirt with some tribal symbols, similar to my shirt are in charge of this store. I show them my sword, commenting on the similarities of our t-shirts; they seem interested but need to bring it to the back to analyze it properly. Ok, I say, feeling a bit worried they might scratch it, and hoping they'll give me something for it.

Someone is standing next to me to my right. I recognize this girl from a dream, she's not someone I know in my awake state – or life as Enrica, since awake and dream awareness can be misperceived. We're talking about the sword, which leads me to the thought of just keeping it and continuing to practice with it. That's when I receive images of me practicing with the sword, remembering the beauty of the training and how it made me feel. Is she helping me change my mind so I can keep it, reminding me of my tools and training? The ladies return, I take the sword back and leave.

Outside again, trying to get on this little flimsy scooter with my backpack. I'm waiting at a street light, while a few other people are waiting too. One of them is trying to get into my backpack, and as I try to get away the motor of my scooter begins to die, it won't engage at all. I'm better off running, but stubbornly stay on the scooter, eventually getting away, securely closing the backpack. The scooter is moving but very slowly. Although I am not scared, I feel totally unsettled having to watch my back and being extra careful. The long road now turns into an uphill, and the scooter just can't make it. It's literally dying, so I leave it to the side, and begin to walk.

Things are clear now. I visited this location before in previous dreams. It is familiar to me, able to recognize some landmarks like a little road with the market-like stands in the streets selling clothes and items of all kinds. There are local people everywhere walking around, shopping. I have to go through a building to reach the other side of the road, walking up the hill, recognizing so many things.

Mom's Cottage

I arrive at a property located on a downhill slope. It's familiar, I've been here before in another dream. I see lots of greenery, plants, trees, and bushes, it's lush and beautiful.

A bright, glowing light emanates from the cottage. I walk in, and mom is there. She is putting things away. Another woman is next to her, it feels like I know her, but I can't place her at the moment; however, she does recognize me. Tears roll down her face, greeting me. She puts something down, then leaves the room to give us alone time. I walk over, looking around, noticing a beautiful quilt on a bench and flowers mom likes to decorate a space with. There are beautiful things all around, it looks sort of like a little antique shop. We make eye contact, she smiles. I don't have the urge to cry because I miss her so much. It's more like, oh, hi, I'm here. This is such a familiar space immersed in angelic energy. She is here, but I know she's always with me wherever I am. There is no sadness in this cottage, it's definitely more like I'm back visiting. It's so lovely to share this space together. Looking around, I comment on how pleasant everything looks - Mamma this is so you, I say. She's telling me this quilt is covering the cushion on the bench because it's full of cat hair, with the usual funny smirk and look on her face, then she talks about some other objects around the room, and shows me what she just straightened out and rearranged, some improvements here and there. It feels like it has been a while since my last visit, so she's just showing me around.

We sit - everything stops. There is a beautiful glow infusing every particle of air and energy surrounding us. The warm afternoon sunlight is coming in through floor-to-ceiling windows; we're in a delightful and enchanting sunroom, bathed in the golden light.

I'm suddenly shown another scene where Jason appears, too. Mom is there helping us figure some things out, as I notice some calculations happening. What are we doing here, currency conversion? or is it clothing sizes? There are numbers, statistics, and some complicated math I do not understand. The scene resembles a situation when one is in a clothing store trying on different size clothes, coming out of the fitting room, and allowing the other person to provide feedback. Jason and I are saying, ok, try this on, see how it feels, and mom is just there watching, being involved but more in the background, without interfering. We're suddenly back in the magical environment, the cottage. Everything looks like Hobbit-town architecture.

There is a very large gathering, is this a family reunion? I don't recognize everyone. Jason and I are walking around, stopping to greet someone, but they look very upset and continue walking past us. I have a strong feeling it's not good to be around this person. We let them walk by without getting involved in conversation. As we let this person pass, I realize he or she represents a part of us that continuously brings us down, but we don't allow them to linger, aware they're moving away taking that heaviness with them.
Jason and I have a sense of playfulness and adventure about us. Growing closer during this whole experience, we are getting ready to head out of this environment. We've been here for a while. It's evening time, there are celebrations, everyone is relaxing after a long day, and mom is hosting. Now I sense this is a holding space, the gathering of many people on a long journey, coming together, recharging, then moving on.

We go through an opening resembling a large antique doorway. I go through it first. Jason pushes me on my butt playfully, and we laugh.

It's almost like an exciting game.

We receive so many things here. Some protection, nurturing energy, and gifts that will help us in the journey ahead. It all feels very loving, like a blessing - warmth, light, and joy.

Reminder of Connection - Fairy and Wolf

I am outdoors. Everything looks black and white, or late in the evening, there is hardly any color. I hear and see something flying toward me extremely close, catching my attention, then flying away swiftly. It's sparkling, reddish orange in color. Quickly ducking, I look around to see where it fled, is this a bird? Once I see it in the sky, I immediately know it's mom. Upon realizing this, I zoom in with my eyesight, noticing the bird is instead this tiny little being with wings, and a human-looking body. She is clapping, saying, yes, yes, you got it, all excited jumping around with her small cute little face and body, and enormous wings - it's a fairy. A song fills the air, it sounds like a popular modern song. I am trying to focus closely to make out the words, knowing there is a message for me here. The melody is great, I love it, but I can't distinguish the words, intently using my ears to tune in. The fairy flies toward me very quickly, then she slows down a bit and shape-shifts right in front of my eyes. I am in awe and a bit of shock. It's rapidly transforming into a big dog-like animal. In an instant, she becomes a massive Wolf, giving me her right paw to hold. Sitting down now, looking up at her, holding her paw, an abundant flow of communication streams from her eyes. I know these eyes. This music and song are still going on in the background.

Covered in Hives

I have been overly consumed with thinking. What's the purpose of so much thinking - I am not fully accepting myself.

There is such confusion in the dream. I can't keep up with all the images going by in front of me. This confusion is about the ongoing internal turmoil. I see myself in bed, in pajamas, with one of my arms out of the shirt. My consciousness is present as If I were this third person watching, just a few meters away, fully aware, looking at myself, in bed, with my arm and shoulder exposed, bare skinned. The

225

self in bed begins to wake up, then realizes something. She's uncomfortable, looks down at her body and starts crying. She's completely covered in hives, noticing it's coming through the pajama shirt, too. There are some shadows of the red spots through the shirt; the part of the exposed shoulder, upper back, and arm are covered with blistering hives and large red spots. Watching this scene makes me sad as I begin to cry, too. I recognize I am making myself sick. Jason comes in, within the dream, trying to comfort me, but I am reluctant to receive any attention. My skin is reflecting how unsettled I feel inside. This is all my doing.

I wake up crying, and keep crying for a while. My body is hurting; the shoulder blade and trapezius are still burning; my lower back causes me anguish all day long, every day. Nothing works. I could drink buckets of Arnica, but it wouldn't work.

Healing with Wind

Waking up with a terrible headache, I sit quietly, reaching for iron rose quartz and indigo gabbro, my companion stones. In the awake-sleep state, I experience the following healing vision.

Spine clearing, dissolving calcification from old structures is the initial message. Water in the form of starlight rushes down. A perimeter is built carefully around my body - a safety boundary where healing can occur at a deeper level. From the lower dahnjon, a disc of golden light expands about 2 meters away from the body, creating a bubble of some sort, but it's not circular. The barrier shield reaches the ground. Earth's energy merges with it and shows me a bond connected through her energy lines - the grid.

Beautiful, colorful streams of light rise from Earth - liquid, transparent, brilliant light, resembling veins, converging with the barrier shield. As these blueish-white light strings merge with the boundary around my body, they continue to move upward, blending with the energy of the cosmos. I see it now – they are creating a woven connection between my barrier, Earth, and the cosmos. It kept assembling itself, becoming stronger and stronger, yet able to clearly see through it, knowing detrimental particles won't be able to enter. My mind speaks, this is a safe place, you can rest here now, and receive what you need. There is no safer place but here. You are merged with everything, connected to the All.

Bathing in these energies for what seems like days, I feel safer, stronger, and more relaxed. A portal opens now, and I hear my voice guiding my lower self through this healing process. This is a bright doorway creating an opening within the barrier – a Seba, the entrance to all dimensions. In the middle of this gateway, there is a vortex, and its center has incredible force. My guidance speaks the words, the vibration quality of this space is the pure source energy that creates your unique vibration and frequency; it echoes the distinctive pulse, rhythm, color, sounds - this is your own song. There is nothing like it.

Suddenly, a shape forms within the center space of the doorway, shooting outward an intense laser-like beam of light, a pure white silvery light. It rushes straight into my heart. Then the voice says, this vibration regenerates your heart portal. Receive well.

Now look, follow the vibration beam being directed to the center of your brain and another to the center of your pelvic cavity. The three beams are working directly on and with your soul dimension portals. Repair is happening, a remembering of this echo. Coding needs to transpire to bring you back into alignment. Just BE; there is no doing, no thinking, no imagining. Be with these energies.

I hear music in the background and feel motion as if getting closer to the sound source, slowly becoming more like an electric-static hum, or vibration. I'm thinking some of my senses are asleep, then the voice immediately says, there is time for integration, let the energies continue to work. The visual given to me includes little light particles working so quickly at a quantum level.

There is suddenly so much wind. Leaves being blown, snow blizzard, rain in the wind, the waves of the ocean in the sun, the dust, clouds in a hurricane, so many wind images; my hair flying around, inside my body a whirlwind of blood cells and oxygen being blown about in spirals through tunnels as if being pushed by a strong invisible current. The voice reminds me, you are the current. Dae Hae, it is your name. Trust the integration time. Slowly, I hear, begin to feel your

227

body.

I wake up feeling thoroughly relaxed. My headache, the pounding sensations from several hours prior is gone, just a bit fuzzy and weak. I am so cold, probably because I did not move for 5 hours, expelling energies I no longer need. Words about multidimensional bodies resound in my mind, my voice guiding me through an explanation about phenomena lived thus far and reviewing the elevating process, transmuting lower frequencies. *It's time. Use this for guiding people. More is coming; more has been coming. Open up and trust.*

Although in a daze, I sense changes in my body and energy. I received a lot. Thank you for this work.

Power Word Chanting

It's early morning, around 4 am. *I am returning to my shield of light, merging with the Earth, then going up, connecting with the sky. At a certain point, the capsule expanded into a vast space. It's like I drop into another space altogether - reaching another area of my field. I can see the bottom as it opens into a large bowl-shaped structure, yet the top isn't fully visible, feeling connected with everything, surrounded by a deep, bright, cobalt blue light.*

Right above my head, there is a vertical, egg-shaped bead of light. Oh wait, it's me. Am I inside the egg-shaped capsule or am I the capsule itself? There is some wording on it, characters and symbols that speak of who I am, evenly disappearing to my left. At first, I sense separateness, but it quickly shifts to an expansive state of blending with the surroundings. My mind receives information through sounds and words. I can hear them clearly, then notice I keep repeating this particular word, over, and over, hearing it reverberating all around into the distance, holding the intention of remembering this single sound and word. In the background is a team of beings, encouraging me to speak the word repeatedly. It seems like a team of light beings, yet I know it's my higher self, merged with many beings all around – thinking, my multidimensional selves, my guides, and companions, not limiting the possibilities to any particular thought-form. The word is diaa kah *– putting it in writing is difficult due to the* *pronunciation. Maybe this way is more like it:* Dia'a Kah.

After a while of hearing this word and saying it so many times, I realize it sounds similar to when I received the name of the guide with the cat face - the beautiful, tall, white being with the veil that came to caress my face a while back. When I was given her name, it sounded very clear, Tiaka. In this dream-vision, the word I am hearing and encouraged to repeat sounds just like that, but the first letter is much softer. Then and there, I got it, hearing the clarification – oh, thank you, this is a calling or title of some sort. It refers to the role, the nature of the work - it represents an order, like a group or board of individuals holding specific responsibility.

This is a power word, an energy word that corresponds to my nature. While the team is sounding this word like a chant, I enjoy resting my mind, knowing more information will be coming forth soon.

Reflecting back, it's been over a year since I met the guides Tiaka and my higher self as the Sirian blue being. I know they are asking me to remember and focus on their guidance. We're always here – you can merge the gap.

16

RETURNING

Embracing Old Wounds

Here is something I've come to realize, suddenly becoming clearer as I come up for air from the tumultuous splashy waves of chaos and turmoil. This current phase of *realignment*, at least in this chapter of my life, is about allowing *being* versus *doing* – presence over a state of constant activity. It doesn't matter what I do. To be complete, I must fully delve into who I am *now*, not what I've done, what I wish to accomplish, or what others want and see in me. Here I am, months into digesting and integrating this diamond of wisdom transmitted through the pulsating vibration of the Earth's heart and my soul.

I came back home and was immediately faced head-on by the strong waves of hidden judgment, displayed by my family's obvious behavior, that was now clearly recognizable - the *not-so-obvious*, the *unsaid*. In the past, I wasn't so hurt by this, probably due to my thick armor, but this time, I could perceive much more of what's beyond the surface. I could feel it right away at the airport the day I arrived, with six suitcases, a Jason, and a Charlie. I am so different, yes, why is that so bad?

Lost pieces of my soul returned like a hurt puppy. Let me clarify, it's not about feeling like the victim here; I want to describe the experience, but in no way, I identify as a victim.

Parts of me were drawn back inward toward the strong magnet - my energy line, as I began experiencing the powerful release of old, outdated information. What happens when old information approaches the edges or the surface, is that one can see and feel it more, and that usually becomes unpleasant, inevitably translating into physical pain. It acts as an emotional explosion of unruly misinformation left unmanaged, just like a bunch of teenagers when the professor is absent on the last days of the school year. There is no focus, no way to get any accurate information out of them; it's complete madness.

When I say waves of *hidden* judgment, it simply refers to whatever I was perceiving not being the entire truth. This is transparent now. What is behind this level of information is the call to focus inward more, and to create a stronger connection with the true self. How can I take care of myself more, accept myself fully, recognize whatever these sensations are revealing to me, and find better ways to move through them? What others are directly and indirectly communicating simply means I need to care for myself *more*? This is the time to go deeper.

Any resentment or sense of lack, instead of directing that outward and becoming immobilized by what's missing, here is the opportunity to fully transform the feelings into gold, the same vibration of gold that I hold in my energy line and mind, reflecting my pure essence. This part of me is the only thing that matters.

In our society, we have been grossly misinformed or mis-educated. Taking care of ourselves, our minds, and our state of being is not selfish, it's not frivolous or indulgent, it's the source of generosity. When we can hold more of ourselves, of the immense brightness that we are, we can navigate all relationships, and see beyond the superficial layers. No matter where we look, there are symbols and guideposts from our soul.

Always feeling like I had to prove myself in the past, I recall all the times, and sometimes still catch myself doing this, when I would want to share some story about my students or, back in the day, some hotel experience of hero-like resolution that saved the day. I simply wanted my dad to be proud of me, so that in turn, I could feel proud of myself.

There was a strong need to make sure my family thought I was doing a wonderful job, yet I have always been quite confident in my abilities. Isn't it normal for a child to want the family's approval? I think so, and still want that, of course, but it is just a want. Who wants that? Perhaps it's the self who was sent away when she was way too small, simply because my parents couldn't handle my sister one summer, and had to work with her differently. All these years, thinking that terrible summer camp experience destroyed me. I should be enough for myself first, 100%, not 70%. This is the real work. It doesn't matter what I *do* in life. Whenever you meet someone, and they ask you, *what do you do?* There may be this underlying, persistent need to prove what you *do* is equal to your value. Isn't that outdated and superficial?

When I was a director in hospitality and had a successful corporate career, everyone important to me acted as if I was a big deal. Now, on the other hand, they honestly still think I lost my mind, and that my mid-life crisis is lasting a decade. They showed me raised eyebrows at my frequent anxiety attacks in the past, strong disapproval of any of my relationships, sharing thoughts such as, why couldn't you just buy a house and have some savings, and why do you have to move so much in the world; can't you settle somewhere and away from here, cause you're a bit much to handle? We don't really know you, and you're the only one at fault for that. You weren't here. What's wrong with you? Do you need an invitation to come over? Of course, you are family; come whenever you want, this is your house – but underneath it all, the thought, why are you here?

Somewhat hurtful, maybe more than a little. Feeling like I'm taking something away from someone, be it attention, support, or love felt intensely agonizing.

Then the sweet voice of my mom, this is how I felt for 30+ years. You feel it so strongly because I carried this myself. I'm sorry you're holding this too. It's not you. You know the truth, release this information, it's not yours; expand and focus only on what you know, and take care of growing within your heart; you will help us finally step into another story.

Redirecting Focus

We consciously or unconsciously make up stories, create scenarios of how a person or situation is or should be, and that becomes a reality. We develop strong feelings and thoughts attached to this reality. Any subsequent interaction with that person or situation is filtered through preconceptions and assumptions. This entire operating system is like a foggy lens, lacking clarity.

When we interact with others, the words we use hold relevance. However, in any conversation, is everything communicated fully absorbed if we have filters based on the past stories we made up? Then, when is it time to acknowledge the limited view from which we see and live life? Isn't there a moment when we internally notice this way of being? When is it time to inspect the filters? Of being brave enough to have truthful conversations with ourselves? I feel the choice must be there first, if not one just fights against the desire to create peace while the other party – whether another person or a version of ourselves - is unphased by the underlying turmoil that needs to be exposed and resolved.

It's very difficult to understand the complexity of a person and of an entire culture. We try to decide what/who/why, which is a process of the head-brain, and in addition, we have this tendency and need to absolutely put everything into categories. Isn't this a consciousness defect? This is operating with the thinking-sense alone, a process linked to centuries of antiquated loop mindset - the grossly incomplete view - which creates separation, competition, and conflict since the *box* is defined by an extremely limited perspective. We've consciously and unconsciously adopted a highly immature and utterly incomplete way of seeing life. When we can loosen up the grip, even just a little, on the need to place things, people and situations in a category or box, our whole world changes.

I don't know how, you may think. Well, if we only consider this conceptually, we must recognize that *judgment* in this form - *the*

234

snapshot becomes the reality - is literally a dis-function and continuously separates us from living an inclusive life instead of everyone-fending-for-themselves life.

We're in *the* time of evolution. We have been for a while. So, this means taking a good, honest, hard look at *how* we think - we need to *be* more complete. Not only do we do this internally with ourselves, putting ourselves in this or that category, but we project this mindset onto others. The more we catch ourselves and self-regulate, the more we can redirect the flow of openness, connection, and expansion both inward and outward.

Pure alignment involves an ongoing reconnection cycle and rhythm, just like breathing and the pulse running through our being. Time and time again, it's a constant call to keep drumming, to continue paying attention to our own rhythm, the vibration that is firing like lightning strikes in our brains, hearts, and throughout our veins. Energy lines merge and fully align with the higher expression of our light.

This is a beautiful opportunity. This life. What I've experienced, thus far, is full of incredibly precious jewels. The unconscious participation in the great plan of soul evolution and expansion was masked by the small-mind/left-brain ego feeling like she was in charge. We must continue to move inward to then expand outward. The alternative is burdened by the obsolete idea of focusing outside to then create a shiny surface persona representing 1% of who we truly are – thinking, the rest doesn't matter since nobody can see it. This was my box too, the way I knew how to lead my life, who knew any different? There is no right or wrong, until we get to see more than the 1%, and then begin to navigate ways to learn more. Who am I? Who are these people linked to me? What am I really being shown here?

Softening my barriers, and allowing for waves to settle down, allowed me to see things from other perspectives. I can see immense kindness in my sister, in my father. I can see the tremendous pain and learnings they've gone through living through so many experiences and perhaps even misunderstandings. There are times where I felt small again, belittled and bullied, which allowed me to see specific patterns and aspects that needed more nurturing, feeling like those neglected, unloved, unruly fractals. When I shifted my view back inside, everything became softer and brighter.

I swim in this immense sense of gratitude knowing I am a participant in a grand plan. That my soul has incredible wisdom and that what I experience with my small mind facilitates a way to look deeper first, then allows me to move higher.

Dreams ~ Visions ~ Journeys

Hanging On Under the Big Wave

I see myself in the ocean, near some large, rounded stones. They are massive, yet I can put my arms around one, hugging it, holding on for dear life. I keep looking back to see when the next wave will be coming. There are others around in the distance, ocean begins making different sounds, and a wave rushes in, but it's not so rough. As I cling tightly to the stone, nothing happens to me, I am fine. Then another wave approaches, it's not too big; able to see my face, I'm relieved, smiling. In the next moment, there is a sense of so much happening all around. Not knowing what's next, I'm immediately overcome with extreme anxiety. My rock seems the right one for me to hang on to, sensing the need to stay here and resist. My attention is pulled toward the right where I can clearly see an enormous wave heading my way. It is hundreds of feet high, unlike any Tsunami ever experienced. This is the one, I hear myself say. As the wave moves in closer and crashes down right where I'm holding onto my stone, struggling in the strong currents, I hear many voices all around - they are all me, versions of me - shouting, you have to let go! It's time to let go! I trust without second guessing, then see myself release my grip on the rock, flowing with the strong current. Glancing back, I notice a part of me is still hanging on to that rock. It's like a projection or hologram of my body. Knowing there is no survival by continuing to hold on to that rock, I absolutely must float away, dive deep, and ride the current under the surface. It is the only way. Encouraging words resound in my mind, you can do it, I can do it! With an intense surge of relief, I finally completely let go of my grip.

I wake up startled, wanting to go back into the dream. Did I fully let go? Am I still hanging on to the rock? What is happening? Did I do it? This is a strong message of resistance and letting go. Instantly feeling sad and frustrated, confused, and startled, asking myself, how can I let go more?

Our Ghosts

I did a lot of training and much has shifted through vibration and accumulation postures. My body still hurts. I went to bed, and something strange happened.

Waking up in the dream, I sensed that what I'm seeing had happened before. I hear myself asking, am I remembering yesterday morning's vision? Two or three days become one, merging all-time. Things seemed different though, so it can't be a memory. I'm seeing distinct smokey shadows shooting from one side to the other of a house. There are many people around a large dining room table. We knew each other, this feels like family. The phenomenon of shadows flying around the room from the floor to the ceiling, from one wall to another, seems very normal, we're just sitting there, watching, and waiting; oh, here is another one, and another, did you see that? In the dream, I don't seem scared at all. These are definitely ghost-like beings, but sensed that they're not hostile or sinister entities, they belong to us, like projections. My ghosts are here too, and we are simply watching them move around like they run the place. While watching this whole scene, we start feeling playful, waiting for the next one to spring out of the wall or the floor and cross the room, making bets as to whose ghost will jump out next.

Then I see a much younger version of myself, running away from one of the ghosts who's chasing me. In this scene, I look frightened. It seems like a larger ghost, a big dark-gray blob-like smoke, and it's coming to get me with not-so-good intentions. I have to stop running because I know it's useless and suddenly feel a firm bite on the back of my hands. While watching this scene from a third-person perspective – me consciously observing at a distance – I'm amazed by what happens next. The ghost and black cloud chasing me transform into this white little fluffy bunny, but then immediately into a mean pissed-off bunny. Even though it looks like this little harmless thing at first, it bites me really hard with its sharp teeth.

My arms are cuffed behind my back, wrists close together, but they're not actually bound. I am running from a black smokey ghost which turned into an evil bunny; my hands are behind my back, thinking they are bound, but nothing is there. In the dream, the other self, observing this situation, looks shocked, and trying to get my attention, she screams loudly, you are free, you don't need to keep your wrists together as if you had handcuffs!

I run to what looks like an ancient washhouse and squeeze the blood out of the holes created by that bite on my hand, trying to get the blood out like the poison from a snake bite. I am not so scared anymore and now realize I can actually use both my hands. They are not bound, and the bunny is just a short distance from me, but now it's no longer chasing me. It looks like it's moving on like a normal animal, just roaming around.

I wake up breathing heavily, focusing on reentering, and what I see is just like a movie. It's me having this dream, I'm seeing the observer, which is me – oh wow, there is another version of me looking at what just happened – me (another self) in the background observing all the ghosts, then running, being chased, and bit by the obnoxious bunny. All the disguises of what seems scary are pretty clear now, in reality I am free.

In East Asian traditions, ghosts represent our ego-mind, heavy emotions - thoughts, and what torments us. We must recognize they are not who we truly are. They catch our attention, creating illusions simply because they tend to be the loudest, most frightening, confusing, and in-our-face, but they are absolutely questionable.

Emptiness - Creating Space

I'm in a dark room, being taken by a man, a dark figure. This person is approaching me, I am very scared, crying and screaming, he's coming to do something terrible to me. I know it has something to do with my face, will he beat me? Within the dream I quiet myself, then call mom and the guides, and start chanting chun kuan chun um chun pha sung (merging divine light, sound, vibration), very loudly.

This is an evil spirit, but while chanting these sacred words and asking my guides to help, the sense of anxiety and fear disappear.

As I turn around, in my half sleep-half awake state, I see countless sparkles of light. Just like when you have your eyes closed but lots of lights are flashing or flickering in front of you. Yes, I can see them with my spiritual eyes, immediately recognizing they are putting a protective shield around me, feeling a sense of comfort and support. Maybe the dark figure is a part of me that wants to be seen, resolved, dealt with - the unseen heaviness that is just behind me where I can't fully see. I ask my guides.

Embrace who you truly are. Everything is guided and you have access to seeing. Don't be so serious; make space, and prepare for what's coming. What feels right say yes to, what doesn't just turn around. This is the threshold to pass through. You have the keys, the codes. You have trained and are walking in the time of deep information clearing. We are showing you the connecting points. Empty and create space.

What Is 'The Big Picture?'

There is resistance. Recognize it and unlock more. Focus on freeing your heart. This is the work. The light body is receiving more light activations. Gain a bigger perspective. What is the big picture? Connect to the crystal spirits of the Earth. Unlock the codes in the Earth. Take steps to create the life and soul path agreed upon. Use life lessons and teach. You must teach. Journey and dream - pull more light in - allow for increased in-gathering source.

Connect and clear channels to receive soul guidance. Inner doubts and conflicts from past wounds are being resolved. Retrieve past experiences in ancient lands to gain clarity over the map of your next phase. Open heart. Upgraded thinking.

Move-Action-Create is the grounding of light.

Sun Energy

Receive a code of opportunities guided by the star ancestors. Trust the direction and soul messages. Bring Sun energy in to purify the heart. Lead with love. Root into the Earth. Become like a tree. Be still, grounding. Become like a mountain. Resilient. Strong. Stable.

Connect the Sun's energy to the Earth to enter the higher perspective senses. See the big map of life with the Eagle as if on top of the mountain. You can strengthen this energy coming in from other worlds into the Earth. Shine the light on the purpose of your life. Burn fears and old programs.

There is more potential than you realize. See the bigger self, and don't limit your mission. Things are happening you don't yet see. Connect with the Earth and allow the Earth to guide the instructions received into the energy of creation toward a joyful fulfillment of purpose.

Leave all notions. Forget everything and dismiss what you think you need to do. All is happening in spacetime. You move to stay grounded and connected to recognize our call.

Tired of Feeling Small

I'm in the back seat of a very small car with three other people. My sister is there, and I'm unsure who these other individuals are. We are talking about some difficulties with the Italian language. It's so annoying, while I describe the example when making mistakes at the post office, not knowing what certain terms are. I look frustrated while speaking, feeling pretty ridiculous and inadequate. We are joking around, then talking about other things, but in my mind, I know they all judge me for the difficulties with expressing myself in Italian. I'm sure of it, and it bothers me because I've felt this way since I was small. I'm about to scream.

In the dream, sitting there in this cloud of negative vibes, these words resound in my mind: I'm sick of talking about superficial things, and tired of having to prove myself to these people, always having to find something to say that shows everything is fine. Why this need of them being proud of me and happy for me. I am the only one that matters and this whole pattern makes me want to scream and stop everything.

What am I trying to build or show? It's just for them. It is not who I am or what I am aligned with.

This is my choice, I recognize and say to myself in the dream. The choice to have these experiences was a collaboration. I asked them to make me feel small and inadequate, helping me see through the superficial layers of challenges in expressing my authentic voice. They provide that opportunity to help me wake up to the fact that who I truly am, and my full expression, is above and beyond anyone's approval. My small mind will surrender and allow opening and expansion. I don't need to be afraid or to stay hidden and small.

Transported Through Layers of Reality

Frightened, I wake up screaming and crying. *I am at the checkout in a grocery store, speaking Italian. The lettuce is coming apart on the belt, things move as if I'm under water, sensing a current, like a stream, moving things in a flow. Suddenly I am feeling very sleepy, within the dream. I actually begin to think I'm having a low blood pressure moment, and may be passing out at any point here. Not really looking ahead or fully alert, I am feeling some contractions and heaviness. I'm about to lose my senses.*

The cashier says something, but I can barely hear her. I'm in a bubble or something, unable to hear her words. Her face seems like she's telling me something funny; she has a smirk on her face. Making a motion to repeat herself, I say something like, I'm sorry I don't feel so good; I'm in a daze. So, she says, where do you think you're putting your salad?

In an instant, I look up fully awake, back to all my senses, and I see her sitting, looking at me, but there is no checkout anything anymore. Turning around, we're in a giant empty warehouse-type building like an empty Costco.

We're speaking English now. A woman some distance away shouts, what is happening? Where did everything go? There are three or more other people in the same shocked daze experience, coming back to their senses. I begin to scream with terror inside the dream. We all find ourselves in another place altogether. Although it appears as an instant transition between the grocery store façade, the vibrations of the transition, and now, being in this open empty space, time has passed – we've been sent somewhere.

In my sleep-awake state upon waking up, I try to re-enter the dream vision with determination. I know there is no need to be scared, and proceed to ask, what is the empty building and where I am? What should I know? The heavy feeling, or low blood pressure again - I may pass out.

Everything is ok, you're fine - the words I hear as I fall into a very deep sleep. Upon waking up, I knew many things had happened, and it was ok to not know. I felt very calm.

Earth Wisdom

You are guided through challenges and supported to seek and remember your dreams, so that they can manifest with ease. Receive inspiration. Enter the space of joy. Journey to this space and receive guidance to move forward. We are with you through all circumstances. Everything is just as it should be. Trust the course of events as the transformative story that you're unfolding. Remain focused on your voice. Seek out to shine your truth. Your true nature is guarded and supported by guides, ancestors, and Earth. We are supporters in all densities and dimensions. You feel the presence more each day. The illusions are more apparent. Let all those old stories dissolve. It is happening regardless. If you allow the dissolution to occur with grace and focus, you may experience less pain. As you seek, push forward with a joyful state of hope in your dreams. You have the energy to hold and remember your strength and use it wisely to expand, to build more effective boundaries of protection, allowing pure light in and out, exchanging in equal sharing of truth and love guided by the Earth's harmonious spirits encouraging growth.

The body is adjusting to these deep releases that have been happening for a while, but now more deeply. Acknowledge how far you've come. See what is being washed away. What have you learned? How can it help you move forward?

With deeper releasing and letting go, there is more room for the soul's voice to be heard. Keep listening and following your highest voice. The call is more available now than before. Keep quieting the old self and rest, making space for new energy coming in, allowing you to see, feel, and hear the vibration of your soul. You're already doing it. Trust that all is good and the right step will be shown. Mom is guiding this path. Deep healing of one area of her life is being lifted. Integration is key. She is here holding you, wanting you to expand your heart more and more. Changing your energy is the message you must share with the world. Change the vibration and create the new. This is what she's helping you see. We are behind her, behind you.

There is not one way. Rest, take time to do what feels good, what fills you with joy and grace. What you need is being revealed and embedded in you gradually. Don't micromanage. This is a good quality that sustained your past roles. Fully trust that we are holding you through these transformations and that things are happening in the background.

Joy. Love. Peace. Grace. Movement. Rhythm. Sound. Art. Connection. Star guidance. Earth wisdom.

The Transition Back Home to Italy

I've accepted, for many years now, that although Italian is my native language, I'm able to express myself much better in English.

I would get knots in my solar plexus and throat when I was trying to communicate exactly what I felt or thought, trying to explain something difficult to talk about in any language, to where I would just stop, hear myself, realize it wasn't exactly what I wanted to say, and felt inadequate.

For example, I can conduct a KiGong class and feel very comfortable, joke if I stumble, and make silly mistakes when explaining something. The same scenario would happen even in my corporate job. When I came to open the property in Rome, it took a lot of work to translate the training onboarding materials. I know the terminology in English; it doesn't sound right in Italian, I would say.

All of this is to say that my discomfort around my family was in part influenced by their behavior, which I've touched upon earlier. You're so American. I would just hear my mom in my spiritual ears, yes, honey, that's right, we are Americans, and we're not trying to hide it, are we? The best way I can describe the discomfort is that I felt like a foreigner in my home country.

We arrived in Italy mid-February but became sick with Covid a week later. Unbelievable! Two years without ever getting sick, it was inevitable, I suppose. I hated that I had to get the vaccine, but I knew I could help my body and my energy bodies handle the intrusion. While sitting in the Walgreens pharmacy back in Prescott, I was meditating, breathing deeply, and focusing so intently on my cells receiving this concoction. I spent time sincerely talking to all of my cells, encouraging them to preserve the brilliant light source within and to protect that brilliance while the vaccine was doing what it was supposed to do without too much damage, concluding by always thanking each part of my body.

I became sick, mainly fever, and a headache that I thought would kill me as well as extreme fatigue. My father contracted Covid too, which was very upsetting and worried me so much. I was also saddened by this strange reality check and odd behavior just a few days after arriving since I was literally dished with a good portion of untrue, taunting statements. These statements were the types of observations based on a fraction of the entire story going back years, resulting in distorted opinions that revealed a deep sense of disappointment.

One evening I couldn't stop crying at the dinner table. I felt so bad for Jason, who is always so protective and loving. Why is this happening? What can I do? What happened, he would ask. I could only look at him with deep sorrow, feeling like this yelled-at little girl. No words were spoken. Anger fueled my tears. Why am I so sensitive? Mom wouldn't allow this to happen, or maybe she would. Why so much meanness? Clearly, nobody is open to understanding who I really am or Jason, for that matter.

You didn't think I would make the jump, leave Arizona, and move here? I was shocked. I guess they really didn't know how good I was at manifesting - if I decide something will happen, I can make it happen, remember? My visit in October of 2021 was the week after the studio closed. I had called my dad three weeks prior to inform him of my visit. It was well overdue. I was supposed to go sooner but couldn't. He asks, are you going to get someone to cover your classes? I respond, no, I'm actually closing down.

I could tell my dad was now paying attention instead of watching TV while talking to me. Yes, I'm closing. I didn't say anything before, but I've been having a very difficult year. I gave a brief explanation and how I came to this decision. He listened, but just like every time throughout the years, I felt I had to make sure he was still approving of me. I knew he was going to be worried.

When I decided to resign from my corporate career, telling him was the worst. I was able to inform him I took a leave of absence first, and then slowly that I had resigned. It was very unsettling for him then, and I think he never accepted it.

After sharing my situation with my dad, I let him know my visit would be about three weeks later. That evening, I got this apprehensive voice message from my sister on WhatsApp. Dad said something concerning is happening with you and that you're in trouble, but he wouldn't say what's happening. Are you ok? Did something happen that I need to know about? We exchanged some messages, then spoke on the phone. Drama! I thought. But I also felt like she genuinely cared about what was happening and was interested in supporting me. We're sisters, after all. It's just us two. You don't talk to anyone, nobody knows what's going on with you, but these things must be discussed. Of course, she said all the right things that anyone would want to hear. She was right, but I was suspicious; are you just curious so you can mock me later?

My visit was a time when I felt I could open up a bit more. I felt uncomfortable with keeping everything to myself and holding it all in. It had been so much for me, but I had been doing that my whole life and it had turned into an unconscious habit. During this visit, I thought it was safe to be fully myself and open up, but I was in wishful-thinking mode. Nothing significant happened, but I sensed this general feeling of, oh, yea, a bit of a mess here; she's like a lost puppy. But I didn't feel like a lost puppy at all; only misunderstood, once again.

It was a good experience to share some of my work with my sister. I had never experienced our relationship like this. We discussed meditation, energy work, past lives, and deep emotions. My heart was full. I can have this beautiful companion I've always wanted and needed growing up. I no longer feel completely rejected for just being alive; I no longer feel like a freak and that I don't belong.

I kept probing my dad about moving to Europe. Why stay in the US? I can live anywhere, why not move closer to a country with a much lower cost of living? My dad immediately suggested Spain or Portugal, which was interesting. I had already considered these options as I began the TEFL certification course. Supplementing my income as an English Tutor with the intention of working online seemed like a wonderful idea, but for him, this concept of online work was and still is so foreign. It's not real work; what does that mean? It's not real income; it's a joke. This is the generation that has difficulty grasping any type of work that does not involve going to the same building for 40+ years and then retiring; there is simply no need to argue with that mindset.

What if I come here? I suggested. I was trying to see what his reaction would be. I finally asked him straight out and clearly explained that I wanted to know if moving closer, whether an hour drive or flight, would be something he would like. He reassured me immediately, saying, yes, of course, it would be great to have you closer than you are now. Why in the world would I doubt that my dad wanted me close to him. I felt such contraction. I had to have approval and an invitation that it's ok for me to return to this side of the world. I did not like this feeling, this smallness, and, at that time, it was simply stronger than the warrior angel energy I have within. Perhaps my family didn't realize that when I set my mind on something, I will make it happen.

As I returned to Arizona, Jason and I seriously began planning this big move. Planning, research, logistics? No problem! This is also when I started applying for all these language schools. My dad instilled in me this worry that I absolutely needed some kind of

Italian work contract to survive.

One day I focused on just applying and seeing what would happen. My goal was always to work for an online platform instead of an in-person school, but applying didn't hurt. Soon after, a language school located in Siena contacted me, and the owners seemed wonderful. I was so excited. I love Siena, mom's encouraging words resounding in my head. I knew it was right.

Shortly after recovering from Covid, we moved to this first-floor apartment of a large country house in a small village just about 20 minutes from lovely medieval Siena in Tuscany. No matter where you look in that region, you are surrounded by beauty. It's incredible. This journey lasted six months. I was in a tremendous rush to move since I had to start working. The school was so patient waiting for me, but as usual, my deep need to please people and not disappoint cost me a huge amount of stress. We moved, and I started working literally the next day.

It was so difficult at first. I was overwhelmed by the lack of training and the newness of it all. I didn't know what I was doing in some areas, while I was doing pretty well in others. It was so uncomfortable, though. I knew I would feel more confident and do a great job with more training and time. It was overwhelming. They assigned too many classes at first, and I didn't object, which was a mistake. I did my best, and although it was overly stressful, noticing my body resisting so much, I pushed through and sucked it up. I would wake up crying and have a deep sense of anxiety. One morning I stared at my crying eyes in the mirror. It was the same feeling as when I worked for the corporate office years before. That feeling I can't put my finger on, but it makes you want to run away.

I didn't want to disappoint anyone. The owners were so busy all the time. I felt like I was at the doctor's office in the States. You better speak in 2 minutes or fewer because they only have 4 minutes, max, for you. Finally, I was able to make it clear. It was too much. I had too many classes and was overwhelmed. I asked if I could please have fewer classes. The situation continued for a while, without any changes, and I kept going.

Many challenges revolved around facilitating grammar explanations. Well, it's probably because I hate grammar, and many people are under the impression that if you don't learn grammar, you're not learning a language. This is somewhat true, if you're a beginner, however, if you've studied grammar for 15+ years and they have yet to teach you how to *speak*, I am convinced that what you need to do is actually speak, and I mean in English, not Italian.

In the meantime, what was most urgent was the immigration paperwork for Jason. The beginning of Summer was approaching, and my courses were ending soon. I asked to take time off to take care of the bureaucracy and paperwork. We agreed upon taking a month off and when I was ready to come back, they would give me more training. I was grateful, but deep down I didn't believe them.

17

HANDLING CHANGE

The Soul Always Knows Better

As things started to resolve and settle, we had to think hard about the current arrangements, taking into account the work commitment. Tutoring online without needing to handle the stress of this type of rigid structure felt like a smart idea and definitely more fitting. The original pursuit of this direction was led by the thought and misperception of increased stability and security, but the reality was that I felt too overwhelmed and misaligned, which usually means I need to take a closer look at what's happening inside.

Getting good internet service in the mountainous countryside was extremely challenging, a process that took over two months. Once I was finally able to get reliable service at home, I resumed my KiGong and mindfulness sessions, which decidedly lifted my spirits, like a breath of fresh air. Many of my U.S. clients joined the first online class and continued to connect for subsequent weekly sessions. Everyone was so graceful and loving. I cried happy tears after I logged off that first Zoom meeting, and said to myself, of course, this is what I need to do more of, for myself and others.

Once again, my soul spoke to me through my heart, my body, the overwhelmed feelings, and chaotic thinking. With the hurricane of nonsensical bureaucratic paperwork surrounding me, being distracted, losing focus, and scattering my energy was a daily occurrence. I simply needed to bring my focus inward, becoming quiet and still, connecting with my mind. What's happening? You know better (in a loving voice) - and it was true, I did know better.

Change affects people in so many different ways. We're all so unique. I have experienced many changes in my life, and several were significant changes, such as moving to another country, with another human and pets. Each time, the experience of change was lived differently.

Looking back at this particular period of transition, and closing my eyes, as if entering a dream, I can see myself overly struggling, trying to manage, to stay afloat, to keep my chin up, even if it was just for others; trying to enjoy the sunflowers every time I drove by the fields, asking my soul repeatedly, show me the heavenly messages, please help me. It's with such compassion, not pity, that I look at myself and send her so much love as if I was hugging my mom with tears in my eyes. I'm sorry you're struggling. I love you. You're doing your best. You will be alright. Please try not to struggle so much; see the suffering from another perspective. You can see beyond this inner conflict. We are helping you. Feel your heart.

Dreams ~ Visions ~ Journeys

Encouraging Words - Be Like Water

Fully awake within the dream, I find myself watching a series of images scrolling in loop-like motion, similar to a slide presentation. Writing appears on a white page, and I am supposed to select slides that look like buttons on a screen. This is a very advanced modern wall board - a screen with digital buttons on one side. The same image of me looking at this one particular slide keeps showing up in my mind screen. I gather this is something I really need to pay attention to. My vision zooms into the slide. Although there was hesitation on my part, unsure about touching the screen and making selections, someone is there to support me, but I have to decide on my own. As I record this experience, the whole sentence is hard to recall, but the word write is vividly clear.

Upon awakening and processing, I ask for clarity. Build a strong foundation of joy and freedom from thought, old stories, and expectations of the world. Recognize they are not your own. Release this hold - that you are to prove something. See how to create your own work. Create without needing to know if it will fit the world's expectations. Create and expand these foundations of self-expression. These will circulate and build the peaceful, harmonious sense of neutrality that allows you to accumulate and hold more light. Teach-learn. Expand to what you are destined to express. Be like water. Creation is possible by fueling joy, then feeling pure freedom in conveying the soul's voice and gifts; these quality vibrations create a much more stable, magical container for manifesting visions and dreams. Be inspired. We are here to bring these connecting strings to you more easily.

Planning Meetings

There have been a series of meetings and planning sessions. Aware in the dream, I'm held in a bubble, a soundproof room like a recording studio, barely able to detect anything from the outside layers. There are voices; they say, oh she's waking up, let's wrap it up everyone, good work.

As I lay in my sleep-awake state I have a clear sense that the guides are having these meetings and I, my soul, am there with them; this looks a lot like a department meeting I would have back in the day at work. I'm trying to reenter the dream to gain more pieces and puzzle them together. There is a lot happening, but can't exactly remember all the details. There are faded images, snapshots here and there, and I have a real, sharp sense that they're not showing me on purpose. The perception is that they're trying to remove some information that's been processed and, on its way out, but still sort of stuck in a loop in my head-brain. The planning meetings revolve around how to present the next set of energy packets – information - for me to move forward.

After fully waking up and recording this, I reach for the oracles, meditate, and receive a clarifying message.

We are readying you to receive. We are supporting your tuning.

Gather strength and build strong boundaries of energy that will help discern where to push through and where to stand by. Acknowledge your own groundedness and connection with Earth. See the way ahead toward the future promise of becoming. The soul vibration - destined expression - is here. Hold strength, courage, hopeful, bright and joyful potentials as beads of light. You are creating. You find a way as you always have. Search the mysteries of All-time. They are held in your body. Soul awareness and remembrance will guide you to find the way forward with the most beneficial tools, skills, wisdom of ancient times. Write.

New Paths and New Ideas

In a very large meeting, I am nodding and acknowledging with a cheerful look on my face, taking notes and paying full attention, hearing myself say, yes, I will do it, I can do it, thank you. There are many beings in the meeting, all there to meet with me, giving me instructions. My heart feels content, full of courage, with a sense of, yea, let's do this! I'm ready!

Once awake, I meditate and ask the guides what is happening in my dreams? There have been so many meetings lately.

You are facing your inner conflicts - the self that sees internal war, the struggle to balance two sides. This conflict is coming to a resolution by looking at what strength you can use from both sides, bringing inner peace and balance. You are gathering strength to neutralize the inner struggle. A space is created where you can then receive the cosmic force to stand tall with a renewed sense of knowing, of fire that brings trust in all new ways, confidence in your abilities. This level and quality of empowerment were lost and minimized in conflict.

The process of creating inner peace and accumulating strength will allow you to in-gather the purest form of power from your higher-self vibration, which stands in the middle to fill you up and provide fuel to move forward with a different type of heart power. Love and heart-mind energy are renewed. This new sense of empowerment is amplifying the heart's wisdom. Love yourself and all your paradoxes. Conflicts have shown you where you are and the value of what you can hold, and how unique your voice is - a strong energy of love that amplifies with a sense of assuredness, of confidence in who you truly are. Balance is restored - old versions of selves passing away. Reconciliation is making peace with those parts of you who hang on to tell you how to stay small. The dear protectors of old wounds, the cautious selves who just want to be heard. But this renewed heart power hears and understands the call to release such strongholds, to be freed.

We made peace and agreements on what is not helpful anymore. These conflicting parts of your being are dying now. We see the beautiful sense of peace and gratitude for all the offered assistance and the intention to help. The time to lay these selves to rest so their energy can be transformed into a source of new beginnings is now.

New paths and new ideas. This is the end of an era and the beginning of a new one. You will see many other options and ways to move forward. Obstacles or distractions will just be overcome with ease. All flows. You are empowered. The courage to find the course will be a lighthouse in the journey. You will feel strong guidance as we are one, and you are us. Now is the era of clear vision and awakening to another layer of truth. Keep going. Pay attention to dreams, visions, and drops of wisdom. Receive well.

Resolve. Refine. Open

Refining self-awareness. Releasing the old - being, transformed into a higher vibration of courage. Courage to see - to love and support all choices and learnings. Courage to move ahead with brighter light, sound, and vibration. Mental bodies, which can only see a fraction of spirit realms' expression, need to be allowed a voice. Not the leading voice. Collaborate with them. Don't let them run the show. Allow them to rest. Mental bodies activities need a reset and a guiding hand. You're the guide. Resolve the sense of lack.

Create the container and visualize yourself in her most expanded version. Joy. Love. Peace. Life flowing in and out. Expanded - constantly exchanging. Bring what is needed to feel safe and comfortable without any deficiency. Inner communication with other-selves is refined. We are here to help you communicate and fully express your true nature. Your mission is to be authentic with yourself and reflect it outward to all others in contact with you. Expand the sense of compassion for all experiences and learnings you hold within. Open up to all moments aligned with the Soul's purpose to flow. Trust the highest self-vibration to create through the portal of love, trust, courage.

All-Light is Oneness Itself

Depths of oneness. Awakening of the access to wisdom codes. See yourself standing with arms up toward the sky, palms, and fingers connecting to the web of oneness. Plug in. Ask what tools are needed now. Open and receive these technologies as they're always available, like breathing. The song of the web of All-Light is oneness itself. With awareness, your frequency becomes more refined, and the web of life of All-Light can fully incorporate your song into its wholeness. Now it's just intermittent inputs. Make it a constant song. Vibration so high, deep, powerful that awakens, shakes, destroys, rebuilds the purest song of the soul.

You can see. Move forward with your dreams. Envision - dream. Play it in your mind and cultivate that vibration as it is blessed with powerful love. A way will be shown. Trust your heart and lead with serenity and acceptance.

Transformation - Alignment

Alignment is the transformation of moving through the fear lens into love frequency. Here/Now - Space/Time is alignment of energy lines, ending a way of being - this is the process of true heart-opening.

Old ways of leading life are smothered by fearful patterns. The unwise way to proceed is to retain the same patterns.

Trust that soul is stepping into increased purity of mind and following guided light paths of a newly recalibrated series of coding. You belong. Soul fragments know how to return to the whole and flourish as one again. Earth connection provides the quality of strength now. Be the tree. Be the mountain. Allow information to reach depths of the heart complex. Divine alchemy occurs. In the

aligned fire of heart is freedom, peace, space, potentials - all that is.
Call on the highest form of vibration. What symbols of trust do you
see?

Rest. Make space. Access the study hall.

Honor All Parts of You

There are buildings everywhere. This is a city, and I'm back in hotel
life scenarios, in an outdoor area, seeing images flow by as if pushed
by the wind. It's a series of memories. Talking to my teams, sharing
tears, laughs, rough times, and incredible bonding moments. In the
dream, I tell my guides: thank you, I understand what you're showing
me - how much I've learned and how much I can share with others. In
that moment, they help me recognize that I have been trying to
distance myself from that life for quite some time. It's almost like I
reject it altogether. I used to despise what that life did for me, and
hardly talked about it in the past, but as they show me this part of
myself, it's so beautifully clear how much this life actually taught me.
All those moments make me melt, in realization there is so much to
cherish, what amazing experiences. There is no need to reject those
parts of myself. Some memories appear in black and white; others are
very dim - are these ghosts now? They show me how much I am
walking away from this part of myself. I hear the word, jefa (Spanish
for boss), and my heart swells. I loved the feeling I got when my team
called me, when they needed guidance, assistance, giving me the
opportunity to fix some problem or just be there to cry or laugh
together. Yes, many mistakes, but so many more impactful positive
moments.

Then I see myself stepping back. The buildings and structures fold
into the Earth as if being swallowed by the sand.

Another person is pulling me - come this way - I hear. It's another me.
An ancient structure emerges from the land where those buildings
sunk into, while strong winds, dust, and sand appear everywhere.
Upon focusing my sight, I immediately recognize these ancient
structures, noticing they're in really bad shape now. I begin to bow
as a greeting, in recognition and reverence, and hear voices chanting
all around. This is a very unique language – the sounds resemble

IMRA - imra - imra. As soon as I begin chanting these words too, I am shown wearing an elaborate headdress, with two long rods reaching toward the sky, and another decoration in the middle holding them in place. The rods vibrate with static-buzzing, electric energy, lightning-like sparkles running up and down these scepters. They are alive, being charged and activated by the sound of the chants.

Honor all parts of who you are. Recalling energy beads from this life experience draws ancient vibrations needed to proceed. The empowered wholeness is already in place. Recognition, and acceptance are the way forward.

Later that day, I reach for the Hieroglyphs Words of Power book, and the pages open to *Ir-Ma'a*, symbol for the visionary, the dreamer, walking in the imaginal worlds; it is about seeing true.

Leaving the Little Shack

Inside a tiny cabin that looks more like a wooden booth, I hear sounds of water, waves crashing on the sand, and wind blowing outside. There are no windows, just a small opening with a flap to close it for protection. Looking out from this opening, I'm not able to see much, just a bit of sand and water. The inside of this tiny little cabin looks familiar, like I have been here before, and while exploring, I notice many of my things are here, pictures on the wall and small items. It's an unsettling situation because the strong winds indicate a huge storm is coming. Feeling terrified, I think it's best to stay inside in order to survive. Suddenly, the strong winds beat on the side walls even more abruptly than before, as water begins to enter the cabin. Looking outside through the small opening, the skies are notably clear, only a bit of wind, not so strong as the sounds make me perceive. It's not that scary out there, it sounds worse from inside the cabin, maybe it's safe to leave. Building courage, I decide to step out and move away from here. As I reach for my phone, and take a closer look, I realize it's recording. There are videos of me in the cabin during this whole time, it's been recording for days. Someone has been watching me! Are they observing me go crazy in this tiny little flimsy cabin? Feeling a mix of disbelief and frustration, I know it's time to get out of here - I've been stuck in a box, life is completely different on the outside.

Things are not as you think. You are living a movie, but what you see is less than partial. Get out of there.

Standing Up to the Obnoxious Self

There are people or otherworldly beings all around observing, it's a crowded space. Mom is here too, but in the background. A few of them begin to approach me, walking slowly to ensure I can see them clearly and not get scared; this is probably because I'm noticeably anxious, overwhelmed with fear and anger - I must protect myself, hearing myself say within the dream. Unsure of what to do, I start shouting and crying, expressing my anger toward them. One particular person comes forth, she looks like me. Wait a minute, I say, who is this? Her facial features look fluid, moving slightly. I get right in her face and shout at her with my whole body, fists clenched and all. By the look in her eyes, and the smirk on her face, I can see that she is challenging me. Everything about her, including her aura, is so intimidating, but I don't budge; instead, I begin to hit her on the chest, except it feels like hitting a ghost, there is no impact. While I'm screaming and hitting her on the chest, she looks straight into my eyes, alternating between locking onto them, then looking away.

I stop, breathe, and hear myself - you are standing up to her. Release the pain. She no longer has power.

Energy Calibration

An energy line of healing frequency reaches you through many dimensions. It holds multiple level-planes sound-light, bringing down unique energy for integration. This happens without you needing to do anything. It communicates similarly to the energy line, while other levels of frequencies and geometry, that you cannot fully see internally, begin to emerge. It is the energy of the 17 through 19 planes of vibration, more refined than what you have experienced before. The absorption capacity is limited to micro doses at the moment. Openness to receive has been activated as you faced your fears, and the residual is still washing away. Most of this fear-based identification is dissolved. We are pleased to see your strong will. You know what you hold.

We are helping you dissolve hesitation to step up and into the new way of operating. You are walking along the edge of the path. You see it to your side, while still walking your current path, with the dream-halo-haze around it lingering. We are patient. We love you. We are here regularly meeting about your experience. You are in a place of expansion in service to all. Step closer to the dimensions aligned to your vibration. See yourself walking in your aligned state - most connected frequency. Healing occurs in your physical spine. The energy lines we hold for you are open - a clear, smooth connection with Earth planes and expanded-highest frequencies. Use sound to connect. Use nature spirits to connect. Use vibration to connect. Rest. Reflect. See your journey.

A Perceived Attack

I see myself fighting with a woman. She's much smaller than I am. I don't recognize her. She has a knife and is trying to get me. I'm fighting hard, struggling so much. Something stops us, it's not entirely clear; there is some announcement, we pause, can't see anything, then we go back to vicious fighting. She's now behind me, trying to stab me from the back. I'm able to get a hold of her hands and bite one of her fingers, thinking it might be hard to break through bone, but the fingers crumble like a hard and brittle cookie. It comes right off the hand without any effort. Suddenly, aware something is off, I hear myself say, wait a minute, this is all fake, then turn to face her and look into her eyes. She looks surprised, maybe even shocked, quickly getting back into character, showing some pain as I just bit her finger off. Noticing this whole scenario, I'm immediately suspicious. A second ago, you weren't in any kind of pain, what's up with that? Ah, I see, you're supposed to show me some form of fear. I understand; well, damn, you scared the shit out of me; I think you got the part for a reason, but I'm not impressed.

Chanting Peace

It's a dark, dry space. There is light coming from a doorway or window. I see myself sitting on a wooden chair. My eyes are closed in meditation while I am chanting. In the dream, my consciousness zooms in with the intention of listening closely to what I'm saying.

My chant is melodic and so sincere. Mhotep, Mhotep, Mhotep - the words spoken. There are two versions of me, both sharing space, repeating these words Mhotep. Becoming aware of these sounds, I suddenly pause and say in disbelief, Imhotep, am I awake? My awareness returns to the sounds of reverent chanting. They reverberate in the room. The self that is sitting on the wooden chair stops chanting out loud. Something is being carefully administered energetically. The observer self continues to chant, holding space. From above, high up within this room, were energy-spirit beings coordinating the experience.

In the dream, the observer self dozes off, as if she was gently dismissed, and sent into a deep suspended state indicating wait here- this time, *you can step back for a bit. I feel I'm in good hands, then notice my observer self rolls over, and falls into a deep, deep sleep. She looked and felt so tired.*

Reference:
Hotep is an ancient word that means peace. The peace we can consciously create beyond the brain needing understanding.

Imhotep was the perfected spiritual child of Ptah and Sekhmet. He was a seer, doctor, architect, scribe, magician, and high priest.

I see this message as a reminder to make peace inside. Peace allows for deep opening and refinement of vibration, allowing our spiritual family to help us heal. They request to be involved, answering our call, we simply need to extend the invitation and then let them. We send the request by demonstrating that we can create and hold peace.

Vision of Upload

The words we use matter. A download is a word that is too often used. Since I can remember, I've always felt words can't transmit the multi-layered meaning of one's message as initially intended, even so, we must use words to communicate.

Let's consider the term *upload* as I share word frequencies from the guides.

Crossing a threshold. A new form of energy assimilation-integration, expression-expansion of the energy system is occurring. Expansion of the energy system to respond, match, express these light spectrums.

Now, see the emergence of new energy points – not new – previously hidden, dormant energy points which act as centers and doorways that resonate and maintain the new light spectrums within the fields. Earth vibration expresses these dormant doorways as gateways within and without, through one-humanity. Now portions of this wisdom are revealed. A fraction of energy information is shown to calibrate the remaining distortions.

The location of these doorways is intended to upgrade cosmic light spectrums as they flow and navigate through the lower frequency minds continuously while delivering packets of codes – light.

Each individual complex will have a unique delivery system process. The cause-and-effect map signature of each individual is the key that determines the specific positioning of awakened energy points and doorways.

External doorways to the physical ears are activating. Heart complex points on the outer edge of the field connect to the ones next to the ears through rising spiral energy lines that are constantly moving as a radar signal, collecting information emerging from the heart complex. Interaction of light exchange between throat and heart complexes is a technology of purification.

Words of the heart are spoken - manifestation of heart complex visions - a union of what is heard and felt. Calibration - Alignment for expression of soul's earthly mission.

Higher mind vibrations can deepen through direct delivery of soul's divine messages without interference as was manifested before. System upgrade regeneration process has been underway, expressing itself now in a form that can be digested and absorbed in a deeper, more profound way.

The emergence of soft activation of energy points, and gateways will allow humanity to mature from low-mind-ego life view to expanded creator view, gradually encompassing higher densities and dimensions within universal mind view, refining astral, mental, causal minds. Embracing all unique vibration signatures of personality gifts - stepping out. Entering space-time continuum of full system communion of activated bodies with Earth, constantly being the bridge between above and below. Thank you.

Dreams ~ Visions ~ Journeys

Lost Soul Contract

So busy, running around like a crazy woman, exactly like when all hell broke loose at the hotel – chaos, people everywhere, madness all around, I am frantically looking for something, some paperwork. Then I notice someone else, amongst all the people, also looking for something, and she looks exactly like me. So distracted by this, back and forth between looking at her and searching, it becomes clear to me this person actually is me. I now realize what I'm seeing is myself helping her - the other me - look for this document, and immediately feel so encouraged because there is help. We're unsure what the document looks like, but I know it's supposed to look like a pedigree or some sort of medical document with detailed historical health information, lineage, etc. As I look at this girl again, she seems very lost, way more nervous and exhausted than I am. It's terrible because I have a strong feeling that it is my fault the document is lost, and she's in real trouble if we can't find it. Aware within the dream of this connection between the two of us, then I suddenly see what this is.

This scene reveals that I've misplaced, or stashed in a very hidden place, my very own soul contract. I chose to make it extra hard to find so that I could experience a more profound realization that would allow me to merge all of my lives into one. Spinning in circles, running around, lost, and lonely, unaware that she is right here helping me, in truth, I'm not alone.

Black and White Metal Tools

Inside a hardware store that also acts as a jewelry store, I'm waiting to pick up an order, but it's not ready. Somehow, overthinking within the dream, I assume it's a ring, probably because I'm in a jewelry store, and get a sense that I'm waiting for something precious, but unsure if it's an actual ring. The cashier tells me the total is $81, as she hands me the order envelope. My item is not ready, but there is something inside the envelope, a white, metal object. The shape is quite unique; it has a rounded top, and the lower half is pointed with two split ends, funneling down. The object's shape resembles that of a metal wine cork screw, except the pointed part has a clear cut separating this section in two. How do they cut a ring from this piece of metal? Maybe out the rounded part? I'm holding it, taking a closer look, and am completely puzzled on what its purpose is, however, I know it's very important that I learn how to use it. Another almost identical object is presented to me; it's a lot bigger than the white one, made of black metal. They both look exquisite, with a smooth, shiny surface.

The people in this store are going about their business and working away while I'm waiting. A long time goes by. Why am I waiting? I get so tired of it that I start screaming, then someone comes right away, while I try to justify myself. I've been waiting a long time, it has been two hours, I am not feeling so good, please be patient with me, and help me. Why do I have to wait? They finally start paying attention and assisting me. Someone is getting measurements for this ring I need – or whatever I'm waiting for, and they're trying to see if they could do it right then and there. I'm not sure if I'm supposed to get a ring out of this, that was my idea as I got there, but I am now clearly getting the impression the ring is not the point. Not wanting to wait any longer, I tell them perhaps I should come back later. What is this place? Then things become clearer.

The white and black metal objects given to me are tools. If drawn on paper, it looks like a head, a neck, and shoulders then funneling down in an up-side-down triangular shape ending with two points, which are next to each other, touching, with a slight cut, almost reminiscent of the Waz scepter.

The Big Still Ocean Wave

I'm on what seems to be a tour, along with some other known people. It's not a tourist group though, more like a spiritual retreat setting. Everyone is very quiet and respectful, behaving peacefully and calmly, while we receive instructions. A dear friend and teacher is there guiding us, Master Han Myung. She's a beautiful, bright woman who dedicates her life to spiritual work, supporting individuals' growth through workshops and retreats.

We find ourselves on a cliff, observing the ocean from an elevated view point. Behind Han Myung, an enormous wave emerges, the perfect surfer's wave, rising to eye level. I freeze, while staring at this incredible wave. It appears to move, although I really have to pay attention in order to detect it at all. It is so slow, the wave almost looks entirely still, time stops completely. Watching the magnificence of the water in slow motion is mesmerizing, I have never seen the magnitude of a wave this big, it's quite remarkable.

Han Myung points out whales, dolphins, and other sea creatures swimming and gliding over the surface. As I turn to see them, they look so small compared to their natural size, and then realize we are actually all very large beings – we are giants. Everything seems so small, except the wave.

I have a distinct feeling to be somewhere else, a different reality, or other dimension as I'm seeing things from up above, knowing this is definitely a place in spacetime where I am being shown a truth to uncover. Then hear, you are so close to seeing, the wave is raised, everything is slowing down, almost stopping altogether in order for you to really see.

The environment is frigid, ice everywhere, and everyone is all bundled up. The waters are dark blue, and although there is a giant wave, I can't see through the depth of the water. With an immense sense of awe, enchanted by the wave in her subtle movement, I also sense that I miss Han Myung and what she represents. The sense of belonging to a community dedicated to high vibrational work, where we practice ceremony and connect to our true nature.

I have flashes of tending to the ancient temple activities, the sacred work I do in another reality.

On the Ledge Facing the Abyss

I'm standing on what looks like a narrow sidewalk, right on the water. It's a ledge, from which I can see the deep dark water in front of me. Everything is in slow motion, including me, flowing smoothly as if the air was a thick jelly-like substance. I am very sad, feeling both alone and lonely. It's dusk with some dark clouds in the sky, and as I look up a bright light catches my attention, is it Venus or Sirius? In that moment, a feeling of being protected or looked after washes over me, calming me down. I walk up and down this sidewalk around the corner and back. The narrow ledge is part of a larger structure, with a tall wall just behind me. Unsure what I'm supposed to do, fear starts to kick in. Everything is in slow motion. Do I have to jump in? Even though it's scary, I feel like this is the only way I can survive - I must jump in the water.

Suddenly, something flies around, it's a huge, bright green beetle, which lands up high on the side of the building. It's so loud it makes a thud as it hits the stone wall around the corner. The beetle starts crawling toward my side of the wall, and I notice it's a very different-looking bug, with a strange form I don't recognize. I'm petrified because there is nowhere to run. If I try to escape this hideous bug, I may lose balance and fall into the deep, dark water. This creature continues down in my direction.

In a flash, I find myself in a room, no longer standing on the ledge. The bug shapeshifts into a bright green cat. I am completely overwhelmed by fear during the transformation. In the attempt to protect myself, I engage with the fire activation breath, just like the initial stroke in healing sessions, with the intention of expelling this creature and have it move away from my space. During the energy movements, I feel there are others in the room, but cannot see them with my eyes; I know they're there watching.

I wake up thinking I should have jumped into the abyss.

264

18

A NEW QUALITY OF CONNECTION

Create a Space for Peace

Early in the morning, I started vibration training, shaking my body, followed by some stretching. After the initial energy circulation practice, my body began moving to relieve tension on the right side of the neck, a pain radiating toward the shoulder blade. It's been bothering me for a while. No longer angry at this pain or my body for requesting attention in this way, I just closed my eyes and asked if I could be guided to move in ways that would relieve the tension. I know it's already left my body; it's just lingering in a few layers of my energy fields. What I feel is just an *echo* and it's been moving outward. In my heart, I sense it is resolved, but my body still feels it strongly as if sitting on the outside patio in the late evening, hearing the town's square event on a summer holiday; they seem so close, but they're actually far in the distance.

Our body is much more intelligent than our thought processes, and we do understand that our bodies know exactly how to recover innate balance. It's actually the natural state of *all* of our bodies - constant movement, a smooth flow, little waves pushed by a gentle breeze, maintaining clear waters and freshness running joyously through streams of light. Experiencing pain of any kind helps us reactivate our sensitivity to energy-spiritual bodies. The body will always tell us, one way or another, it never fails. Our job is not only to pay attention, but to dig deeper, to go beyond the surface. Where the mind goes, energy follows. This is a universal law. When we become still and allow our heart-mind to focus, in a relaxed state, it's like turning on a laser beam, shining a new light, and uncovering the true message. By becoming still, I allow my body to move in ways to help me release these sensations of discomfort. It only takes a few minutes of mindful, focused awareness to see this is the echo-heaviness. It's being dissolved, messages such as, thank you so much for helping me focus. See, it's moving outward, but time is needed to process. You became accustomed to it. It's an adjustment period, trust, and rest. You are participating in this process and waking up from the numb groves of distortion.

After the holidays, something shifted in a big way. I can describe it as if I was missing some essential pieces of clothing, but now I'm finally able to wear a top coat. A new level of protection and guidance unfolds, after shedding what seemed like a steel cage around my heart, specifically the back.

Following a challenging winter, another small move was preparing to manifest. It became very clear that it was more beneficial for me to focus on creating a space of peace, light, and creative expression, instead of allowing intense swings of outdated misunderstandings to push me in this or that direction. Who's in charge here? I would ask.

The lightness I feel in my new space is precious. The town is small, but it has all the conveniences one can ask for. The landscape is lovely, and I look forward to continuing to explore the bordering regions of Umbria and Tuscany even more. I feel deeply held by the land restoring a specific quality of resilience, stability, openness, and strength. This time is really special.

Ascension: A Circular Process

I see *Internal Alchemy as a circular system*. We tend to visualize the process of raising consciousness or elevating our awareness as being in an elevator and someone pushing the top floor button. This may happen when we only consider our internal 7-chakra system, which does give us a beautiful path to transformation and learning, however there is more to this, much more. I always felt that the evolution we experience through our energy line is only one phase of remembering or returning to our essence, it's just one chapter.

In ancient Taoist texts we are given the path to Soul completion through KiGong practices such as the Microcosmic Orbit, and other internal transformation training. Here we see a profound parallel to the teachings passed down to the ancient people of Khem (Egypt) which we now know as Hermetic principles, and this is because they had the same wisdom teachers.

We cultivate the Fire in the lower abdomen energy-complex, known as the Mind of our physical Form. Once activated, it rises to purify and restore the qualities of the Soul's Mind, the heart chakra complex; then it continues its journey through Soul's gate, the narrow passage of our throat chakra complex, into the instrument of consciousness within the Head Brain, the home of Spirit.

Each one of these processes has various cycles of refinement, it's not a 1, 2, 3 short-stop and done ride. Soul merges with Spirit and vice-versa - through the body. In turn, we must bring this wisdom, the upgraded frequency and vibration, back into the physical body, and connect these vibrations to Earth's wisdom.

Instead of one line connecting these portals, we can think of this process as a pyramid. A strong foundation to hold and sustain elevated light – the square representing the Earth, the triangle representing the higher elements of our essence. The pyramid generates a circular movement within and around it which allows us to access our multi-dimensional being, the various levels of Mind. Interesting enough, the ancient Taoist symbol for *hu-man* looks like a pyramid, a *completed being* merging the above with the below, and the ancient Egyptian god *Hu* was known as sound, light and breath or spirit, also represented by the sounds of taking a deep breath in and out, light, breath, circulation, bringing refined Spirit back into its zero-point, and just like breathing, this process keeps going.

The brightening process is not an elevator, it's an ever-turning wheel, expanding even further into a growing spiral.

Meetings with the Guides

The Study Hall

Asked to access my study hall, I am immediately brought into a very large room with many ancient books, a grand mystical space. There is an elderly man who looks similar to Gandalf from Lord of the Rings, he is the guardian of my study hall. I know, with unmistakable perception, that this is another version or aspect of myself, part of my soul that chose to be in charge of my study hall, appearing to me as this old wizard-type person. Suddenly, a tiny, small version of me comes into view, next to the elderly guardian. The wiser-self guides me by hand, walking toward a particular section of books. The dust is made of golden sparkles; I feel like a kid surrounded by the most magical atmosphere with all these beautiful old books and scrolls everywhere. There are many of them on a large desk, one in particular is smaller than the others, and it's sparkling white. I am encouraged to select that one. The pages open on their own, and I'm able to look through a few of them here and there. There are pictures, but I don't actually see anything inside the pictures, until suddenly all these images flood my mind, like a quick breeze.

Animals come to greet me. There is Lynx, my companion, and the sweet little Tito is here, too. There are birds everywhere, I see an elephant and caress his forehead, then a tiger and a panther, and a whole bunch of animals in the immediate area. As I lift my head to look forward, a massive aquarium-type scene is revealed. It's not an actual tank, more like a portal within the study hall, providing an opening into the deep ocean. Whale approaches, and I feel a beautiful energy coming from her through the water. There are strings of light coming directly from Whale into my heart and another on top of my head. She is connecting with me so I can feel and recognize her.

I sense mom, and see her come forth from the ocean – a radiant light floating, surrounded by a brilliant cobalt blue glow. Her eyes and smile emanate pure energy, I recognize her. Lynx and the puppy are at my sides. The Tito is on my right side, lying down at my foot, and Lynx is just sitting next to my left, purring strongly, and rubbing on my leg. Whale sounds and music fill the air, and Wolf can also be heard in the background. Light language sounds and symbols dance through the entire space.

We are always here for you, they say. You have the knowledge, and everything you have is within you already. Other beings wearing beautiful white-purple-blue gowns appear next to mom, there are so many of them, part of a distinct group of beings.

One particular being comes forth from the background, surrounded by a blue glow, with golden sparkles all around her body. I am amazed, having an intense sensation deeply within my upper chest - it's me, a future version of myself. She has such joyful and enthusiastic energy. This is wonderful. We make eye contact, and as I look into the blueness of her enormous eyes, I travel through them, seeing snapshot images of me, some of which I recognize. A Native American wise woman, a non-earthly tall and beautiful being, teaching, and leading people, healing and assisting groups. There is a lot of information streaming into me through the eyes of the future self, the radiant blue-golden light being.

Even though the images are coming in so quickly, having difficulty keeping up, I know only a glimpse of what's happening is enough to help me remember my experience as a soul. Mom, along with my soul, tells me they have something for me, and presents me with a glowing rectangular object resembling a box; I open my palms to receive it. Inside is the gift of the golden key, they say. Upon looking down, in my palms appears a glowing gold, old-fashioned key that dissolves into sparkles of light, seeping into my palms, traveling through the arms right into my chest, immediately creating an intense sensation of energy flowing around my heart.

The resounding words from all of the beings, the key is your heart, giving me a wonderfully comforting feeling as tears flow down my face. My mind tries to understand, asking questions such as, I don't know what to do next, how do I proceed? The messages reach my heart, don't worry, stay calm, you're doing it, you're on the right track, you will just know. We are always here when you call on us. This key is the way into the doorway, your gateway, where you can find us. You are now stepping through it, it is time. You have the key.

Immersed in light language and enchanting whale songs, I can sense the presence of all the animals, and beings showing me so much compassion and love. Some of them are holding me, offering protection. The energy makes me stronger and brighter.

It is soon time to go back. The little puppy and Lynx appear next to me just like when I first arrived and sat on the big chair in my study hall. The guardian-wizard approaches, I know it's time. Before leaving, he wants to show me the study hall a bit more, so that I can get a better understanding of what is here. This is a very large, bright, and comfortable space. It is my space, where I can come and renew myself, study, and connect. Here, I can visit magical places in nature, share time with ocean beings, and meet my guides. It's very clean - no surprise here - I am safe and feel joy. I will return to the study hall and commune with all beings here. Thank you.

Healing Journey into Another World

A powerful light shift is happening - a clearing – enhancements to quality of energy occur. Sounds and light from another spacetime. Healing and light upgrades. My body is feeling it through current pains and severe discomfort. Arcturians' blue light energy beings presented themselves. Mom is here, and a vision of energy exchange appears. Guides are helping with digesting upgrades, the process of expansion. They encourage to think of the future spacetime, to recall the source-power. Write the future. You are releasing the ancient blocks from the land people. We are here to show you the light power within, and guide you forward. Connections are stronger for you now, as you can see.

You are more aligned with our vibration, being activated through the golden key you received. Use it well to envision your path and soul destiny, then manifest it. The heart chakra complex receives upgrades through the golden key. The light expanding is the doorway to deepening the inner alignment. It's a transformative vibration of love, acceptance, encouragement, and expanded view. Nature will help you ground and stay strong in order to integrate this transformative energy. Hold this light, and move it forward as you prepare to share. The high-heart golden light complex is the doorway to fully *expressing the authentic voice, the true vibration. Alignment with the destined agreement occurs now. The way forward is here. Unconditional love embraces your golden light. We say, trust and be in serenity. We are you. You are us. We love you. Love yourself.*

Naming the Stars

I'm awake in the dream, floating in the cosmos, speaking these words in Italian:

- *Castore e Polluce (Dioscuri - Gemini constellation - divine twin horsemen - rescuers and healers).*
- *Ganimede (the Eagle - Aquila and Aquarius constellation) e Callisto (the Bear - Ursa Major constellation).*
- *Pleiadi (Taurus constellation).*

Knowing they are moons, and constellations, I ask myself, why are these important to me? Why the twins and the sisters? Analyzing within this vision, saying, usually, something like this is an invitation to review the mythology of celestial bodies.

I find myself floating in the cosmos, receiving instructions. My brain is unconsciously processing, while information is being shared. As I let go of wanting to know, wonderful music catches my attention, I recognize it. It sounds similar to Fado, the passionate heart expanding Portuguese music. The incredible singer Maritza is now singing with such passion it melts my heart.

Here it is, in the heart. Just feel. You are ready.

Pages of the Book

A young girl is playfully running around in nature, surrounded by trees, flowers, animals, grass, sunlight, and joyful sensations. It's me, and this is happening now, it's not a memory. I appear innocent and joyful, full of courage and curiosity. There is no fear as I walk through the forest. Guides are watching from a distance. Some have the role of protecting, and others are just observing how I put in place the teachings. There is so much love and support, feeling so comfortable and happy in this environment. There is no sense of urgency, or time running out, instead there is a warm feeling that everything will be ok. I hear myself ask, what can I be shown that could help me in this period?

The little girl shows me an ancient golden book with thick pages, telling me, this is all we need, then opens it to a specific section. She's got the best little smile with big bright eyes, a playful, innocent demeanor, and so wise at the same time. The book is so large it sits on a tall stand. She gives me a nod as an invitation, or permission to take a look. I'm almost afraid and intimidated, but her eyes and warm smile reassure me that it's ok. Not knowing what to expect, I look down, and try to focus my eyesight. The pages look like fluid, shiny, metal plates. I immediately know this is my book, and I'm the only one who can actually open it and read the language in it. There are different types of signs, and many forms of writing. I know this information because I'm the one who wrote it. Characters begin to emerge from the page in a light form, they are moving and floating off the page. There are symbols to the left and three others catching my attention toward the right, just lifting off the page, floating toward me. This is not a modern language or writing style, it resembles shapes, scribbles, a code-based language - similar to hieroglyphs or East Asian kanji.

This is the message from the codes. Renewal process. Remember the experiences of service. Suddenly I am shown a temple where my responsibility is to manage temple operations, training the people who will serve here. These are very ancient times, based on my clothing and nature of ceremonies.

In the next image, I'm shown on the deck of a large ship. The seas ahead are very rough. I am in charge but not the captain, and carry weapons on my body. There are both women and men on this ship. We are bringing goods to an island and its neighboring large peninsula. Many people are waiting for us, they are friends, and we help them as they help us. I am especially tall, along with everyone on the ship, and the people we visit on the island and peninsula are much smaller than us. Not little persons, just smaller. We belong to a completely different race.

I'm able to see myself more clearly now. A warrior-guardian and teacher of the ancient order. Through my eyes, the energy is transmitted and directed. During ceremonies and rituals, my energy field creates beautiful sounds. The vibration emanating from my being creates a magical melody. Some can already hear this frequency, while others can't, they need more training. Those who want to learn how to develop coherence come to ceremonies and rituals to improve their connection to the inner source of fire. All light beads, within and without, assemble in a specific way to create magical frequencies. When the sounds are created, a unique quality of healing occurs. Specific sounds activate instant healing and recovery phenomena.

Alaleia - Alaleia - Alaleia is the sound I repeatedly hear as a beautiful song dancing with the air.

Beamed to Sah - Orion's Belt - Mintaka

There is a spark and lapse of consciousness as if losing my senses for a split second, almost passing out, then coming back online. In a bright flash, I see myself being transported back up to Orion's belt, specifically Mintaka. The experience can be described similar to when the power goes out, causing the lights to instantly turn off, then quickly turn back on. In a split second, I find myself back here, looking up at the stars, knowing a part of me is currently living there and comes down to guide me and provide instructions. It was an unmistakable experience, fully aware of being there, then experiencing the return to where and who I am now. An amazing feeling.

Sirian Guide

Awake in the dream, seeing myself as an observer, the scene shows a magical, beautiful being – a Sirian guide - holding me dearly, cradling my body as I sleep. Upon a closer look, she looks exactly like a wise teacher I know. There is another guide here, holding the role of assistant to the Sirian guide, facilitating a proper introduction. We are in what looks like a hotel room, and it feels so comfortable. The warm and loving mind of the Sirian guide shares a message with me, this is an invitation to slow down and rest together. Although I am enjoying this moment, my brain starts to analyze, within the dream, the stream of energy emanating through the images. I hear myself say, how clever for you to show me your presence this way. I am so grateful you are connecting with me as this particular teacher I admire and resonate with so much. The sense of reassurance that they are working with me makes me feel held and accepted. We know and see you. Keep going. Thank you.

Temple of Dendera

In and out of awake-dream time, I hear myself ask the guides to take me back to the temple of Dendera. I am instantly drawn back into the dream, seeing myself, with a surprised look, realizing what I just asked. Then I see it, the ancient site, and hear myself say with excitement, oh the Hathors! I know this place from a time in the distant past.

A seer-leader guarding the temple operations, and managing temple affairs. In service to the Hathors, connecting the Light of the Sun and the Love of Venus through Pleiades' healing experiences and principles. Your power is held in the memories of times before Khem, where the Hathors influenced a specific portion of the leadership. We worked with Djehuty as mentors for the elevation of purpose. We began the mysteries in a series of courses through schools and formal educational environments, including temples, and practical evolution experiences, to create more impactful leaders by activating the love-lead healing quality of leadership - a technology sourced by few, the activation of soul-voice co-creation with ego-matter gaining focus. Student leaders in service to the Hathors could activate the heart and mind to lead individuals in seeing the most balanced approach to any situation. Leading from the heart through devotion to service, communication, connection, continuous learning, and responsibility in sharing.

As I see and hear these messages, I am recalling my roles in this life.

Message from the Hathors

You know this with the thinking sense perception - what you see is incomplete. Everything is ever-changing. There are aspects you cannot see clearly. You are not designed to. Distractions appear through the thought forms, which prevent you from the larger view.

Acknowledgment of illusion and distortions is not only a mental-body function, as this is very limited. Abundantly receiving spirit-soul merged energies through the energy line is the next phase for all. The energy line provides the essence of softening and releasing in order to expand this new creation of the minds. Spirit light moves outward from the depth of the inner source. The purity of quality depends on the acknowledgment of the distortions.

We are showing you new paths and directions. New thought forms become more suitable tools for the following tasks and phases. The time of living past distortions is evolving. Trust what is presented as the area of focus - now.

Emerging as a new source of creation. From the chaos of lost pieces, fractals of soul-spirit, and mis-information, you can settle into a new beginning - a new way of life. It will be fully and clearly seen as you step into it with dignity, and complete trust in your aligned mind complex.

Inspire to inspire. The new way of being appears as there is a new focus. It is returning home to your most powerful mind. As you shift the previous focus to the new, experience a breakthrough. The old projections, which created armors and missing pieces of powerful light, dissolve. Elevate into a protective shield that breathes as it constantly moves and adjusts, deeply rooted and vastly expansive, as the spirals of wisdom create ripple effects in all directions. This movement has regained its rotation.

The body suffers, but it's a necessary destruction path of clearing. The resentments of choices are left behind. The shades of memory are to lay to rest. The sense of lack and scarcity intensely packed in the dungeons of the body and soul are lifted through trust alone and by shaking and breaking the distortions. Wisdom will show you how to lay this heaviness perception in the transformation chamber for the new production of light. This is the inspiration for others. If one can do it, everyone can do it. Live a new creation.

The steps, path, and direction are already laid out. The experience is

*happening now. You are on the path now. You are your future you -
now. With determination and reverence to your heart-soul, find the
lightness of your own guidance and love. See your lessons clearly as
direction pointers. This is how you can bring back some of your light.
Call in the guide messengers to the energy line from which you can
see and share. Purity and clarity are already in and out, swirling
around in motion.*

*You are this motion itself. Transmit this to the body. Inform the body
it is this light. There is difficulty accepting the new light. Help her
remember. You are doing it already. Focus deeper. You are loved and
held. Trust and be the peace you already hold. Dignity in your eyes
and fire in the belly to lead and push through all un-truths.*

*You are the dream that awakens, the movements of connecting waves
between the realms - the current of connections, seen and unseen. Be
the wave. Receiving and giving. The heart-mind regains mastery. This
is the expansion of the new energy line. Heart wisdom is the refined
light-mind-intelligence. Be her expression. Here is the map. The heart
holds it with its compass in place for safekeeping. We love you. Thank
you!*

Inward Journey - Waking Up the Cells

In a wonderful self-training session, I was guided through deep
cleansing, brightening, raising vibration, then laid down and started
toe-tapping practice, while listening to drumming music, going at a
nice comfortable pace for a little over 50 minutes, then stopped and
laid completely still. I earnestly stilled my mind, watching all the
swirling of incomings and outgoings, including my thoughts, of
course. Bringing my mind back to the beautiful energy movement
sensations along my legs, arms, and spine, allowing my body to
breathe and relax more and more. Experiencing the merging of
physical and energy breathing processes is blissful and always
creates even more space in the minds. The healing journey now
turns inward, expanding into the inner worlds.

*I have quite an intense feeling of inward movement beginning in my
forehead, sensing a tight tunnel spiraling motion. It becomes such a
strong pull that it almost turns into a headache. I'm not startled by*

the discomfort, just feel a great deal of pressure from the forehead first, then throughout my whole head as if the center of the brain turned into a potent magnet causing my entire head to experience an intense pull toward its core. I focus on emptying, and relaxing more, then suddenly I'm shown as a tiny version of myself floating inside my brain, directing where to flow next, weightless, and so comfortable.

I hear myself begin to give some commands, not too bossy, just direct, and assertive, but also joyful, just as I would normally speak and encourage others. This is a wonderful experience of witnessing me directing the show here, instantly feeling so proud of myself. So, I begin informing the brain of what's about to happen. Ok, everybody, here we go, get ready! There are some intense swoosh sounds and motions of sweeping side to side, up and down, and bright flashes of light creating circuit explosions and sparkles. Some of these particles of light haven't flickered in a very long time. Finally, everyone is getting quite excited. I am cautious about entering the throat gateway, this is a special, delicate place.

The tiny version of myself floats down and begins to change position, standing up-right, facing backward, toward the spine. I begin to unhook some form of rivets from the base of the head where it meets the atlas and axis. This motion, almost resembling when you take a hanger off a rack, creates a release that ripples down and out. I see myself turning around, observing a flat ring expand and shift outward, resembling the shape of an old LP album. I look so excited, singing loudly and joyously. It's actually getting a bit hilarious from my point of view as the observer, watching this whole scene with such interest, not getting in the way – fully aware of me, the witness, thoroughly entertained and in wonder, and the tiny version of me, completely in charge, doing the work. This is so amazing, I say to myself.

We're now diving into the chest area. I am so extremely loud that it's almost over the top. The observer self is totally cracking up at this entire scene. My goal is to purposely awaken and stimulate all of the cells. It's a collective wake-up call. So here I am, floating around, jumping with joy, and dancing a bit, moving around like a very charismatic public speaker at an uplifting convention. My cells are the *audience here, this is awesome. I am reprimanding them but also so sweetly and lovingly encouraging them to clean things up and get back to work. I'm so overly pumped that I even make a side-high kick to my heart, not with the intention to hurt, more like an assertive encouraging nudge - here you go, take that, let's wake up everybody. The heart begins to stream another rhythm, along with my regular heartbeat simultaneously running a different pulse.*

Coming down to my shoulder blades, I make strong wiping motions as if thick spider webs covered an entrance. I then place a silky, lightweight veil across the shoulders, trapezius muscles, and upper back, realizing it looks more like wings, offering protection. After placing this veil on the shoulders, holding it in place with beads, it immediately attaches itself to my body and the beads are absorbed into my skin, being fully restored after having been removed long ago.

I'm now proceeding to the solar plexus area. There is some serious clapping here, just like a sports coach at an important match, making loud sounds and crouching down to ensure I get to all the cells, even the ones stuck in the dark, back there. Many fat cells are covered in a slimy substance, an unpleasant sticky goo. I am telling these cells, you know what, it's been enough of this, what is this? Let's clean this up, c'mon. Noticeably, a few are actually beginning to respond, then more and more follow, twisting and stretching, wiggling a bit, as if emerging from a spell. Waking up, they become entirely filled with bright light, rippling outward to affect all the neighboring cells in the entire abdominal cavity, reaching all of the organs here.

Now facing the kidneys, I bow to them in reverence, with a grateful mind, encouraging them to feel that loving vital energy from before birth. Whispers are appropriate here, they don't need me to shout or make loud noises, just a quiet, loving voice of encouragement is what they need. Seeing myself as if I was in front of two enormous elephants, they look at me, so tired but strong, extremely grateful I'm here. It's quite emotional, but my tiny self is full of explosive love, and they can feel it too. Reaching for the adrenals, I caress them as if they were cute little kittens with such a soft, loving touch.

My tiny self turns around and opens her arms like an orchestra director. Let's go, everyone. Here we go again. Please, she says, you absolutely must be your best selves. Mediocre doesn't cut it anymore. What is that? You can do it, and you must. This is our job. Then I see this blob-cell approach and realize this is supposed to be the supervisor of this area. His shirt is wrinkled and a bit dirty. As he comes up and tries to straighten out, I can see right through him. I know what you're doing over here; it's been too easy, and lazy, but it's ok, it's time now, c'mon, we can do it. You can do it. Some cells make faces of discontent and say, oh man... ok, fine, but most cells don't even rebel. They actually know better that this is what it's all about – do your job correctly!

I'm fully aware, within this journey, my mind is showing me references to hotel life. Mediocre conduct and service training have always motivated me to make a positive impact, and create significant change.

The motivational speaker self continues to push the cells, you know better, what is going on; let's make her more comfortable; you're making things more challenging; you must help make things clear and smooth.

As this chaotic, cleansing hurricane is happening and I see everyone hard at work, my tiny self floats down to the bottom of my pelvic floor. It's nice and quiet down here. I sit in a half-lotus meditation posture, close my eyes, and become very still. Surrounded by a very subtle transparent bubble of protection, I begin to pray, asking that the vastness of who I am, come down to fill the voids. As I step into emptiness first, then expand into spaciousness, I feel that pull in my head again. **Continued...**

Connection with the Council of 11

From the top of my brain, a waterfall shoots down my energy line into where I'm quietly sitting, in my lower dahnjon - rushing waters of liquid light of extraordinary intensity. Instant alignment through a flash of lightning packed with information.

In a state of complete presence, opening to receive, master-teacher El Morya steps forward from what seems like a cloud. Telepathic communication begins. We are so happy you detect us more now.

There are 11 of us. We are the Council of 11. Yes, answering my silent question, you know this group, as you connect through Serapis Bey. Some of us are entire groups, representing more than one but acting as one, the Hathors. Eleven of us, as companions, including you. You serve with us, and we serve with you throughout time. We must work prominently together. Now is the time to merge the teachings, as you know, for you carry them in unique ways. The process has been evolving for a very long time.

I then feel this significant pressure on my temples, above my eyebrows, and a very intense contraction on my forehead. I ask him if this is a signature feeling so I can recognize him when I reach out to him; he says, sure, but you have other feelings you've experienced before and already know when we communicate. You don't have to work so hard, just need to release the doubt protection mechanism. We are all here, all the time. You are here too; a portion of you is where you are now, and a portion is here with us, supporting this connection.

In the next instant, I'm shown all these beings in a joyful, party-like mood. They're jumping up and down, hugging each other, like they just won a trip around the world or something. So much joy, high-fiving, kissing each other on the cheeks, and celebrating. Then I noticed they are hugging, kissing, and hugging me, as in this being that is also me there with them, with the 11. I see myself smiling and almost laughing. They are so hilarious. They're celebrating that this connection is happening in this way. They are cheering because I am paying attention in a new way now.

I ask, what do I do? What should I do? He says, more will come. Don't concern yourself with what. Just write. In writing, it will come. Your unique way is unfolding, and you are moving into alignment. Rest assured, what you sense and hear, what you intuit, is in destined alignment. It's us and you, so trust and just follow the guidance because it comes from you. We are creating together. I suddenly get flashes of what looks like an island. I immediately know it is Crete, hearing I must review the ancient language codes, rituals, and ceremonies.

It will come lovely, and he tells me so lovingly, you're already aware of your habit of wanting more information, which sometimes prevents the natural flow; you don't need to know. He is so kind and gracious. Guidance will come, he says, no need to overthink or overwork. Why, I say, I want to see it all now. It may be too strong, he says. You have to function and not fall into distractions and distortions. He shows me an image of physical impairment, a little at a time, otherwise, the body may suffer. What is needed has already all been delivered and is currently stored. It will become more apparent as things unfold, offering the energy space to be delivered when it is needed. The work is communicating the heart vibration.

I sense space, silence, and peace. I come back to a more awake state. Something changed. I feel full. As I begin to feel my body, apparently nothing has changed, but change has indeed occurred. There is brightness, no longer tension, and a sense of returning from a pleasant visit with my best friends after ages of not seeing each other. Such a sweet feeling in my heart. There is work to be uncovered that will nourish me and others. I am so uplifted and grateful.

My body begins to move and stretch, fully awake, I follow the nudge to go count the newly collected feathers placed near some of my instruments. I count them, there are large ones, one tiny one, a hawk, a mug pie, doves, white and gray, colorful combinations, and they're just perfect. There are eleven feathers. I smile and say, ok, you guys, so clever, and hear them through my heart-mind. Just trust. We're here all the time. There is nothing to worry about. We got you. Thank you!

19

THE NEXT PHASE OF THE SPIRAL

Walking through a Threshold

What felt so triggering before is like watching some awful commercial for a new reality show. It's a bit disturbing, but completely powerless in piercing through me, in being fully absorbed, energy and vibration no longer drawn to my center. It's loudly visible, I'm entirely aware of it, but passing by in such a way that I just don't even go back to it as I would in the past. It is neutrally dismissed as an external phenomenon that doesn't belong in my field and doesn't benefit me anymore.

Mentally going back to those triggering thoughts, ruminating on what was said, how it was said, the underlying misunderstanding, beliefs, and judgments has gradually become a less intrusive, tormenting, and unsettling process.

The beginning of Summer felt like I've been emerging from a cave. I word it this way because I physically feel as if I've walked through a passageway, and I've also experienced it in dreams.

At the edge of an opening, I won't look back, having a feeling of satisfaction for what's back there, behind me, curious and hopeful about what's out there. I crouch down on my knees, looking outward.

Gentle voices say, it's ok, now is a good time, we'll help you. A beautiful, peaceful sensation came over me upon waking up.

Old, heavy feelings had been processing for a while, and this phase now felt complete. I stepped into a new field where I was presented with opportunities to go deeper, to see myself in greater light, to embrace everything and to enjoy life more, by doing what I genuinely felt was in my heart, following inspiration and inspiring others by just being me. I've always had a strong will, sometimes very imbalanced, yes, but I know what it means to have determination. Adjusting to a new way of living, a new way to align the fire in the heart and body with the fire of the spirit, represents a new beginning. It is the beginning of a more profound way to trust and connect, and to live within a new quality of alignment, of balanced will.

I have experienced smallness in aspects of my life. When things show up even more, it's an opportunity to become more present. This is a good sign. It means the contracted feeling, the smallness, gradually moves outward, like pain. The neutral observation of the same behaviors, all the unsaid, unseen, unheard information is captured and processed. The processing system developed new, upgraded filters, which are now more engaged than before. What felt like another dagger, it was now received and quickly processed into another form of fuel. My inner pendulum swing has returned to a manageable ebb and flow. The quick spikes, the more significant swings, are swiftly caught and reminded to return to their natural rhythm.

The process of alignment through the three soul-portals continues its evolving refinement. Alignment beyond this circulation system is happening with a considerable amount of information exchange between each layer of energy-spiritual fields. I know all kinds of things are happening behind the scenes with the full direction of the higher self. The small mind, which likes to organize, coordinate, micromanage everything, and often take over, actually needs to let this alignment expansion happen. The higher self is way wiser than me, Enrica, in this life, so why should I worry or concern myself with the need to know everything? There is no point, actually. It's not my place anymore. Needing to know is an extension of control, a symptom of contraction, and I see it as the opposite of trust and presence.

The focus is directed toward continuously up-leveling awareness - the beautiful, bright information I'm swimming in, accepting the process as is, opening to the guidance system in more ways. Anything else presented is a distraction, including my struggle with rude people, as a simple example, is just another clever indicator to turn the spiritual eyes toward the inner teacher-healer. Why is this triggering? A simple answer will be received, and then we must move on. There is no need to dwell. Dwelling equals over-thinking, another symptom of contraction - the small mind.

We all possess the desire and will to *create the life we are meant to live*. Often, we suppress this mindset due to survival, who doesn't? We're people. Throughout life, we are shown so many different types of experiences all designed to help us create our best selves. This is true for everyone. I think we genuinely know this to be a rediscovered truth within. However, we continue to be swayed in many directions, away from alignment, depending on what holds more magnetism and what's apparently stronger, louder, and more logical, in line with the rules. We forget our own magnetic energy and power is a force to be recovered and refined, and this work alone is what will help us regain trust in our inner compass, clear our lenses to detect the experiences designed just for us, by us, to create what truly brings us closer to our higher self.

We are an encyclopedia of information packed with irrelevant pop-up ads. We tend to perceive pop-up ads as our own intelligence. This is the small screen we're focused on without noticing the immense 360-degree Omni max outdoor movie theater experience behind it, surrounding us, as we're stuck on this small tube TV device. It makes me smile with sweetness in my heart as I see myself fixed on this little TV watching the ads that, apparently, make complete sense, but in truth, it's exactly like taking some painkillers – make it go away, never mind communicating with the root cause. We should be tired of numbing and looking the other way, don't you think?

Venting about suffering is not expressed to perpetuate victim consciousness, it is intended to circulate feelings and thoughts so they can move in whatever direction they need to, solely to undergo purification on all levels of sacred fire energy. The fire of the body, the heart, and our soul-spirit merging. Movement prevents stagnation, and when there is stagnation, the heavy muddy waters in the swamp must go through deep cleaning. When cleansing becomes a regular daily spiritual practice, after several deep initiatory experiences, stagnancy may only accumulate on the surface, and consistent gentle cleansing is all it takes to return to a natural flow.

Movement, including internal and external training practices, have supported me in understanding more who I am and what I want to create. I purposely use the term *training* because it's continuous. Daily spiritual practice of connecting *is* training.

Our role is not to suffer. When suffering shows up, we need clarification about what *we think we want and need*. Everyday life situations, even the mundane and superficial, are just opportunities to help us return to who we are.

Returning to my homeland presented me with resolution, closure, and the opportunity to move forward. Creating healthy boundaries, opening my heart to hold more compassion for myself first, then for others and the Earth. Releasing the hold on distorted ideas of what I want, like, or need. Continuing to build a stronger foundation and structure for myself, not because anyone told me it's what I should do, but because I recognize a deeper alignment and choose to follow that. Alignment now seen as a sense perception, like neutrality and presence, all belonging to our soul-spirit mind complex.

When I faced challenging situations that made me feel small, I knew very important work needed to be done here, to honestly embrace more aspects of myself, including my triggers, and of course, accept all the people in my life. But that's not the complete picture. As I tried to describe earlier, the work was more about recognizing how much tension I held inside, keeping some of my armor lifted for survival. Why is all that still necessary? It's no longer the proper way to operate. Dissolution and transformation are a new form of evolution, how life wants to be experienced, and resisting is denying ourselves more light.

Furthermore, the guidance system has repeatedly delivered clarification that I'm physically here in this part of the world to absorb the ancient beads of light that I stored in the Earth back in ancient times. A confirmation signal of this guidance is the fact that, even though some of the challenges would have made anyone say, forget this, I'm leaving, I actually felt and feel a deep contentment and connection with why I'm here. There is a teaching, my teaching, being transmitted through the Earth. *Preparation is key. Making more room in the mind is the way.* I'm putting more and more pieces together, fascinated by how messages are just there catching my attention, speaking.

Here is what's really happening. This is just another turning point, another sharp turn upwards, catching the next step up the spiraling staircase. When conflict between the small self, or left-brain ego, is at a standstill, when it encounters the true self, the true nature. It's happened before and recognizes its effects. A whirlwind of contraction, then the quiet space, which is the eye of the hurricane, a chance to see what's happening, to in-gather through the tall funnel connecting the above and the below, then allowing the strong winds to pass, this time standing stronger and more resilient than before. It's when we can realize who's really communicating. The lower-self mind or, the higher-self mind, and within these are multiple aspects - sub-layers, we can say. It's a beautiful process of paying closer attention.

The sharp curve, which seems like a rough uphill slope, is the feeling of moving against the current - there is so much pressure. This contraction may cause internal turmoil, pain on all levels, and stagnancy. We are taught to shy away from this, that it's a clear sign that *the universe says no*, but in reality, what's happening defines the moment right before we can see the beautiful, natural flow that magically unfolds. Like twisting a wet rag soaked in water, we compress and contract, holding tension, then we wash and cleanse, using our pure intention to move forward, gaining the ability to see through it, reaching the quiet, still place in the center of the center.

The sharp curve is only a perception. When the base of the spiral is vast, we can hardly tell we're going in a circle-like motion. When we go higher and higher, the circular turns and spin become tighter; this appears as contraction, which creates a resistance phenomenon as the ego feels squeezed and fearful of death. Death is exactly what's happening here. The squeezing of the old through the container, which is the body and mind, to allow for a purge and spacious flow as we go through the tightest point. It's not one-single point; it is a continuation of the spiral, just becoming small and compact, like the apex of the pyramid, then widening more and more to its other extremity, the widest point - continuing into the smaller and tighter concentric circle until it comes to the smallest point. The multi-dimensional progress, which in 2D may resemble a series of triangular shapes, creates interconnected diamonds - the pyramid's base is connected to another base, rising through the apex, which is connected to the next apex, and so on.

When we come to the tightest point, the left-brain ego, which has a partial, restricted view of the incredible waves of transformations, wants to stop and stay behind; why is she doing this again? There she goes reading that stuff, practicing this and that mantra, chanting, singing, dancing, again with the instruments, that's a waste of time, nobody actually cares, you need to go back, we were really happy then, you just couldn't see it, let's go back.

Here is the moment where our soul is right in front of us, the two apexes touching each other, nose to nose, eye to eye. I can see you, do you see me? The perception of the small space, the tight passageway, is, again, just a perception. As spiritual energy refines with each word we speak and each breath we take, we pass through the quantum particle onto the vastness of what is, which is more of our true essence.

We continue stepping forward, and this is the work - keep going. When we think we got it, we must carefully ask, what can I do to integrate all the learnings so that I can keep going to see what's next?

When I see this series of spirals connecting and creating through All-time, I also see other sequences occurring simultaneously. There is clear insight of at least one other spiral moving side by side with the one we are participating in, with this personality in this life; the others contain fractals of our soul. We experience these energies as guides, angels, and ancestors. They are expressions of our unique vibrational essence, our own soul and spirit united, also experiencing and creating in All-time. The wiser me in thirty years from now, the fresh new baby excited to be a second child, the adventurous traveler, and so many more *me* that are ready for me to connect with.

When asking about physical pain and what it needs, there is clarity in the message: *focus on the soul light, not the ego restrictions, through continuous purification training and continuous evolution to refine your light. Create something you infuse your vibration and resonance into; this is the true calling. Through this body and ego personality, you're elevating the vibration to meet your true center. Communicate balance and peaceful resilience, expanding through the center of the heart vortex.*

The body shows us simple messages. It acts as a portal. It is a doorway surrounded by scary creatures, darkness, and fire. We usually tend to stop, turn around and find an apparently easier passageway, or we try to numb the urge to walk down the path of increased connection. The path may require entry through mysterious doorways, making us return to old mental patterns, the left-brain ego wanting to feel safe, happy to present disguise remedies and solutions, the fast-acting medicine, the tiny box of the old and outdated notions, creating intricate unseen distortions. Truth is shown when we can fully discern the information presented to us, and recognize our internal healing power. Messages arise such as, this may be good for me, but I need to be gentle and try to relax enough to listen to my body and make sure I don't strain myself while moving forward focusing keenly on what the body is telling me. I can understand her messages to help me move and navigate in ways that will open up blocked energy and allow me to fully unleash the divine heavenly power of true light - my healing superpower. We all have it, not just a select few.

This superpower is what we're made of. We must fully embrace it. Healing messages differ from: no, this is stupid, and my body hurts, which probably means it's not right, and I shouldn't do it. I refuse to open my mind because I already know it's not the way. All the info I gathered online and from the experts tells me ancient wisdom doesn't help, they must be right. I will go with what my friends and doctors say. I don't want to move forward, why is there a need to change anyway?

This entire back-and-forth phenomenon of trying to find clarity is challenging. The difference between these two messages can be subtle, maybe even undetectable. It requires energy and spiritual senses to work closely with the physical senses, like the nerves in our physical body, as they are communication antennas. The brain won't know any better if the communication is distorted. This is why the brain filters must be clear, polished, and refined, otherwise the soul-spirit connection is intermittent, unstable, superficial, and three dimensional, which is downright incomplete.

This *is* all about communication - who's talking, and who's listening. To trust our physical senses is one thing; to trust the complex encyclopedia of wisdom that combines and complements all types of communication *in one* is another. This is my study and work, which for me is the most important direction I can dedicate focus to. Within the physical senses, which are six as they include thinking (brain-processing), there are many more dimensions to them. Internal dimensions are found living deep down into the smallest particles of our nervous systems, endocrine systems, blood, and water. Communication expands to include the energy senses, another vast sphere of sense perceptions, some of which are coming back online as we brighten our awareness. Spiritual insight represents another grander sphere of perception, which effortlessly communicates through all layers and vibration in our expanded fields.

The empowering phenomenon occurring for all of us, whether we are consciously participating in it or not, is that our inner communication technology merges with a universal mind that has the capacity to hold the dimensions of all of our sense perceptions - therefore essence, intelligence, minds, and fractals of self, in addition to all other aspects of universal mind expressions.

We are all experiencing this expansion and upgrade. What we can do to prepare is up to each individual. There is no right way, just your own. Continuing to move inward before we can expand outward, gives us brighter insight and a greater opportunity to discern the quality of information we are receiving. Let's connect and communicate with the messages of pain, confusion, or bliss and joy; additionally, notice and carefully consider if messages represent another band-aid and disguise, such as a pretty ornate carnival mask, interesting and attractive but not the truth.

Dreams ~ Visions ~ Journeys

Frantically Going through Motions

I had gone to the osteopath to see if he could help me with my back and neck inflammation. He worked on my head, my jaw and sacrum. I could feel more space and he clearly felt the shift in tension being held. I felt a surge of energy and I had to hold light language and a strong movement through the spine. I had received an activation just like during a healing session, after initial activation fire strokes. I allowed the energy to flow throughout and also experienced some vocal cords dryness and cough. A good clearing sign. That night, here is the dream experience I had.

My whole body feels like it's hooked up to an electric power grid, nerve pain down my legs and arms. I am aware an adjustment is underway, working away to help me through this phase. Some old wounds are coming up. I have such conflict inside and deep frustration. I am in the kitchen, busy over the stove, cooking rice, some vegetables, pasta, and salmon. I must be going mad because it's not even 5 in the morning. Why would I be cooking all this food? I look frantic going through the motions, but I also feel I'm losing my mind. My nerve condition takes over and I start crying. Jason comes in the kitchen to confront me, which helps me quiet down, although I can't stop crying. I then start screaming in the empty space, crying, and screaming at the top of my lungs calling out for help. Screaming for my mom, I shout, Mamma, aiutami (help me)!

Preparing for a Big Trip

I am preparing for a trip. Some people are here, they seem like family. Mom's energy and personality as in this life are clear, the others, I'm not sure who they are. There are clothes everywhere, while going through them, I recognize the pink Korean blouse, the purple sweatshirts, and pants sets - training uniforms. Neatly folded clothes lay on the bed, while I go back and forth to a suitcase, clearly packing. The people in the room with me are making jokes, laughing, remembering moments in time, being very playful and joyful. I get a sense this is a decisive time, embarking on a new journey, and my family, in spirit, is there helping me. My face looks a bit serious, only smiling here and there, recalling what they're sharing as a group. I don't look so impressed and happy about the outcome of some of the stories being remembered; on the other hand, they are more cheerful and joyful, joking around, and being totally relaxed. They truly love and accept me, trying to make things lighter for me. I know I won't see them for a while, and enjoying this time together before my trip is important.

There are many pieces of clothing for me to choose from. As I sift through them, I select the few key pieces that are more important for this trip, the purple sweatshirt, pink blouse, and training uniforms.

We are now in a parking lot. It's an open empty space with just our two vehicles. Mom and one other person are with me. I now have to move my things from one vehicle to this other little, tiny car, which will be my ride from now on. Everyone is standing here, hanging out as I gather my things. I now realize what that heavy feeling was. It's melancholy or nostalgia. I'm about to leave, and I knew it was coming; it's definitely also exciting, but sad at the same time.

The selected pieces of clothing call my attention. I'm supposed to wear the pink blouse on my journey. I actually need it now, it's time to change. Mom says to just change in the car, which I do. After slipping the blouse on, I'm finally ready. As we start to say goodbye everyone acts as if it's a casual farewell, then I turn toward mom and the other person close to her, connecting one last time. Although reluctant because I don't want to leave them, I do feel ready and prepared.

I wake up feeling very heavy. My whole body is so heavy as if it was 2 in the morning, and I haven't slept in days. I look over, and it's 7:30 am. My body feels incredibly heavy; this is incredible. In my awake-sleep state, I hear my inner voice saying, it's because you were just *there with us, and it's so much denser over here.*

The Big Feast
There are many people sitting around a very long table. I'm next to a giant being, a guardian and wise man, who is on my left. Compared to him, and everyone around me, my body looks so small. He helps me by explaining what is happening around the table, the different languages spoken, all the different kinds of people, where they came from, etc. I am quietly observing, taking it all in. There are lots of different things in front of me, all kinds of dishes I'm not familiar with, some soupy substance that was so delicious, and something that looked like giant shrimp, but another form of crustacean. I haven't seen anything like this before. Noise and laughter from the gathering filled the room. It's very joyful, like a bunch of friends coming together for an occasion.

I stay present and enjoy the food, watching all the interactions around the long table. The guardian next to me is paying close attention to me while engaging with someone else simultaneously. He's focused on me, ensuring I'm alright, checking in with me in a loving way. I feel so grateful and stunned that I can sit at this table of higher realms beings who look like giants. I'm so little in comparison.

Receiving Scientific Instructions
I am saying words I don't recognize. I think some of the terms are scientific in nature. Something about time, but I'm not sure what they mean, unable to understand the concept. In a classroom setting, writing with an old antique calligraphy pen with ink, I am taking notes and instructions, agreeing, and nodding in approval of what is being said as if I totally got it. Coming out of the dream slightly, I can see myself looking back toward me, here, waking up, and I say, she's awake, we have to go and continue another time. I see myself gathering my things and preparing to return to my body. The work isn't done, but I'm awake, and totally interrupted, then hear myself say out loud, no, please go ahead, I'm sorry, please finish.

Going Through a Tunnel - Accessing Another Dimension

Curling up like a ball in my cocoon, I can see in my inner eye the bright lights coming toward me, and then flowing from me outward in front of me. Moving a small glowing ball toward and away from me, back and forth. It starts making a swirling movement, a spiraling tunnel. I recognize it as I often experience it. In a flash, I can see the other side clearly, and in another flash, I am going through the tunnel. Everything is so clear. I suddenly jolt back to this side of the tunnel, with a surprised look. With the intention of going there again, the swirling tunnel appears instantly as the thought of walking through it comes into my mind. My vision needs to adjust, and just like that, upon thinking about it, my sight improves, zoomed in and crystal clear. It happens in a flash, lightning fast.

There are lots of flowers on a pillow. Although it's clear, I'm trying to understand what I'm looking at. I am aware that I can create this tunnel with my thought alone. As I get closer, visualizing it and intending to go through, then boom, there it is. I say to myself within the dream, wow, I must practice this more. As I try again, I hear a conversation. I hear a woman's name, Laura, and another word after the name, which I can't recall. There are two words, a name, and a last name or title. I feel like I need to remember this name.

I wake up with a sense of excitement. I must practice popping in and out of these worlds. Nothing else is important. Who is this Laura? What does Laura mean? Who is she?

Laurus in Latin is Apollo's sacred tree, symbol of glory and wisdom - the laurel

Bluebird Visit - Inspired Message

A small blue bird lands on my hair. I've seen him before; last time also landing on my hair, on the right side of my head, this time he's more toward the back. I jump a little, not expecting it, but don't feel scared. The spirit messenger tells me I hold something important that I need to fully accept and share. As I upgrade vibration and teachings, there is something new. I do not fully understand what this is or what it looks like for my life moving forward. But I do hear and know intensely that all I need to do now is flow, surrender, and allow, all

Yin aspects of the self.

For 40+ years, I've been a major Yang-ruled person. More balance is what aligns me with my purpose. This is why my whole right side feels pain - manifesting through inflammation. I am being pushed into alignment toward a center I've compromised as I've been operating with my entire right side of the body, the yang fire-dominant energy side. Now it is time for the left, yin water-dominant energy side to lead.

Inspired message: healing is afoot, dear love. You are moving and flowing as you should. We are so in love with the offerings of your heart. It will manifest according to the Earth Water flow current that runs and connects you to your own code crystal portals. You can see. Make a plan - prepare and listen. We are here to encourage you in this next phase. Study to reveal ancient laws and mysteries of wisdom you are ready to open back up to. The love-light color spectrum has already been delivered in the center and around layers of energy bodies as they process the healing properties for the recalibration of energy lines, vertical axis, and horizontal lines. You have been given a code to share. Revelations follow the purification and void. We are always guiding. You are here with us as you too are guiding. So it has been in the All-time. You are us. We are you - together. We move oceans and stand with the mountains. You are the key to us evolving together. Let us open. Let your light move. Thank you.

Destruction and Heavy Burdens

It's a dark room, looks like a pantry, we're in trouble. Next door are people, they make me think they're mobsters, as they're planning how to get rid of us. Others are in the same room as them. I'm scared and keep my head down. I feel like I can get out soon and have to try to get provisions. Jason is somewhere else; he told me he needed peanut butter, except I only found bread. There's another cabinet in the room where these terrible people are, but I may be kept as a prisoner and don't want to risk it. They open the door, and everybody in the pantry steps back, afraid that someone else would be dragged to another area and probably sacrificed. One of the leaders recognizes me, and I ask if I could get something from the cabinet in their room. I thought, in the dream, wow, so gutsy! He agrees but looks at me as if I'm pushing it. I can't find peanut butter, and I'm able to leave.

Suddenly, someone says they detected an upcoming earthquake. I am able to walk away from this place carrying three heavy bags. It was so hard. The earthquake occurs, followed by severe flooding, the end of the world scene, it's terrifying. These damn bags are so heavy! Somebody tells me to go that way because it's safer. As I proceed, I realize it's an angel suggesting the best way for me. The water is coming, but there is a small opening I can go through. It's best to drop a bag and try to push it through this opening, then go after it, but it doesn't fit. On the right, there is another way down. One of my hands is free, I must have dropped a bag or two. Reaching for my phone, calling Jason, I start to cry, telling him what is happening. Hearing my words is heartbreaking, I'm so tired, I think I'm about to die, I can't keep going, that's it.

Light Beams on Ancient Maps

It's a dark evening, and I find myself in my own quarters, with a lovely balcony and lots of room. This is a large hotel that looks like an old-fashioned mansion. I am here for an event with many other women, all part of a family, getting ready and preparing the space for this event. I hear the word becoming *as I explore my surroundings; everyone is busy taking care of many details revolving around this occasion - the event of becoming. Some of the women seem very young, others more senior. There are no male figures. I keep coming back to my room, needing to be alone, feeling a bit disoriented, not knowing what to expect.*

I then see myself in what seems like a doctor's office located in the same building. Everyone has to go through this visit before the event. It's my turn. I realize that compared to all the others, I'm a foreigner here. The lady doctor makes some comments regarding my origins and where I have lived before; she then gives me a full check-up. Several world maps cover the walls of the doctor's office, some I cannot recognize. She keeps looking at the maps while she examines me, going back and forth as if searching for something, or making comparisons between what she sees on each map and me. I sit up on the table and look toward the wall, but focusing my sight is quite difficult. One map in particular stands out. I do not recognize this place on Earth.

Then the doctor realizes she needs to change maps. From the ceiling, she pulls down another map, which looks like the South Pacific Ocean. It has some islands like Australia, but it looks different from present-day maps. I am momentarily shocked, struggling to believe just how far I am from what I consider home, on another continent altogether. It looks like Australia, but only because that's my reference point now, it doesn't seem right, it's another large island. The doctor is using maps to show where I'm from, and this particular map is a very ancient one with unique writing all around it. There is a big island and some surrounding land masses in the sea. I am totally doubting my geography knowledge within the dream, feeling entirely confused, but also mesmerized at the site of this very old map. The doctor acts like everything is normal, looking over at the map, then back at me, carefully watching where beams of light appear throughout the map. She realizes perhaps we need to look at another one, and pulls down this other ancient map, then instantly says, oh yeah, here it is. Light beams appear all over this other map. It's the same location, but this last map was of another time altogether. My light is sourced from an ancient land and residual vibration is still fully present. The maps not only indicated location - space - but also time.

As I begin to wake up, I naturally think of Lemuria/Mu as it was in the Pacific Ocean. It could be another planet and star system complex with a vast ocean like the Pacific or another time on Earth.

New Energy

The new sunlight energy, the yin aspect of fire, provides a new source for moving through blockages. The three portals align with the one Will. You can find the soul-spirit/spirit-soul complex expansion through discipline. Upon receiving, allow the energy to fully move through you. Communicate it well. An aligned, light heart and an open gateway of the throat complex can deliver pure vibration.

The yang quality of water energy is the power of flow. The current that moves the ocean, your name-vibration. New life appears. Accept this flow to and from you. Record the signals. The old must be washed away. See the new view of the laws - time, space, light, dark, open, close, up, down, in, out. A new understanding has been delivered and must now be shared.

The foundation is strong. Follow the rhythm of the universe. Listen. Record. Be. The vibration of creation is occurring. Your instruments are ready. Remain focused like a laser beam. Relaxed, open, stable, and focused in order to create and spread the new fire/water light frequency to others.

Door to Infinity - Meeting a Helping Friend

In a series of flashing images presented to me, I see myself rebelling against some form of injustice. Flashbacks and recollections of leadership scenarios where I had to stand up for someone. The feeling associated with these memories is that of heaviness and conflict. I'm in a dark room. At the edge of this dark room, a door is opening, which allows me to see the bright, colorful room on the other side, and can see people out there. The only light source comes through this doorway. Many people are casually chatting away, then I see my dear friend Theresa. She turns, recognizes me, then comes toward the doorway into my dark side of the threshold. I begin to cry as we share a long loving hug, I'm so happy to see her. She then goes back to her side of the threshold.

I return to the feeling of being around low vibration thickness with all the energy of those conflicting moments, memories of unfairness. I scream to express my grief and resistance to how terrible things are on Earth, venting about how asleep we are as people. Too many don't care at all about the Earth and humanity. There is such a strong urge to scream, and rebel; something dramatic needs to happen to help people wake up.

Theresa is a dear friend who passed away two weeks after this dream vision. She was in the bright room full of joyful people gathering and catching up with each other. I could see her through this doorway. She saw me and could communicate with me. We hugged; she was so loving with her angel-blue eyes and sweet heart. I could feel her deeply. I knew in the dream that she was transitioning, and she was just showing me to be myself. She was a creator, an artist, and a fun-loving person who truly lived. She suffered, and her heart was so big. We've shared so many laughs, as well as tears together. In the dream, she was my bridge helper. I was on my side of the door, the dark room, struggling with all the conflicts, resistance, narrow-minded, old ideas, systems, mentality, and the shallowness of everything. On her side of the threshold, the infinity room was another thing entirely.

The dark room appears as this little box, while outside the box is the boundaryless infinity. How narrow-minded can we be to not see or know this? Why?

I am so grateful Theresa came to help me, hug me, and show me the infinite loving light of our true nature.

The Boat with the Gods - Writing Fish in Greek

In a large learning hall, I'm being instructed on several subjects. Through a large modern wall screen, I'm remotely communicating and chatting with my teachers, who appear as Egyptian and Greek gods on a boat. Is this the solar barque? One in particular, Ast-Isis, is so loving and encouraging. I show her that I could write the symbols she gave me last time, and I'm doing my best writing them correctly, taking a snapshot and sending it to her. She is so happy to see it, showing the others. I feel a little inadequate, but she makes me feel wonderful. She then places this image on her upper chest area, which becomes a tattoo on her high heart entrance. I see it more clearly now, it's the word ichthys *in Greek* ἰχθύς *- fish. I know within the dream that the fish is Osiris. It's the body, the khat, symbolizing death and rebirth. This is what's happening, dying, and becoming. The process is supported, and I am loved.*

I show the gods on the boat that I'm on an island, able to get on a boat all by myself. There are a few other boats out at sea. They seem happy and satisfied. A few other women are present on my boat, and each has a specific task. We are strong.

The gods are joyful, loving and encouraging. I miss them so much. Ast-Isis is sitting there so excited about my news and updates. This is a full-on catch-up conversation. In the dream vision, I recognize that they already know everything, but I see how amazing it is that they're lovingly checking in on me and allowing me to show them what I'm doing, what I've learned, offering such interest, and showing me how happy they are about me, just as I am. They are genuinely huge fans.

My Subconscious is a Hotel

I walk in the entryway of an old downtown building, with an ornate ceiling and marble everywhere. Right in front of the door is a large table, resembling a church altar, it's a lobby. The entryway consists of two sets of white door panels and one set of brown panels. I find myself walking through this entryway twice. Upon walking in, the first time, I realize this place represents my mind. Startled at the thought, I hurry right out, not wanting to be intrusive or make too much noise. I'm feeling a little scared, but curious at the same time, determined to go through this initial entryway and see what else is there. Giving it another try, I push the doors open and walk into an open space with a massive staircase going down. The scene resembles a hotel with many doors along the halls, and I find myself in the back of the house, the service area. The stairs heading down are more vivid and transparent, suggesting I should follow them. It's a very long staircase leading to unseen areas of the hotel. While trying to be cautious so as not to make too much noise, I hear something. At the end of the staircase is a long open space, with a wide doorway on the opposite side of the room and a heavy-set person at the threshold, holding something in their hands. Focusing in, I can now see it's a spray bottle, thinking to myself, this is someone from housekeeping. The person is dark, and facial features aren't visible, it's more like a shadow; due to the size, I gather it's a strong, shady side of me, on the edge of this large doorway.

There is another door on the left, and a little man with a strong negative attitude comes to the threshold. He wears an apron, making me think he's from the kitchen. This is who prepares our food? Damn, I hear myself say. He has such a bad attitude, and is being pretty obnoxious, rambling, talking under his breath; you're lost, this is not where you should be. He gives me such a bad feeling I turn around right away and run up the stairs, returning to the initial entryway. Another person shows up, startling me, but I soon realize she's the Human Resources manager, which settles my mind, knowing I'm ok.

As we walk down the hallway, she starts talking about an issue and wants to help me. I am telling her I need answers and she can help me navigate where I can find the information I'm looking for.

So, we walk down what resembles the back of the house at the San Diego property, down toward the accounting office. We walk into an area with large office spaces where three people are busy at work. I recognize one of them although he seems different, and see myself joking around, talking to him, like old friends. I am waiting for something, unsure if I'm going to receive information or if it's time to go back. Sitting here, contemplating these images, I'm given a glimpse of my subconscious mind. There are lots of departments, rooms, hallways, doorways, etc. Some areas are accessible, while others I cannot enter, and need to be very quiet and careful.

I wake up and say, I must know this hotel in and out. I'm determined to go back there.

Healing Vision - Through the Gateway into Light-Land

Traveling through the Seba, my consciousness gateway, I experience a large passage through many light purification layers, resembling a car wash, slowly walking through these layers of light. The movements of these washing-light-layers is very powerful, feeling the pressure as I'm going through a tunnel of shimmering thick, liquid light, an important preparation prior to walking out onto the other side of the gateway.

I'm now emerging into a new environment. It is the space of light, my own view of Akhet - light land. Today it's appearing to me as a tropical beach. At the shore, mom is waiting with the little Tito; as we make eye contact, I begin to cry, and Tito jumps around, so happy to see me. She takes my hand, and we walk toward the beach pine forest, then walk in. The animals and sounds of the forest welcome me back. We arrive at an opening where I see a glowing stone with a flat top. Mom places my left hand on it, and holds it there, while I am being infused with a specific type of energy emanating from this stone. Messages are running through my mind; a conversation happens at fast speeds. That which you think you need, you already have, now.

Meanwhile, the energy infused in my body is now flowing from my spine toward my whole right side. Like brush strokes of light washing outward, covering the right side of my body. Simultaneously, three or four beads of light drop from the top of the head; they are golden, rose, bright, orange in color, trickling down, one after the other, each falling further down.

A circle of light connecting brilliant energy points around the belly begins to run counterclockwise. As it creates circles, it proceeds upward toward the neck, then draws a t-shape at the base of the neck area. The liquid light movement of circles around the belly, moving up the spine then creating a horizontal line across the high-trapezoid level is repeated many times. The messages transpiring are, share, keep returning, this is one key, a new light and life energy key. The key has your signature, in turn, you alone can bring this to life. Live in flow.

There is a lapse of time, finding myself on the way back to the shore. Mom and I still hold hands. Whales and dolphins are singing, beads of light floating. We are walking in the Sun, communicating. The air is filled with encouragement, love, reassurance.

It's time for me to go back now. The little Tito is jumping up to say goodbye. He's so cute. I can see both his little eyes. Then mom hugs me, I love you, she says, and I respond in Italian, pure io - me too. I am reminded to come back anytime to connect, receive light and inspiration.

They walk toward the trees, looking back a few times. I'm at peace, I'm ok. It's just a see you later. A little boat is ready for me. The sea beings are there to help me back. The big whale is next to me, it's magical. Looking up toward the sky, the sun warms my face, and I start to feel the transition back, needing to return through another Seba. As I reach a shore, going through some thicker layers of air-atmosphere, I now walk out onto the sand, and up a few steps through a doorway. My body begins to feel itself more, sitting here, and I'm fully back.

Mission of Balance - Inspired Message

What you experienced is the teaching. Merging fire and water into waves of light, harmony, balance. Rising waves, descending winds, flowing as one river – the currents of water-fire, fire-water - flowing wisdom. New vibration quality presenting a new awareness, which is a new set of sense perceptions, a new knowing and light spectrum beyond the linear. Another consciousness, moving through layers of awareness and color-light into a new simultaneous dimensional construct. Realize the process of merging into a different quality of vibration sustained and guided by the higher bodies, instructing this convergence recalibration into a new landscape, this is a new way of perception. Resistance is pushing the minds to allow the opening, it is the inevitable movement forward. The past submerges. Dream into the new phase of seeing through the source mind consciousness self. Float into the renewed winds, water-fire waves. Simplify as you see the meaning of missions move clearly. Reach for the expanded senses again - this is life. Thank you.

Two Types of Hospitals - New Reality

Inside a hospital with chunky, colossal cement blocks, a person is giving me instructions. Not really belonging to this space, I'm just here to receive information and a set of supplements and food, shown some kind of medicine and ways to take care of my body.

I suddenly move to another building that seems much larger, not as thick as the previous structure. The transition from the first structure to this other one is very interesting. Going through some serious wavelike motions, I see my body move in as if being pushed by strong winds or going through a vortex. As I try to walk through, I have to hold myself up. It only lasts a short while, just the transitional time between the two buildings. There is a lot more room here, with people everywhere, while in the other structure I was completely alone. Here too I am given specific instructions, but on a whole different set of supplements, food, and medicine. This space feels really good, like I belong here. In the other structure, with the thick cement walls, I felt stuck, it seemed an insane asylum. Here, on the other hand, there is a sense of opening, much more comfortable. There is one person giving me instructions, and someone else in the far distance, watching after us.

I doze off into deeper processing for a few blank moments. Then, I see myself wake up within the dream, in another structure this time, a building clearly resembling a hotel. Talking to a housekeeper, I ask her to use the bathroom, and she takes me through some crazy back way, passing through some small corridors and caved-in doorways behind curtains. I get to a small dressing room with several ladies doing their makeup, getting ready for work. They recognize me, smile, and nod, encouraging me to keep going. I follow my guide, she's moving so quickly, taking me through a passageway into an opening, a large room that looks like an old-fashioned ballroom. This part of the building is inaccessible from the other side of the hotel where I was earlier. Although feeling exhausted, I'm able to notice many details, the wall condition and tall ceilings, the large windows, a big rug on the floor, and no furniture. I see my face, and I understand, hearing myself explain; these are angels, and I can interact with them. They are showing me a part of myself that needs more light. There is a connection between the hospitals and the hotel. The first structure, the chunky small hospital, represents the old ways. The second larger structure is what I've entered now. The threshold vibrational waves are the portal I am going through, the gateway to another density-dimension realm - another aspect of myself. I enter a portal of merged realities that then split.

I physically feel the same, still noticing some pain, but also aware of a deep change. I am so grateful.

Floating in a Green Energy Field

Smiling, feeling so comfortable, I hear myself asking who of the seven rays is here to help me today. I am instantly embraced by a lavish green aura. I'm lying down in a meadow with lush green grass surrounded by a radiant, bright, intense green light all around.

I look up and see what looks like an old-fashioned TV monitor. It's me on the screen as a teacher. She's in the middle of a lecture with two scrolls depicting a familiar ancient text with East-Asian characters right behind her. I am mesmerized by the similarities with this person on the screen; it's me, after all. I have a strong sense I'm seeing myself in the future, and become a little anxious about this realization. What is this unsettled feeling? Not being ready, misunderstood, or wanting the teachings to be accepted?

The Aquamarine Stone - CRENON

I am completely alert in the dream, admiring a beautiful stone. As I ask what kind of stone this is, the word crenon comes across my field of view as a label. The beautifully polished stone has a large oval irregular shape; the color is dark blue, a deep turquoise. I immediately recognize it as an actual being, having something to do with my birth and alignments during my creation. The type of stone looks like a large dark aquamarine, but I get a clear sense it's a stone from another Earth.

The Spirit World DMV

I'm in line at the DMV, my number is 9. I am called up, the person seems very nice, as she recognizes me. While filling out a form, doing some paperwork, I look back and see myself there waiting again. Another me, at the end of the line. The people at the counter look toward me, smile, and go back to their work, they know something I don't. Before, when I was in line, I couldn't tell these workers recognize everyone in the room and look out toward us; only when I came up to the window to do the paperwork, I became aware of this. There I am, back in line, number 9 again. This time, I do recognize that I was just up there at the window and the scene is repeating itself. However, I am also confused because people keep going in front of me, these numbers are not in a row. Did I miss my turn? Is there another line?

Suddenly I understand. Guides and angels appear to me as DMV workers handling everyone's paperwork. These guys are joyful, though, which is something that makes me smile. I knew they were angels the moment I went up to the window when it was my turn. They are there, and we're just not paying attention. But as we come up to the window, closer to them, then we can actually recognize them.

Confronting Lower Emotions

At the new house, I wake up in the dream screaming and crying, but more like shouting angrily with tears of anger, not sadness. It's so intense, surrounded by all these strange people who look more like shadows. There is a dark light in the background. I can't see through them, they're everywhere, appearing out of nowhere. It's scary, like a bad movie. Wanting to confront them, I approach them and start to scream out of extreme frustration and anger.

I realize these are my limitations, and they are showing up out of nowhere, walking all over the place, so disorganized, it's extremely annoying, I've had enough. There is so much work to be done, for sure, I'm saying to myself in the dream, but that I can recognize these beings of low light, going right up to them with an attitude feels so good and empowering. I wake up with a sense of hope in my heart. I got this.

Memory of Siblings

I'm visiting a very large mansion. Nobody lives here anymore, but the house is still full of belongings. It's a family house from long ago. I haven't been here in a very long time. The reason I'm here is that there is a special gathering in honor of someone who passed. While walking around alone, I begin to remember, and soon experience a strong melancholic feeling. Headed outside, there are many family members greeting each other as they arrive. Confused and startled, I look back at the front door, it's open and this older lady is looking around. She looks like she's snooping around more than just looking. Although I assume she's part of the family, I become agitated, picking up on her intentions, getting this terrible feeling. She's after something. I'm going out to see if another family member can speak to this lady. She's definitely up to something, maybe trying to steal.

As I walk out there are three people at a picnic table. They are my siblings; it's been so long! Two sisters and one brother, I'm so happy to see them. We are all in our seventies. They look so lovely and peaceful, joyful, and nurturing. They see I'm upset, and try to calm me down. My brother and I are very close, and we look so alike. Here is where I see myself, resembling an older Nicola Tesla, physically, I mean. It's incredibly clear; my brother looks just like me but a few years older. I'm venting to them about this lady who's after something; she doesn't care about the loss and other people here to *share moments together at this event. How can people be so vain and shallow and only care about stuff and not see reality as it is? I am so frustrated and hurt, angry and sad at the same time. I start crying, and my brother hugs me, feeling such a strong connection to this place. My heart swells up.*

This really happened, I say in the dream. As the memory becomes more vivid, I cry uncontrollably. I miss them so much! I wake up because I'm crying so hard. The feeling lingers for a long while. It's so strong, I keep crying, seeing their faces, and feeling their heart.

At that moment, still in my sleep-awake state, I know this was a past life event, feeling so grateful to be able to see this, to experience these feelings and understand and begin a deeper phase of uncovering some of my heaviness. This empty house, the people there. Someone had passed. I was there to meet with the family members. Primarily my siblings, who were apart from the rest of the family. We had a special bond. We didn't belong to the superficiality of those other people's reality. We were light and loving. This was a time that represented an ending. I was so upset because I could see how shallow people sought stuff not honoring the person who passed.

As I reflect, this also shows me another ending and another beginning, something to process and release as complete, and something else to process and release as it unfolds.

In today's training, I will focus on honoring all that is passing away through bowing, then welcome floods of the new energy, the new light, and new creation showing up, moving forward with offerings of prosperous, hopeful, joyful, abundant next phase. Letting go. Being. Openness. Flow. Harmony. Love. Thank you.

20

FINDING A NEW DIRECTION

Calibration through the Spine

Often, when I wake up, my first thought is how much my body misses the dry Arizona weather. The humidity, even in the warmer months, is not so pleasant, especially when one deals with joint and lower back pain.

After reviewing the MRI results with the family doctor, he immediately sent me to a neurosurgeon. His sense of urgency and reaction while reviewing the results made me slightly worried and anxious. My sister was so kind to come with me to see the neurosurgeon at one of the major hospitals in downtown Rome. Upon entering his office, I sat quietly, waiting for him to analyze the paperwork and the MRI disc. Without even looking at me once, he started writing a prescription for a specialist in pain management, telling me the only solution was to manage pain through injections and subsequently undergo spine surgery.

He kept writing and talking as if I wasn't even in the room, then I stopped him quite abruptly asking to please explain both options in detail. Although I had done my own research, and was familiar with these treatments as some of my own clients had gone through similar situations, I knew with all I had in me that these options were absolutely not right for me; still, I wanted him to take the time to explain them. I asked if there were alternative therapies before taking what seemed like drastic measures, but he thought injections for pain were perfectly normal. I was pushing it a bit, feeling frustrated that Western medicine is so black and white about only addressing a few symptoms and quick to prescribe drugs.

Walking out of there, my body reacted as if I had just heard some good news. A sense of calm and complete relaxation washed over me. The entire way back home, sitting quietly with my palms over my lower belly, I was lovingly reminded that there was nothing wrong with me, that my focus had shifted and simply needed to be redirected inward. My mind showed me all the instances when I could take care of my discomfort through my training. Pain drove me back to the wisdom that comes from going deeper. The key lies in finding the balance between processing new energy and allowing the necessary time for energetic and physical integration.

I experience absolutely no level of pain during training, and when I enter a state of presence and emptiness, my body shows me what she needs in that particular moment; internal and external movements arise through visionary journeys, KiGong, and light language, clearly showing me where the realignment is taking place.

The pain has significantly decreased and is barely detectable most of the time. When discomfort shows up, I know it's because I've neglected my minds, recognizing I didn't take time for myself yet. Perhaps I sat too long, or my thoughts took over, scattering and depleting energy, which resulted in feeling overwhelmed with superficial tasks. Just like most people, I too get lazy and sometimes become stubborn, with the usual, *I'm fine!* It's ok, we're human, but after timing myself, allowing whatever is happening to just be, I do something to help me come back to center, reset, and recharge.

I spoke about being self-disciplined and training ourselves to be good stewards of the minds; this is the diligent work of healing and growing. It does take focus, which we may sometimes think takes so much effort and time. Look carefully at the perceived obstacles to self-care. I can go on-and-on about what ten minutes can do if we genuinely choose to give those ten minutes the sincerest focus you can muster. Even when it takes more time to increase energy circulation, to soothe inflammation, to extend ourselves time to slow down. It is very important to calm the nervous systems, and it is all absolutely worth it. When the mind is trained, those focused ten minutes translate into a full battery charge, restoring the ability to operate at your best. Occasionally though, the body does need more time, as we are processing more information than ever before.

Recently, in a conversation with a dear friend about self-care, we remembered that it is exactly like plugging in your cell phone when the battery dies. There is nothing to contemplate; when the phone starts to die, we simply reach for our power cord and plug it in. As I described in an earlier chapter, self-care is generosity toward ourselves, not an indulgence. Self-care is exactly the same as reaching for the power cord and plugging in. No thinking, no believing; we are technology, and we need to be charged. The quality of the charge does matter, but the emphasis here is just a reminder that, above all, we must choose a different story, the one where self-care is the most important activity we can do each day.

Alignment and calibration showed up for me through my spine, revealing another source of direction, insight, and wisdom within the ongoing language of transformation and growth. Although an uncomfortable process, I'm extremely grateful for its teachings.

Returning to the Origins

I am often reminded of this concept: returning home - returning to your origins. In Taoist SunDo philosophy, *returning to the origins* is not only a profound philosophical topic, but it also refers to physical and energetic activation postures that focus on supporting the kidneys, engaging the powerful vital energy we are born with, the pure balance between yin and yang energies, known as primordial water and primordial fire - the essence and vitality of the root of life stored in the kidneys.

For me, *returning to my origins* translated into a physical move back to my home country, even though it may be temporary. Who knows what the future will bring, as I do like to have multiple plans out there floating in the air.

Everyone experiences, at some point or another, a form of *returning home* - returning to the origins. I don't mean physically, which can undoubtedly be the case, but spiritually. My guiding compass led me home for specific reasons mapped out for me, by me. I keep tuning in, staying open to receiving insights as I continue to move forward, releasing any expectations of specific outcomes, as I manage my need for situations to be in a particular way. Returning to my origins, for me, means absorbing the *beads of light* that I both deliberately and unconsciously left behind, drawing back in the precious jewels that create peaceful wholeness.

I see the powerful gifts given by my higher self were preserved for me in very safe places. I envision my brightest, star-infused-self capturing with the most nurturing, loving mind those particles of light that escaped from my energy line throughout time. She carefully stored them in light blue glass jars, sealed them tightly, and sent them deep through the various Earth layers, into a reservoir of inner Earth's lakes and streams, near a shore with loving beings singing beautiful words of peace and harmony. A magical world where the purest light is safely stored for a while until we're ready. There are magnificent beings of cosmic wisdom here, who chose to be guardians, teachers, and healers of light. They nurture and protect the beads of light as if in a nursery, in an *orfanotrofio* (orphanage). There is no right or wrong in this place. Particles of light stored here receive teachings, and they keep growing and maturing, coexisting alongside the life our persona-self perceived in what we call *real life*. There is a time when the pure brightness of our beads of light regains the original radiance, emanating enough strength to be able to push through thick illusory boundaries created by the self-perception mechanism - what we think is our *conscious mind* - revealing itself to be a mental thought-processing construct, the personality we identify with. I use the term *conscious*, but it's not really conscious.

Let's consider the self that is aware of the minuscule fraction of what life is, living this life ruled by the incomplete array of sense perception, by the information received through the six senses alone; in addition, let's also reflect on the self that discovers there is a lot more to life. That self, the one who *starts* to feel restless, *starts* to notice severe imbalances and patterns and *starts* to look for ways to understand the inner workings more, *this* is a more conscious self. These *starts* are signals, part of an intricate communication system, a specific language, that is being transmitted through the universal quantum intelligence field.

This phenomenon is a natural law, occurring throughout all-time-space, regardless of our focused awareness. We absorb and interact with this type of language just like breathing, most of the time misunderstanding what it is and where it comes from. It may hold many disguises, leading us to simplify and minimize the true meaning, thinking, it's just a coincidence, that was only a dream, what a nice person back there, did you see the writing on that billboard on the highway - I needed to hear that today, my body hurts, I think I'm sick, I can't believe I twisted my ankle running this morning. There is no such thing as a coincidence, not even the twisted ankle, the accident, the billboard or license plate message, the dream, or the nice person you randomly meet.

Empowerment is enlightenment. We've seen these words together before. What does it mean to you? The lost *power*, which is *light* - our true essence, wants to be found. It's like the *ring of power* in Lord of the Rings. It wants to be found and seen by its master. What type of master do you choose to be? What is the condition of your filters, your lenses?

Returning home refers to a way of creating enough magnetism deep within, through our energy line, by fully opening our soul portals and continuously purifying our energy-spiritual bodies, the minds, so that our power - our light essence - can return and safely dock onto the command center platform; anchoring, ready to be fully integrated, reporting back on the adventures, exchanging and sharing beauty and true light, true information; hearing of the experiences of our other light particles, providing profound reordering and calibration for a realigned, fresh vessel to comfortably flourish in. The inner environment begins to radiate a slightly different sound and light that resonate with our soul-spirit unified frequency more closely; a frequency existing beyond the known physical spectrums, including shapes and colors that vibrate with our own name.

The next phase is symbolized by sitting on the throne of empowerment. It is a metaphorical throne representing dignity and courage, exuding stability, and resilience, lifting the skies with the top of our head, radiant and open with extended arms, expressing confidence to do the work originally intended, standing or sitting tall, suggesting a deeper connection to the wisdom of the ancient angel-light rhythm of the Earth, holding all the tools we stored and will ever need, knowing who we are.

We receive from our higher selves and the entire universe through the Earth as a filter, a transfer device, a transmitter-receiver; and just like the Earth, we, too, are transmitter-receiver devices. The key to expansion is clearing all of our filters, not only physical but all levels of energetic-spiritual filters. Although we constantly receive through our energy line, we also continuously give, and more importantly, this is not a linear movement. The never-ending spiraling movement phenomenon is the infinity sign expanding and contracting ad infinitum. As we grow, we expand to *in-gather* more of our own light. We are the infinity sign.

The evolution movement flows into faster spinning contraction, reaching a point of extreme pressure, where we create another pure bead of crystal light, recognizing this intelligence and allowing it to expand into brightness. In this field, we consciously grow, learn, share, exchange, purify, and mature through refinement, to then move on to the next round, continuing through the movement – consciousness – which is infinity itself.

Beads of Light – Restoring Lost Pieces

Savoring the journey of embracing the unknown, making friends with it in every respect, I fully trust my power, my light-essence shown to me as beads of light. They guided me to certain physical locations and through the experience of coming back home, to finally float back onto the grand flight deck, the docking station - my core. This inner world is ready for a welcome home event and the joyful, explosive celebration for a job well done, informing the rest of the sister beads of light of the teachings gained with the help of the ancient wisdom keepers; the guardians, and teachers of the inner Earth worlds, infusing the purest light directly from the source.

As these beads of light approach, a peaceful feeling is accompanied by the coming back online of upgraded awareness. My soul and spirit were so thirsty for this feeling. Beads of light belonging to my own soul-name vibration are making their way as I walk toward that seat of power, the light that the soul-spirit represents. It is with understanding and compassion that I recognize when I lost or abandoned them, knowing that it is not about remembering. I do not fully remember many things about my early years, and feel it's unnecessary to retrieve and relive some memories, as that may turn into a way to control the flow of energy, obstructing the natural communication exchange between our multidimensional minds. I no longer want to control out of necessity and survival.

Instead, I want to master my own seat of power, to be more complete and walk around in all aspects of life as one being - the union of physical, ethereal, astral, mental, spiritual selves, and so on - for that is definitely not *all* we are. I long to be whole, not only when I meditate, teach, and learn, experience active dreaming, visions, and connection to my guides, but all the time. This is who I am. This is who we all are.

It is my choice to fully accept and embrace those parts of me who struggle and resist as she is pushed by the strong winds of the tightening spiral. I gain more profound acceptance and love for myself as the leader that I am, able to use my strength and resilience to step up and out from victim consciousness into space-ness consciousness. I fully invite and embrace those beads of light carefully stored and nurtured by the guardians of wisdom to return home as the expanded-self relinquishes control and expectations.

I hear different sounds, see different lights, and walk around as a vast encyclopedia of symbols continuously opening to the next unfolding pages, allowing the lines, shapes, and characters to impart teachings that can benefit all of us through the bright angel-light rhythm of Earth.

We are on the way forward, from within, deep inside the docking station – the center of the center. The beginning and end which is never-ending. We are the Shen hieroglyph, the never-ending circle where the divine drops of wisdom descend and ascend, as we are the holders of Mind-wisdom.

Interestingly, the Shen in ancient East-Asian languages represents the energy of the heart-mind, divine presence, the seat of consciousness - the seat of power, the core of light. The master of the seat, the master of the house - the temple – refers to the name vibration of the ancient mother, companion, leader, warrior, mystic, healer, and goddess, who steers us back into wholeness, who nurtures new beginnings, who guides us in retrieving our power to create, our mother and sister, Aset - Isis.

Let's emerge into our light, our seat of divine presence, walking into our own unique empowerment as creation energy lives and burns in all of us.

Dreams ~ Visions ~ Journeys

New Fire - Inspired Message

Inspiration of new Sun-light vibration burns all limitations. This is the yin aspect of sun/fire. The seen and unseen light is at work. Run these vibrations thoroughly through the energy pillar and create a vibrational ripple effect on all planes. Change, shed, burn. Renew the flow. Vibration through the pillar creates new light. Earth receives and transmits these vibrations through you. Yang aspect of earth energy is production, manifestation, expression into matter. The light of your fire creates the devotion and reverence of the work.

Keep your life, your bodies, including thoughts-emotions complex, pure and continue purifying through flow. The fire, water, wind, and sun through earth consciousness reveal wisdom rising - feel the roots. Step out. Lead. Peak outside the door, then step out in confidence, empowered, in-light.

Feel the soul calling and strength of infinite light-wisdom guiding you forward. Hold her hand. You are safe this time. Passing through this passage is the mission as the opening to the land of light within. The dimension of translated light into a new language, a new body. New for the lower human mind but eternal for the true identity of soul. Matter and energy of different quality of vibration rising and descending at once. You create-receive like the container you are in and have prepared. Time has come to step out of the smallness you claimed. The gift received must be shared. Diluted light is of another time, not the focus moving forward. Purified streams flow in the higher awareness, and this is now the focus.

The distortions in the pillar, your back, are residual of lineage and unconscious hurts. It is not yours. Grow up and out of this new burning-fire purification reconfiguration for this is what it is. It's the new fire. This is in your strength to resolve. Hold the intention. Clear it and complete it. This is the gift to share. No need to know. Be, share, write, sing, move, smile. It will come. Thank you.

Forgotten Purse - Found Wallet - New ID

On a long road trip, I stop and use a very dirty and disgusting bathroom, like in most gas stations off the highway. At one stop, I remove my purse, which is a crossbody bag with a thick strap made of canvas material similar to the bee-bag my wonderful friend Jennie gifted me before leaving Arizona. My wallet is in there. Having to use the bathroom, I place the bag on the paper holder, then after washing my hands, I just leave, unconsciously walking out without it.

This is a long journey, having traveled everywhere. I come to a stop again, and when entering this gas station bathroom, it seems as though it's the same exact one I stopped in a long time ago.

How could this be? Did I unconsciously return to where I was before? The bathroom is the same, but there is even more dirt and filth this time, it's disgusting. There are brown smears on the trash cans, which I move away to the side, feeling like I should start cleaning, or straighten things out. Unsure if it's a good idea to wait until the next stop, I use the restroom, then wash my hands and move over to the paper towel holder.

There it is - my bag, just hanging there, exactly where I left it. Years must have gone by. There are three other little bags over mine. My bag is the biggest, it's quite visible. How could it still be there? After a few moments of complete shock, I reach for it, remembering the contents of the bag, and assume the wallet must be gone. My hand finds the wallet, and I can see my face with a look of disbelief. Overflowing from the main wallet compartment are about seven tea bags. Incredibly, taking a closer look, I pull out my ID card, it's my Arizona driver's license. There is also another type of ID and an American Express. This must be very old, I say; I don't even remember when this card was active, it was long ago. The few other cards in the wallet resembled passes or membership cards. One of them has a different shape and size and it doesn't really fit in the wallet. It's a laminated, yellow card with large writing on it, that looks like a library admission card or a pass. I know it's to access a particular place, like an entry card.

Within the dream, I realize with amazement the meaning of these images. I am finding myself again. It's an indescribable feeling of immense joy and gratitude for finding parts of myself again after so long. Having traveled long distances, I felt tired and unsettled. I walked again in the same shit hole, and I found the purse – my body - and within it, medicine, the tea bags - Earth resources - and my identity - a pass, an access card. I put the bag across my body, looking proud and confident, then say to myself, I will never take it off ever again. It doesn't matter what's on the outside, it only matters what's inside, and I have everything I need, right here.

Rainbow Umbilical Cord

There is so much contraction within as I wake up crying. Still inside the dream, but aware of what my body is experiencing, hearing myself cry loudly. Seeing myself from up above, I am curled up into a little bundle, a small, tiny baby, smaller than a newborn, with a very long umbilical cord, knowing it is still attached although I do not see the source. The umbilical cord is clearly glowing with rainbow colors. Seeing this image brings tears to my eyes and such a strong reaction down to my core. The rainbow includes the seven known colors, detectable by the physical eyes, but there are other colors, too. I'm aware these colors are coming from within the umbilical cord, connecting me to the mother, the Earth and through her, I connect to the rest of the cosmos.

An angel's voice is singing beautiful sounds, then I see her on what looks like a modern, large screen. She's in disguise, appearing to me as this awesome akashic record reader I had a session with years ago, Debbie. She's joyful, smiling, overly loving, and happy. She starts to sing a beautiful song, and in the background, music and other angels are singing the chorus. It's magical.

The music has angelic sounds with a chill EDM (electronic dance music) flair, just what I love. The music sounds so familiar, it almost sounds like the song, We are the World, something legendary like that, a classic, but not quite the same, though is similar. The lyrics were, you are me, I am with you, we have each other, we share this light, we are one. The energy I received was so loving and warm, I was very comfortable, while my body was buzzing and vibrating intensely.

Inspired messages: The rainbow connects to the core, the center. The vagus nerve connects to the heart-mind and head brain, which becomes one level of energy line. The next phase of the rainbow connection is the pillar of light - expanded energy line. There is a third bridge and level of connection. It shows itself as a spiraling moving entity, a consciousness and intelligence.

It's not a singular, more like an inclusive body. The straight line can be fully captured with the senses, but it involves another range of senses, functioning as antennas or tuning forks, expanding to the next phase. The third bridge represents the dimensions at the smallest quantum particle form to the largest scale fathomable - the Atum, the beginning and the end, and the Amun, the unseen wind of evolution. Until now, the process of awakening to the energy and spiritual senses involved activating the energy line, the second bridge. It's now the beginning of activating the third bridge of development - a spiraling circular system of connection - evolutions as a series of completions.

The number 9 is the Hu energy, breath connection. In-gather, be in-spirit, and allow further development. The number 10 represents the revolution. As the 9 of awareness is reached, an upgraded spirit breath enters, pushing to the next revolution, the next cycle, moving through the spiral of dimensional expansion. With the potential of becoming sluggish and tired, a slight push to reach the 9 comes. Spirit moves to the next revolution. It shows the limits in the current energy pillar perception, with the senses belonging to this level. Sense perceptions, or so we call them, are ready to reach further landscapes. What you think you can achieve is a glimpse. Such is the wondrous spiral connecting to Mind, showing itself in visions and dreams. Enjoy the rainbow. Thank you.

The Work of Refining – Inspired Messages

The old is lifting, you feel it in the body. A time of limitations is ending, not only your own limitations, but those of others passed. The left-brain ego has stepped down. A change of leadership team members is occurring. Lead with the right receptor, the right brain. Direct with your left side of the body. Shake things up through sound, vibration, and rhythm. Alignment and joyful creation run through your energy line. The heart-throat energy complex creates what you hold. The true essence of eternal wisdom lives in this exchange. Purification on all levels continues entering the land of light, merging with Mind. The purest intent is to funnel this vibration through the body into Earth, continuous grounding. You are the roots and line transmitter to the center of the great being. The light of wisdom is a current manifested. Collect and store this light. Transmit vibration as the house tunes and sounds. Through voice vibration, express and create. Exchange rhythm and resonance, infuse purified light with what emanates from the wisdom light of Mind. Merge - this is high doing.

Alignment - calibration - is the work of refining. There is new light showing you. You can see and in-act with high vibration what you receive and exchange in the heart-throat complex. It is not new, just unknown, newly revealed. Energy centers previously unseen are coming back online. Heart-throat complex expands as a ring-disc around shoulders and collar bones. It is vibrating, drumming like a heartbeat, a neon fluorescent light, pulsating, gaining recognition as it expands. It resonates with the land sounds and vibrations of Earth wisdom. Guides are protecting this attunement as you are releasing old leaves and branches you've carried for too long. Trust and cultivate joy. There is more in-gathering as you recognize this vibration. You can center and receive more, clearing sight for brighter vision and integrating with fewer pain distortions.

Trust the approach. There is much to do. Prepare. Receive these words, although the left-brain ego may not capture them entirely. You can see the layers beyond the symbols. This is your work. See all around you. Receive well and share well. Be at peace. Stay in the heart-throat complex. Hold your hands over your high heart to connect, then center in your lower portal. Ground through your zero-point and strengthen the core and pillars of light. Create light, sounds, vibration, rhythm. Thank you.

Chanting 'Om Tare Tuttare Ture Soha'

Every morning, for days on end, I wake up hearing myself sing and chant the Tara mantra. It's so beautiful. Within the dream, my higher self is singing this chant in a loving tone. The higher-soul vibration, through this mantra, echoes and resonates filling the air. It's a song for me, the self that is lying here sleeping, requesting clarity.

Then I see a beautiful place in nature I often visit, and this time, there is a new path for me, and only a few others venture through it. It's very peaceful. I'm walking in wonder, absorbing the beautiful surroundings. Looking around, it appears as if I'm searching for something, and then a sense of knowing descends. The universe is providing, I am safe and wanted. The mantra soothes my heart and makes me feel so peaceful once more.

In the Emptiness

Today's training led me to practice bowing, vibration, and energy breathing, holding kyanite and indigo gabbro stone companions, accompanying messages.

Seba opening - gateway - access in lower dahnjon, ascend through the energy line, and walk out into the land of light. I meet and communicate with vast spheres of energy-spirit. Cobalt, violet, periwinkle, and blue. In complete emptiness, there is no movement of thought, no low-vibrational body senses. The spheres share, be joy and share joy - unfolding new energy lines in this time of infinite space-time. There is nothing to fix. Focus. Connect. Hold it within.

Swimming with a Prehistoric Whale

I am underwater, close to the surface, right under a boat. There is a whale that looks like an orca, but the colors are not so clear. It's faded, or I'm still wearing some filter, my sight is not entirely focused yet. The whale is emitting a song, a sonar-like sound similar to what we hear from whales and dolphins, but different at the same time. The whale also has a snout, a long extension about half a human arm's length. I'm a little scared but also curious and excited. Jason is with me.

The sound gives us a welcoming feeling. The whale swims right under us, twirling. Jason swims closer, reaching out to her. He gets close enough to notice the beautiful sound is coming from the snout. I reach out too, and through the snout we feel there is a transmission of some sort, a distinctive sound accompanied by a warm feeling. She is gentle in her approach. My view is still foggy, which makes me feel unsettled, so I swim back a bit, thinking, what if she's an orca instead, she could open her giant mouth and eat us. One side of me is so happy to meet this beautiful familiar creature communicating with us, another part of me feels terrible about my hesitation and fear of dying. I should know the difference, but my eyes are still a little clouded. Nonetheless, I have a clear sense that she is a prehistoric whale or an ancient creature due to the snout appendage and the incredible wisdom she holds. The high-pitched sonar sound is reverberating everywhere. This is the sound of primordial waters, it is ancient. I am so happy to see Jason is here with me in this experience of contact.

When I woke up, I did some research and found information on the Narwhal. I had never known or seen pictures of a whale like this. The Narwhal is a magical unicorn-like cetacean. What appeared as a snout is a tooth that grows in a counter-clockwise spiral forming a tusk, usually the left canine. Fascinated by this vision, what transpired is that the half-tusk represents the broken or interrupted receptor, an antenna-like sensor. I will continue to connect with this messenger.

Overlay into Larger Fractal

I keep waking up with the echo of a wonderful feeling. This is very important for me. The most joyful and content feeling indicates I am on a path that allows for deeper alignment with my higher selves. It's an amazing sensation because sometimes the daunting unknown can make me feel heavy and worried. Instead, I know everything is ok and will be ok.

I am seeing myself skipping around, playing, and interacting with dear, nurturing friends with whom I can truly be myself. They are my guides and companions, meeting with me daily, here to continuously support me.

Inspired messages: Nothing else matters but to see what is in the heart, to feel her power and strength, to let her flow in her own way. The power of the heart, deliberately using the sound vibration HER as a feminine-Yin aspect of power - of light. It's a different quality of vibration that announces the beginning of a new wave of healing and seeing. It brings new levels of spiritual senses within the deeper mind, opening into a dimension that is just an overlaid moment of time-space.

Here, in this overlay, you are managing and directing. You participate unconsciously but fully receive glimpses as they appear one raindrop at a time. The overlay is also you. More you than this participating self - who is a fractal of intelligence with another design, another set of lists, directions, collection of information, including shapes and colors. Record the flood of connecting beads you receive. Drops of light between the overlays are constantly exchanging knowledge. Analyze what is on the border of the overlay-reality, who's at the edge, and what you need to smoothly pass through.

You can direct the perception of the participating self from the other overlays, which hold a larger fractal of who you are - the light of the cosmic waters. Everything in your perception layer is a raindrop of wisdom. Look around you. Look deeper. In and around every raindrop is also the overlay into a larger fractal. You see with one perception, one set of impressions. You are designed to hold the stars both inside and in the entirety of the overlay's complex, the fields. Listen to the sound of the stars. In an instant, become the entire fractal to perceive the song of stars. Every raindrop light bead is a string of sound vibration here to support your nourishment on the way to complete alignment, providing a system upgrade, a pulsating ignition.

The outer overlays live in all space-time. Move inward to expand senses. As a result, you expand outward to fully see. Be space, with equal exchange of flow in all directions. You guide the harmonic process. This process must awaken in you as the lighthouse you are. This is the calling of the Earth now. Thank you.

I asked for clarity. Transcending sorrow. Acceptance of true balance. Heightened awareness. Self-restoration. Empowerment is being true to yourself. Soul expression is true joy. Joy of creation and transformation, lightness, and awareness. Spirit and Soul nourish the pure mind, truly empty of controlled outcomes. Nothing is missing. You already hold it. Seek balance in everything. Opposition shows you where to focus. Move through distractions with discipline. See your light in everything. Dream and lead. Let imagination guide the blossoming of the way. It is here.

We hold the sacred power to transform from the illusion of loss and heartbroken, small, contracted energy into the radiant explosion of truth that we rightfully are. A truth that is a transpiration of our own unique sun fractal expression. Living the brightness of a star, shining, and expressing joyfully. We are constantly guided in this direction by our higher self and guides, including ancestors, angels, and cosmic families. They help us replenish our resources and fuel us to start new every day. Our job is very important, difficult, but simple - shaking the walls of illusion. The walls appear thick. We usually cannot tell if there are walls unless we feel resistance. The indication is a sense of contraction that makes us uncomfortable, distorting perception. The degree of contraction is influenced by how numb we've become to our spiritual selves. Contraction is our realized-self hitting that wall. Then, we too often bounce back and move on as if it's the nature of life flow. We say things like it is what it is, but it's not like it is, for what we see is actually an incomplete picture.

Moving through contraction and feeling pressure against a wall is like pushing the door of a store entrance where the sign clearly says pull. We are stuck on push when we must pull, unable to identify the difference between these words - push *and* pull - *although in plain sight.*

So, pull! Flow any way you can through contractions instead of settling for what is incomplete. We hold an abundance of divine wisdom and gifts. There are gifts we cannot name, for they are so unique to each individual that language cannot fully expand on their spiritual meaning and vibration. There is no other way to be - the mission is to be in balance as when we move between worlds and exchange equally. Receive and give, give and receive. Learn, teach, teach, learn. Be. The doing is secondary. Thank you!

Receiving Instructions

Waking up in the dream, I see a sequence of words on a piece of paper. It looks like a series of instructions. Starting from the bottom, I go through the words, searching for something specific, pausing about halfway up the page. The feeling is that I'm searching for a particular word that is important for me to study. Something suddenly becomes very clear. I know this list, because I'm the one who wrote it. Some letters begin to appear, one at a time, from left to right, para...something. I hear myself starting to sound the letters, para...sailing, para...phrasing, no, that's not it. As I record this, the remaining letters are no longer clear, but I pause, breathe, center, and calm myself, then ask to be shown. As the letters begin to spell out the word, I hear it, *paranassus.*

Paranassus or Parnassus is a sacred mountain of ancient Greece. The mountain was home to the nine muses who dedicated their lives to the oracle of Delphi in honor of the god Apollo. It was also known as the home of music, poetry, and learning. This is another whisper pushing me to remember, as I've been shown the ancient oracle sites and omphalos throughout Greece, Anatolia, Crete, and Cyprus many times.

New Energy Healing Modality

The following description is part of a series of initial journeys that reveal a new energy system emerging within Earth and humanity. A brief overview will be outlined here. Moreover, another body of work will delve deeper into key aspects as further initiation and exploration is underway.

The Five and the Seven Create the One.

Five is represented by the two kidneys, the spine, and the two hemispheres of the brain, which are an extension of the kidneys. The two pairs create the pure quality of alignment between Yin and Yang energies, and the balance runs effortlessly through the energy line. Seven represents the internal chakra system. As we strengthen through our energy line, we expand into a new energy system where the five components of alignment and balance with the seven internal chakra systems emerge into one circular system. The vibration of the five and the seven creates recalibration of new incoming and outgoing sources of light.

This shift creates the return to the one source, the light that is the immeasurable fire inside. Oneness is expressed as an expanded version of mind, rising, choosing creativity, and effecting change, an elevated state into a new life.

The alignment of Truth, represented by Ma'at energy, lives in the heart. As the center of the seven-chakra system, it is the nucleus of expression, work, and mission - the nucleus maintaining balance. The seven-chakra system moves into a horizontal line - parallel to Earth bringing the energy centers now on equal plane - the three, the one, and the three, representing the upper energy centers, the heart, and the lower energy centers. This can only occur if a stable foundation is in place - a strong pillar of light - which is a combination of multidimensional spiritual lines merging as one. This foundational pillar of light exists beyond the previous dimension of the energy line composed of the chakras along the front of the physical spine. The heart will maintain balance, order, the lightness of right and left oscillations, through purification and upgrade of the cosmic connecting lines.

The upper chakras relate to balance between thoughts and connection with the higher mind. The lower chakras connect to action according to the highest will. The heart is the center, moving from a vertical axis to a horizontal one. An equal amount of giving and receiving is the key to maintaining a high balance, that of a higher nature - where we are elevated to a frequency more in tune with our higher selves. A new level of illumination arrives. Seeing the beauty, the light and power of all aspects as part of the one mind. The completed self comes to light. It is the light body - the Sahu, or diamond body - now upgraded, accepting with courage the journey through the realms of consciousness, of movement.

The body, which is the intelligent being serving as the temple - holder of the offering of light through matter - is the perfected healing instrument for the work of alignment and calibration. Interestingly, the hieroglyph Het is the temple; one of the symbols included in Het is the menorah, the instrument of light. Through purification, we understand the equal value of gain and loss, of light and dark, of space and time - the laws of the universe. Dissolution of lower vibrations, and elevation of realized-self through purification processes beyond thought, allows for the coming to light of the next phase of the energetic-spiritual system.

There is a stronger need to center and focus on the pillar that holds the balance system. New creation is afoot. New light generates new bodies. This is a new level of transformation. Deep work is happening here for everyone. Keep moving forward, elevating the quality of work and connection to the purest vibration, of self and selves.

The old is no longer relevant or useful. Resist wasting energy on obsolete ways to handle the mind. What you call mind - thought processes through brain filters - is not the primary focus. The balance of incoming and outgoing fire-light source vibration is the focus. Seeing it through the reconciliation of the three is the focus. The three being the soul-spirit complex portals that create the multidimensional cosmic line. Collapse the three into one - the brilliant cosmic pillar that you are.

Maintain the seven horizontal focal points to create the energy of eight, harmonious flow in the moment, creating a new vision. The star body has emerged through the gateway of the vertical alignment. It has completely shifted. You are able to hold the components that make the one.

The diamond body era, the way the Earth evolves, is with the breath of the higher mind spiraling in and out. You are the offering of this eternal flow, gaining insight, able to participate, awakened, as magnified instruments, as beacons for many. See the nine-spiral appear and move up to the next evolution and revolution.

When we see everything on one level plane, on the one horizontal line, it is clear. The spiritual light, the heavy dark shadow, the desires, the wills, addictions, wounds, trauma, the thought patterns, the blockages, the potentials, and all-time wisdom. There is no longer a need to work so hard in going backward in time, living from the past-brain processes. For too long the incomplete brain processing systems have hijacked the forward movement of pure light sparkling explosions. Expand the use of the brain so it can properly do its originally intended job. Reflect on the knowledge of your own tools and resources within.

Become the warrior-angel-light vibration itself. The highest essence-in-action of co-creating allows movement beyond living in a past framework to heal old energy. More is now visible as the tools for this journey are in the light of the higher mind. Spirit-soul, soul-spirit unit-complex merge inside and around your physical body as one. The time of being so separate from our other selves has ended; the small mind wants to prove and establish existence through differences, periodically finding the high of spirit practices and phenomena, and basking in it for a while until low vibration pushes us off kilter, again and again. This system has proven to be highly unsustainable. We've become so good at managing the small self, the distorted ideal of holding it all together, unnaturally moving against the current, when it's not an entirely accurate or complete perspective, and the reason for short Earth life and disease. Too much swaying, not knowing where to look, where to go, what to do, what to believe, distracted and scattered.

Now we're in a new era. The one internal energy system is propelled sideways, which raises all kinds of cobwebs-like neglected energy that is out in the open. It is inevitable work. We didn't do anything wrong. This is simply the next phase. Now the work is to recognize and really see through this revelation, to see beyond thinking. Thinking is now on the same level of the root. It is no longer more important, as we have been made to believe, for the ideal of the mental bodies is fragmented. Too much thinking has hindered true seeing.

Ir-ma'a is the hieroglyph for true vision, depicted with two eyes, a mouth, and a tool for working the land. Seeing truth allows its ripple effect vibration to manifest in the creation symphony, by merging the above and the below through our soul's expression, perceiving beyond the physical eyesight, surrendering to the realities of the imaginal realms. True seeing, then doing work of the highest nature is the new direction.

We are now in the readjustment era of what is our truth, our unique voice and vibration. What holds the balance is the source of the truth, and the work simply revolves around this source. The pillar, which is of new cosmic light vibrating, is the focus now. You must hold the center to fully see and navigate with broader sight as you maintain constant movement and flow. The cosmic pillar fuels the accumulation of aligned will power, as we move beyond all distractions of old ways.

Meditation with Symbols:

DAE — vastness — depicted with the IN symbol, representing humanity (two diagonal strokes, one begins from the sky, the other from the Earth, resembling a triangle) with a line across, near the apex - the human who merges the above with the below within. Dae is the expanded self with a strong foundation that becomes the perfected human, the diamond body, the Sahu, the five-pointed human figure in a golden circle.

SHIP — number ten — completion (symbol resembling a cross with a higher horizontal axis) represented by the horizontal alignment of the seven chakras completing the work in the current cycle, ready for the next evolution.

TAE — represents the harmonizing energy, composed of the Dae symbol with an additional stroke in the center of the triangle. The stroke is the center creation point from which we can harmonize the five points. This is the even more expanded source self, generating multidimensional patterns of connection through the spiral movements.

Final Thoughts - Alignment, A Purification Process

We are always supported and receive inspiration from our guides and higher self, whether we consciously know it or not. They are us, we are them.

They guide us toward our dreams, our soul's destiny, and our mission of creating peace, harmony, brightness, and change. It doesn't matter how we create - the work is recognizing that we are constantly led to walk our path, following the steps that allow us to live an inspired life. We do that by deeply reflecting on our sorrows - reflecting, not dwelling - asking ourselves the right questions, and becoming brighter, rising in consciousness.

The surface must be questioned impartially, with a neutral stance. There is always something more as we are only presented with maybe 1-5% of what actually is. Appropriate questions could be, what can I use from this experience? What is the truth for me now, beyond what I see? versus, why is this happening to me?

Our true nature dances with all of Life. Running joyfully toward all experiences while our persona-left brain ego may freeze or want to go back. Constant movement to become the movement itself is our nature. Movement being the intelligent, *conscious Life.*

Alignment, to me, involves the continuous cycle of purification. Through sincere devotion to ourselves, through deep, meaningful understanding, and continuously moving through internal and external processes, we become the best dancers with *Life* we know. Understanding by transcending what folds us or splits us in two - looking for all the opportunities and taking time to reflect, being honest with ourselves, making friends with our higher energy-spirit minds and with our guides, expanding into trust, and lastly making friends with the parts of ourselves we *think* don't deserve to see, honoring them instead.

Alignment is purification beyond what we prepare for in what we consider waking life - the most significant alignment is the purification of the world inside.

Let's keep going, each deepening our own unique process. We must keep going, identifying the harmony within ourselves first through deep commitment to our inner balance and compass, then fully recognizing the connection with all beings, including Earth.

We are constantly guided, protected, loved, and accepted.

About the Author

Enrica Ferruzzi born in Rome with a dual cultural upbringing, thrived in a successful corporate career within the travel industry. Despite achievements, an inner yearning for deeper meaning emerged. After two decades in the corporate world, Enrica defied norms, resigning for a life attuned to her core. Her journey, marked by loss and restlessness, led her to rediscover ancient healing arts. Guided by spirit allies in restoring lost pieces of her soul, she became a teacher and healer, sharing timeless transformation practices over the past decade and training individuals in unlocking healing potential. Ferruzzi has now authored *Beads of Light*, detailing her profound alignment, a testament to embracing change through empowering spiritual practices.